SUBALTERNS OF THE FOOT

Three World War I Diaries of
Officers of the Cheshire Regiment

"A mere nobody, sir, a subaltern in a foot
regiment, or something of that kind."
(Oscar Wilde, *The Picture of Dorian Gray.*)

2/Lieut. T.L.C. Heald.   Capt. W.A.V. Churton.   Lieut. E.J. Bairstow.

         Capt. H. Caldecutt.   2/Lieut. N. Holmstrom.

"B" Company Officers, photographed in ruins of Ypres Cathedral, April, 1915.

SUBALTERNS OF THE FOOT

THREE WORLD WAR I DIARIES OF OFFICERS OF THE CHESHIRE REGIMENT

Anne Wolff

A Square One Publication

First Published in 1992 by
Square One Publications, Saga House
Sansome Place, Worcester WR1 1UA

© Anne Wolff 1992

British Library Cataloguing in Publication Data
Wolff, Anne
 Subalterns of the Foot: Three World War I
 Diaries of Officers of the Cheshire Regiment
 I. Title
 940.4

ISBN 1-872017-55-x

Typeset by Avon Dataset Ltd., Waterloo Road, Bidford-on-Avon B50 4JH
Printed by Biddles Ltd, Guildford

ACKNOWLEDGEMENTS

I am indebted to many people for their generous help during the writing of this book. First to the late George McGowan from Australia, who, with warm encouragement and kindness allowed me to quote from his letters and memoirs. Equally, I wish to express my deep gratitude to Dr. John Hodgkin who generously permitted me to use the material from the outstanding diaries of his father, the late Adrian Eliot Hodgkin, whose factual and lively sketches so enhance the text.

In particular I owe an enormous debt of gratitude to Lieutenant General Sir Napier Crookenden, not only for writing such a moving forward, but for his kindness and patience in reading the manuscript. His helpful suggestions have been invaluable.

In addition, I wish to thank Mr. R. A. Suddaby and the Library Staff of the Imperial War Museum for their outstanding assistance and unfailing help at all times.

The following have most kindly furnished me with much valuable information: Lieutenant Colonel R. C. Peel, Regimental Secretary and Major A.F.W. Astle Secretary the Cheshire Regiment Association; Mr. Tom Sharp, The Headmaster of Repton School; Mr. Martin Middlebrook; the late Mrs. Elise Briggs; Lieutenant Colonel J.H. McGuiness; Mr. John Terraine; The Archivist, Bass Brewery Co.; The Archivist, Greenall Whitley and Co; Mr. Philip Winterbottom, Archivist, Imperial Chemical Industries PLC; Mr. Frank Strahan, The Archivist, Melbourne University. I would like to express my appreciation to Dr. J.E. Vaughan of Liverpool University, and Mr. Alan Wilson. My very grateful thanks go to Mrs. Pat Brooksbank and Mrs. Pauline Taylor who typed the manuscript.

Finally, my husband, Edwin Wolff with seven years of war experience helped me with military terminology, accompanied me on journeys around the Belgian and French trench sites, and took numerous photographs. I owe him a great deal of gratitude.

There still remains controversy about the numbers of casualties incurred by Allied and German forces in the First World War, therefore most of the figures mentioned are approximate. Throughout the book I have kept to the use of surnames, as that form of address, except for intimate friends was normal for the period.

MAPS

CONTENTS

FOREWORD

Lieutenant General Sir Napier Crookenden, KCB, DSO, OBE, DL.
Colonel of the 22nd (Cheshire) Regiment 1969 to 1971

Books on the Great War stream from the presses and will continue to do so for centuries to come — just as works of antiquity are published every year. Yet this book of Anne Wolff's gives so vivid a picture of life in the Ypres Salient during 1915 and in the Somme Battle of 1916, that it holds the attention and stirs emotions, as few other books do.

The letters and diaries of her Father, Tom Heald, and two other young officers in a Territorial Battalion of the Cheshire Regiment, Adrian Hodgkin and George McGowan, are linked into a coherent narrative by Anne Wolff's detailed research and effective writing. All three men won the Military Cross; all three were quite different in background and character; and happily all three survived their four years in the trenches.

The contrasts with today are striking. The stress, the casualties and the conditions of the Somme, far worse than anything experienced by the British Army in World War II or any subsequent campaign; the harsh but readily accepted discipline, whereby men were sentenced to be shot for desertion or for sleeping on sentry post; the mud, the rats, the corpses — nothing seems to lower their morale for more than a day or two and there is no talk of "counselling" or "psychiatric care for the rest of their lives."

The only real discontent shows, when the battalion are "mucked about" by their commanding officer, a long serving Territorial Officer with some pernickety and annoying ideas on discipline and when, at the end of 1915, this same officer accepts and appears to enjoy their conversion to a Pioneer Battalion. This new rôle was highly unpopular throughout the battalion. Everyone thought that it was very much a down-grading of the battalion's status, although it was in fact an arduous and dangerous job, involving continuous work on trench construction, often in No Man's Land between the two front lines. They remained armed and equipped as infantry and frequently had to fight as such. Yet because each company went into action attached to a different brigade, they never again fought as a battalion.

This is poignant reading for those of us, who served in the resurrected 5th Bn. The Cheshire Regiment in World War II. Here again was a body of splendid Territorial Army volunteers, augmented by some of the best of the 1939-1940 Militia, who by the end of 1940 were one of the best trained and most effective machine gun battalions in the Army and yet were kept in England throughout the War.

There are many highlights in this book. George McGowan described vividly the 30th Division's attack at Montauban on July 1st 1916. As the 90th Brigade's Signals Officer he saw the whole battle. He tells of General Steavenson's frequent presence in the front line — not always said of divisional commanders in that War. He describes the 2nd Royal Scots Fusiliers losing all their company commanders, killed and wounded in the first wave, and pressing on with unaffected fighting spirit.

On that same day, July 1st 1916, the 46th and 56th Divisions took part in the diversionary attack on Gommecourt — and because it was a diversion, little attempt was made to conceal the build up of troops and guns. The 46th Division were held up by uncut wire and suffered terrible losses in front of the enemy's first line and the 56th Division, in which the 5th Cheshire were the infantry pioneer battalion, got right through to the enemy's reserve positions, only to be hurled back to their start line by massive German counter-attacks.

Tom Heald was taken ill with a high fever a week before the battle, luckily for him, although he was clearly distressed at "missing the show". Anne Wolff herself describes graphically the desperate nature of the fighting and the part played by the 5 Cheshire companies; each of them attached to an assault brigade; all of them heavily engaged in bitter, close-range fighting; and yet none of them mentioned as a battalion or even as a company in the history books.

Tom Heald was back with his battalion in time to see the misuse of the "land cruisers," as they called the first tanks, at Bourlon Wood in September 1916, when the 56th Division were allotted six tanks, all of which broke down. A year later he was lucky enough to watch the near triumph of the Cambrai tank attack — and there are many other fascinating accounts of the battalion's part in furious battle or heavy continuous work on the trenches in mud, rain and shell fire.

It was not all mud and blood, however, and there are vivid scenes from their life behind the lines, in billets, in those longed for showers, in hospital, at the base camps, and on leave in London. There they watched and sighed over Moira Mannering and Haidee De Rance, laughed at Leslie Henson and George Grossmith, took Turkish Baths and forgot their imminent return to the trenches. The whole book gives a very real picture of what it was like to be subaltern in a foot regiment in that Great War.

For the Cheshire Regiment, the old 22nd Foot, this is an invaluable addition to our three hundred years of uninterrupted history; and for everyone it is a reminder of the sort of men our fathers were.

INTRODUCTION

When my father, T.L.C. Heald, died in 1980 aged ninety-one, I found in the attic a shabby black case fastened with rusty clasps and formerly used for holding old 'seventy eight' gramophone records. Attached to the handle was an old luggage label yellowing with age on which was written simply 'My War'. Inside, there were a number of small khaki cloth bound notebooks with squared paper, containing an almost daily account of his experiences at the Western Front from February 1915 until early 1919.

In later years my father hardly mentioned the war, and I always felt that he had tried to bury the remembrances of it in the unconscious as being too painful to recall. For a long time afterwards he suffered recurring bouts of 'trench fever' and endured vivid nightmares. These nightmares were to return in full at the outbreak of the second world war in 1939, after he had raised and was commanding the 6th Battalion of the Manchester Regiment (T.F.) His diary entries, factual and at times laconic, only occasionally betrayed his deep feelings. Throughout his long life he was a first class games player, and therefore was an obvious choice as a 'grenadier' or 'bombing officer'. He recorded on June 4: 'Had a good day's sniping'; he became an expert at lobbing grenades and firing trench mortars on target. As the war drew to its weary close, like many others his mood became deeply depressed. On August 16, 1918 he wrote: 'My birthday. I am 29. Good heavens nearly thirty and no prospects and no wife. The longer this war goes on the worse it will be for me. What chance has a man of thirty, untrained in business, of getting work at a decent rate of pay when the war is over'.

A.E. Hodgkin, whose diaries were illustrated with fine pencil sketches was quick to see both the amusing and absurd side of army life. Only recently having left Oxford, his accounts were detailed and punctuated with dry humour, they included battalion orders and states of affairs regarding the enemy lined up on the opposing side. Hodgkin also commenced his diaries when the 1/5th Battalion of the Cheshires crossed to France in February 1915 to join the 5th Division. Hodgkin was wounded in the back by shrapnel on the evening of July 19, 1915 and was invalided to England. After five months he resumed active service but did not participate again in trench warfare. The concluding entry of the fifth volume of his experiences reads:

> I have kept this Diary throughout with a fixed purpose: to wit, that my son, if I am lucky enough to have one, may read it, that he may have some idea of the nature of a Great War such as this, and that he may know to what he is about to commit himself when his turn comes to serve the King.

Both my father and Adrian Hodgkin were outspoken about the C.O., Lt. Col. J.E.G. Groves who had commanded the battalion since before August 1914. Born in 1863, Groves was fifty one at the outbreak of war, an age when it would be hard for a man to endure the strains and hardship of trench life for lengthy periods. A generous contributor to the regiment in the old volunteer days of the previous century, he had been appointed Chairman and Managing Director of the prosperous family brewing company of Groves and Whitnall in October 1914. A father of seven children when war broke out, he found that he had under his command not merely officers from a tight local circle of the chosen Cheshire few, but a mixed bunch of youthful civilians who had joined the Territorials, motivated by duty and patriotism, but who did not hesitate to comment on anything they thought stupid or a waste of time. There could be no doubt that the extreme privation, shellfire and the endless fatigue to which they were immediately subjected only served to accentuate the tensions. In trench conditions age mattered more for regimental officers than for other categories. In 1917 an order was issued that no one over the age of thirty five should be given command of a battalion, but after the peace, fifty six again became the limit.

Deeply religious, conscientious and of a serious turn of mind, G.M. McGowan in apprehensive mood also embarked with the battalion in February 1915. Before war broke out he had been an apprentice with Siemens in Manchester and wrote of his experiences in long and frequent letters home to his father and stepmother at their home in Altrincham near Manchester. As he regarded these missives in the nature of narrative diaries, he requested his parents to safeguard them, and not to divulge their content to anyone. McGowan came to prefer the laborious work of trench construction to garrisoning the front line, and it became obvious that Groves, formerly educated as an architect, whom McGowan described as 'a bit of an engineer himself' was in sympathy with that view. At the end of 1915, the 1/5th Cheshires was turned into a 'Pioneer Battalion', a move that was extremely unpopular with all ranks.

Much has been written about 1916 and the catastrophic battles of the Somme. There are far fewer accounts of 1915, a disastrous year which saw the dissipation of the original Territorial Force. By July 1916 there remained only about one quarter of these men in any given battalion. In a spirit of cameraderie these volunteers, friends from the same area, had joined the Territorial Army in or before 1914. Before they were adequately trained, they were flung into the trenches to fill the breach caused by the casualties of the previous year.

An introductory note to the War Office Manual of 1913 stated that the plain of Flanders consisted almost entirely of low lying meadow. From October 25, 1914 to March 10, 1915, there were only eighteen days without rain and on eleven of these the temperature was below freezing. During that winter, the clay subsoil held the water two feet below the surface, so that the trenches were nothing more than ditches following the original field drain system of the countryside. In these conditions, it was virtually impossible to excavate more than eighteen inches without coming to water.

Living outside in these conditions, many personal accounts reveal a sense of euphoria. Harold Dearden, a Captain in the R.A.M.C. wrote in his diary: 'Mud is simply everywhere, we laugh at the feeblest jokes, drink out of mugs of whisky and chlorinated water which has a subtle taste of death in it and smoke incessantly, yet it's a fascinating life and I am very happy here; I frankly can't imagine how or why'. And Lionel Crouch, killed in July 1916 on the Somme while serving with the Oxford and Buckinghamshire Light Infantry wrote home: 'Personally I like the trenches, there is always something doing', even though he had described conditions there as being knee deep, sometimes waist high in liquid mud with dead bodies lightly buried underneath. Euphoria however, alternated rapidly with depression caused by utter exhaustion, and no chance to change verminous clothes or even to wash, the never ending discomfort of little sleep and with no major victory in sight to uplift the heart.

Rumours abounded, as men usually had localised knowledge only of their own small section. Letters home often requested news of the general state of the campaign. Harold Dearden wrote: 'For of the war itself, of its subtle momentous phases, I knew literally nothing'.

As private diaries were expressly forbidden, there is no doubt that those who disobeyed that rule left behind much that was poignant and valuable. Often written by candlelight, the keeping of any kind of daily account required much will power. For posterity the Official War Diary provided only the barest facts, sometimes it was compiled days later, and often when the confusion of battle reached its crescendo, there were few left to tell the tale.

When they left England with the Battalion in 1915, my father (Tom Heald), Adrian Hodgkin and George McGowan had been posted to different companies. My father was in 'B' Company, McGowan in 'C' Company and Hodgkin in 'D' Company. Nevertheless the dovetailed accounts provide a composite picture of trench warfare in 1915, a calamitous year, when over two hundred and eighty-five thousand men (not including the sick and wounded) were killed. In the year following, Heald and McGowan endured some of the worst fighting of the Somme battles. By some inexplicable fate all three officers survived, all three were awarded the Military Cross and two were twice mentioned in despatches, my father being one of these.

The climate of opinion has radically changed in seventy years. What was acceptable then is no longer tolerated. The reverse also applies; many of today's attitudes would not have been acceptable seventy years ago, and subjective judgements made with the benefit of hindsight on the attitudes of our predecessors must be discounted as being merely superficial.

War, above all is a matter of chance.

CHAPTER 1

PRELIMINARIES

In January 1915, the 1/5th Battalion of the Cheshire Regiment (T.F.) was stationed in Cambridge and under orders to proceed overseas. Battalion Headquarters was in Magdalene College and the rest were billeted at Chesterton.

2nd Lieutenant G.M. McGowan found himself sharing a room with 2nd Lieutenant P.B. Bass, whom he said was of the Bass Brewery family.[1] The latter had volunteered for the Territorials while still an undergraduate at Oxford and had been at camp at Aberystwyth with McGowan on December 12th 1914. It seemed that the complement of officers had not been totally finalised and one vacancy remained to accompany the battalion to Flanders. McGowan, Bass and 2nd Lieutenant A.H. Joliffe from Chester all volunteered and after a stiff medical McGowan was selected. McGowan was relieved that Bass, whom he thought intelligent and highly strung, had not been chosen immediately for active service, and he therefore urged Bass to apply for a transfer to the Intelligence Service. One day before they were due to leave, Bass accompanied McGowan to do some last minute shopping when they happened to encounter an old friend of McGowan's a fully fledged lieutenant in the R.F.A. Looking at McGowan's badges, his friend said in jest: 'Poor bloody infantry I see, I give you three months'. At this, Bass was horrified and nearly wept. Later McGowan wrote: 'Poor Bass followed me out to France about three months later, he was killed by a stray bullet, what a wasted life'. (Philip Bass rejoined the battalion on May 5th and was killed in a German trench in the attack at Gommecourt on July 1st, 1916).

Bound for France the battalion left Cambridge on February 14th. It was bitterly cold. At the station the men were divided into three trains which departed at times varying from 5 a.m. to 9.30 a.m. Lieutenant A.E. Hodgkin noting wryly that there was a certain amount of confusion over the arrangements, as his company, was detailed to travel by each train and that even the platoons became divided.

Arriving at Southampton, the troops embarked for Le Havre in three awaiting ships. Hodgkin found himself on *S.S. Oxonian* which he reckoned was a good omen. The others were in the *Manchester Importer* and the *Glenarm Head* which 2nd Lieutenant T.L.C. Heald described as 'an old tramp with its head line at Belfast'. As everywhere was shrouded in darkness and there was nothing to indicate where they were, the officers ran a sweepstake on the likely port of disembarkation and Le Havre won. Heading

---

[1] Philip Burnet Bass, son of Col. P. de S. Bass of Ealing, London.

for the French coast in convoy escorted by destroyers the crossing was moderately rough. Heald thankful not to be ill on the *Glenarm Head* even managed to get some sleep on a sofa in the captain's cabin. Fearful of his responsibilities as a raw and unsophisticated junior officer, McGowan owned that he was nervous, but his depression was forgotton with the bustle of their arrival at Le Havre. In February 1915, the main points of entry into France and Flanders were Le Havre and Rouen. Boulogne was used for individual passengers, mail, ammunition and the wounded. Neither Dunkirk nor Calais at that time were generally made available to the British, although arrangements were made to use Calais in about the middle of June that year.

In the extreme cold, the battalion disembarked and proceeded by companies to a large rest camp two or three miles away on the heights above the town. There, in a freezing wind under canvas the men spent an unforgettable first night on foreign soil, as owing to the non-arrival of the transports they had no kits to comfort them. On the following day the transport eventually arrived having negotiated the steep hill to the camp in wet and muddy conditions.

Although there were motorised vehicles in 1915 the Army depended heavily on mules and horses; many of these unfortunate animals were to perish hideously along with the men they served so well. On February 14th the 1/5th Cheshires transport establishment contained thirteen riding horses, twenty-six draught horses, eight heavy draught horses and nine pack animals. In addition, the battalion had been issued with a complete new set of transport vehicles which included three limbered wagons, four general service wagons, six small ammunition cars, three cooks general wagons, two water carts and one Maltese cart (a small two-wheeled vehicle drawn by a pony and used for general purposes). There were also nine bicycles.

During the next two days, as some protection against the cold, all ranks were given goatskin jerkins. Of a type issued in the first winter of the war, these garments rather resembled those worn in the Arctic Circle. They were bulky, very hairy, and caused considerable amusement even though they added to the weight already carried by each man. Taking the opportunity on his second night in camp Hodgkin went to have a last civilised meal at the Hotel Moderne before marching to the station on the following day. A bleak journey lay ahead. On February 17th at about 4.30 p.m. a French troop train largely composed of cattle trucks each carrying about thirty-eight to forty men transported the Cheshires to Bailleul, at that time in the war a pleasant enough little market town. Clustered around the old gothic church and tall belfry, the attractive houses and shops with characteristic long pointed gables displayed a variety of lace for which the place was famed. Le Havre to Bailleul by troop train took over twenty four hours via Rouen, Boulogne, Calais and St. Omer, the men mostly being without any kind of food or drink.

But Hodgkin happened to spy the C.O. getting out at St Omer. for a drink and was left behind, an incident which he described: 'Had all the elements of humour and none of vulgarity'.

Tired, stiff and dirty the battalion marched up the main street of Bailleul to find that their billets were allocated in the most gigantic series of greenhouses. It was dark and cold on arrival, Captain N.B. Ellington of 'D' Company with several of the men fell over the shallow walls situated in the middle of their greenhouse. Luckily no damage occurred, especially as there was a rumour that the inside walls had been poisoned by the Germans and on inspection it was found that most of the vines were dead. In the previous September the British had devoured most of the grapes and in consequence the claim on the British Government was for £40,000. As McGowan said: 'This gives an idea of the size of the vinery'.

Only cold supper was served in the dark that night, but on the following morning Heald managed a hot breakfast at the local inn. It poured incessantly and to aggravate matters when the battalion marched to the village of Neuve Eglise nearby to join the 14th Brigade of the 5th Division, around 5.30 p.m. they took the wrong road which delayed their arrival:

> All that had been said about Flanders, mud and rain is perfectly true.
> The roads are horrible, paved in the middle and all worn into holes and
> soft at the sides with ruts eighteen inches deep. En route was passed
> some of our 1st Battn. and a lot of our 6th, the latter have just had nine
> days in the trenches. They have had about three months out here and
> have only had twelve killed, about thirty-five wounded but about three
> hundred sick from exposure.
>
> (Hodgkin, February 19th)

The 1st Battalion had been at the front since August 16th, 1914 while the 6th arrived in November, and had been frequently up to their thighs in mud and water. A list of casualties published on December 12th, named nineteen suffering from frostbite. Standing in the cold and wet, the feet swelled and went dead, then started to burn. In serious cases when the limbs became black and rotted, amputation was necessary.

Arriving in the dark, once more confusion arose about their billets in Neuve Eglise. Presumably any habitations still standing were in short supply as two platoons were crammed into one farmhouse. Formerly occupied by the Germans, the village was a dangerous place attracting a good deal of fire, though the rather unattractive dark red angular church was still intact. This was odd as the Germans often used the churches prominent on high ground as a target for their guns:

Subalterns of the Foot

The village church at Neuve Eglise in May 1986

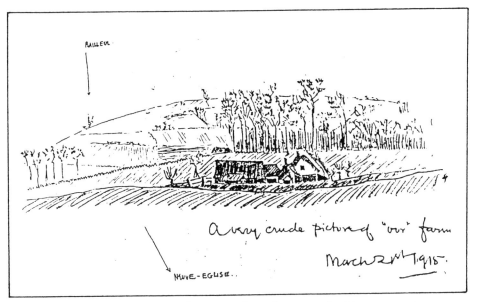

A very crude picture of "our" farm
March 2nd 1915.

Our landlady was robbed of a cart and two horses and a big wagon when the Germans were here; true, they gave her vouchers but they will not be much good I fear. The English came in at one end, and the Germans went out at the other and her wagons were used as barricades and suffered accordingly. The E. Surreys most kindly provided us with rattling good soup tonight, so we go to bed warm but still very damp. The next day was spent in censoring the men's letters of which they write hundreds; they tell the most frightful lies: 'this I write in the trenches and the paper is quivering like a jelly in my hand, there is not a window in this town unbroken'. Generally speaking they appear very cheerful.

(Hodgkin, February 19th, 20th).

Censorship was operated on a unit basis, one or more officers, usually subalterns, being detailed to scrutinise the daily letters sent home by the other ranks before the mail was taken to the Field Post Office. In March 1915 these highly unpopular measures were gradually changed, and green envelopes were introduced for private correspondence. The writer had merely to sign a certificate on the envelope stating that the contents referred only to private and family matters.

It was not an agreeable sector in which to be. The whole sodden countryside had become a wasteland, pounded and remorselessly destroyed by war at a time when the Somme area was almost untouched by shells.

During the first nine months of war in the inundated area along the Ijzer alone some one hundred and twenty thousand corpses lay submerged, unburied, lying for weeks between the trenches. After the saturating winter rain, the trenches badly positioned and in deplorable order were overseen by the enemy who had dug themselves into superior positions on the upper slopes of the 60 foot high Messines Ridge after the first battle of Ypres in 1914. The small river Douve (a tributary of the Lys) no more than a muddy stream ran roughly parallel to the ridge turning the surrounding terrain in the bottom into a soggy marsh.

No time was lost in plunging the battalion into its baptism of fire. Heald with 'B' Company was detailed to dig trenches on the second night of arrival when he was nearly hit by a sniper. So early in the war there was no 'bull ring' such as on the plain outside Harfleur or at Etaples where newly arrived drafts were 'put through it' drilled in their hundreds on the dunes and given technical instruction in a model system of trenches. Territorial battalions such as the 1/5th Cheshires received little if any lessons in England in the use of the 'make do' trench mortars, and hand grenades. Lance Corporal Henry Thomas Bolton of the 1st Battalion E. Surreys who had disembarked in Rouen on February 20th had never had training with a pack or even equipment.[1] In the trenches, ammunition was so short in early 1915 that old tobacco and jam tins inserted with a no. 8 detonator, a short length of fuze, were filled with miscellaneous metal, old nails, bits of iron, and shredded gun cotton were sealed up with clay, lit with a match, pipe or cigarette and lobbed over into the enemy lines. Financial parsimony and general unreadiness had prevented the expeditionary force being properly equipped. The early spring and summer of 1915 when the best trained officers had almost ceased to exist and the Territorial soldiers only starting to arrive was probably the most dangerous time of the war.[2]

On February 21st Hodgkin, two N.C.O.'s and four men were sent down to the 17th Field Coy. Royal Engineers for instruction:

> Sunday and a very odd one... It was most exciting and more like a
> glorified fifth of November than anything else. The trench mortar
> consists of a section of ordinary pipe about 2'6" long blocked up at one
> end with a touch hole in the manner of the old muzzle loaders. A large
> canister of gun cotton with suitable detonators and so forth is dropped
> into the gun and then fired with a small charge of black powder. The
> canister hurtles through the air, drops to the ground and then goes off
> with a fearful bang, the time required being dependent on the length of

---

[1]*MS. Diaries of Lance Corporal H.T. Bolton, Imperial War Museum.*
[2]*Military Operations*, 1918, p. 592.

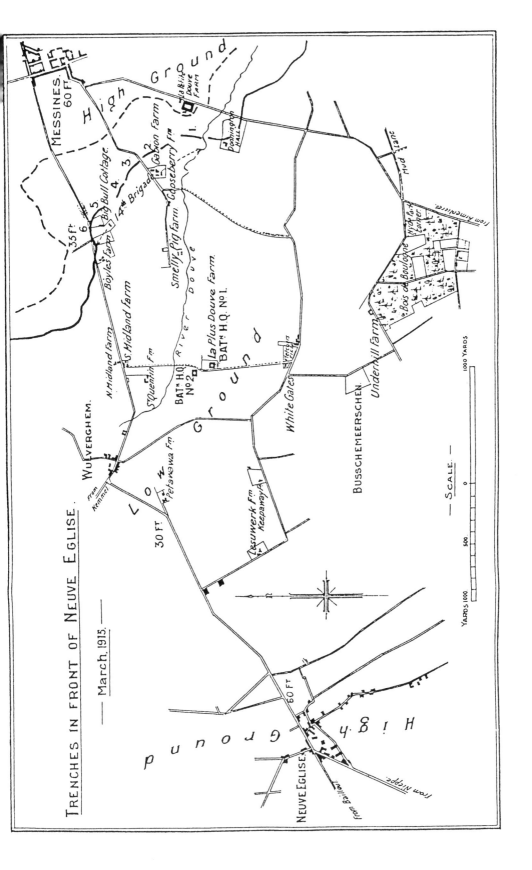

TRENCHES IN FRONT OF NEUVE EGLISE.

— March, 1915. —

MESSINES. 60 FT.

High Ground

La Petite Douve Farm

Gabion Farm

Gooseberry Fm.

Donington Hall

Big Bull Cottage.

14th Brigade

Boyles Farm.

35 FT.

Smelly Pig Farm

S. Midland Farm

N. Midland Farm

St. Quentin Fm.

River Douve

La Plus Douve Farm
BAT^N H.Q. N^O 1.

BAT^N H.Q.
N^O 2.

Low Ground

WULVERGHEM.

From Kemmel.

30 FT.

Petawawa Fm.

Esuwerk Fm.
Keepaway Ft.

White Gates.

BUSSCHEMEERSCHEN.

Underhill Farm.

Bois de Boulogne

from Armentières

Mud Lane

High Ground

60 FT.

NEUVE EGLISE.

from Nieppe.

from Bailleul.

SCALE.

YARDS 1000   500   0   100 YARDS

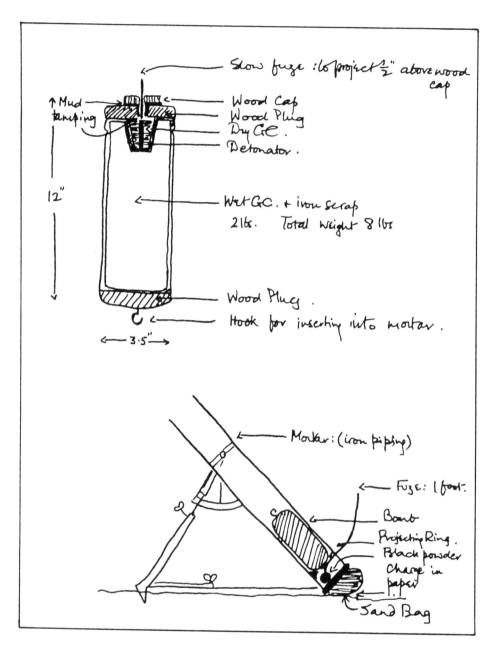

Trench Mortar.

fuse attached. It blows a hole in the ground about 4ft across by 1ft deep. The extreme range is about 250 yds. and of course the accuracy is very low. However, I'd rather not be near one when it bursts. The hand grenade is great fun: the pictures of it in the official books explain it sufficiently. The great point is to avoid hitting the back of the trench with it as you throw it. If this happens you will be unable to relate your experience to your friends. 30–40 yds. is a very good throw. There was a voluntary Church Parade today. In the afternoon the Brigadier inspected our billets and seemed very pleased at what he saw. Later I and Ellington went for a short stroll and saw the Germans fire no less than 63 shells at one of our aeroplanes. It was not hit. The effect of the burst and then of the setting sun on the smoke-puffs was quite beautiful.

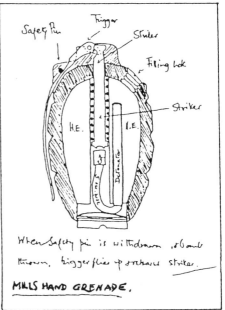

(Hodgkin, February 21st)

In the dusk of February 22nd, accompanied by a noise resembling a shaking blanket from one of the German guns, Hodgkin with his Company Commander Captain G.W.C. Hartley were guided for a pow-wow to the headquarters of the Duke of Cornwall's Light Infantry at 4.30 p.m. The Battalion H.Q. mess in the firing line was located close to the muddy river at a little farm called La Plus Douve. Acting as a target, the farm was frequently shelled, but the splinters did not do much damage as the shells usually landed on the roof where they were cushioned by a large stock of grain. Having waded through the appalling slush, Hartley and Hodgkin found their C.O. in the act of 'taking over' from the C.O. of the 1st Battalion East Surrey Regiment units of which were to take them up for instruction to the fire trenches:

This ceremony having concluded with a libation of rum & hot water I was detailed, with my C.S.M. Sweeney & Sgt. Cross to go with D. Coy. & Hartley & his NCO's with C. Coy. D. Coy is at present commanded

9

by a Lieut. Beren. He slowly managed to disentangle his company from the seething mob of all sorts & conditions of men struggling outside the farm & we struck across country for our section, No. 1, of the fire trench. On our way thither I tried hard to analyse my feelings on first coming under fire, but without much success. There was a sniper enjoying himself on our left, apparently loosing off shoots in the distance on the off chance of bagging something: either he or some other one got a Sgt. later on, shot through the side & rather badly hurt. There was a brilliant moon. I don't think I was exactly scared by these tactics, but I must admit that I saw no reason why he should not turn his attention in our direction. The trenches in this part of the line are not trenches at all, but are built up of sandbags: the reason for this is that the ground is too water-logged to dig into. At one particular point, where I am writing this, the Germans are precisely 130 yds. away, so that one has to be careful when relieving the men in the trenches. Beren said that he never could understand why they did not turn a machine gun on to the relieving force; in such a case of course we should be wiped out en block. My bivouac was 5ft. by 4ft. by about 3ft. high & was very comfortable, besides being waterproof. The German rifles make a much sharper noise than our own, & sound horribly businesslike. The next day was spent mostly in the bivouac listening to the trench just behind us being shelled with high explosive. This kind gives me no time to think; the rushing noise is almost simultaneous with the burst, 8 casualties was the result. In my trench nothing much occurred & I left about 7.30 p.m. & went back to Neuve-Eglise. I was not sorry to get back!.

(Hodgkin, February 23rd)

In addition to occupying higher ground the German fire trenches were very narrow and as deep as possible. Often their sandbags were particoloured to make it more difficult to spot the loopholes. Shellfire was not something to which they ever became accustomed; after five months of trench warfare, Heald wrote:

Shellfire has a very peculiar effect on one. No one seems immune either. It, at first makes one tremble so that it is an awful job to keep one's hand still. It is quite alright if one has something to do. You don't notice it if you have not time to think. The great thing is to keep a real grip on yourself and not to give way to it. If you do you are hopeless. Today's shelling lasted from 5 a.m. to 6.30 a.m. and we got a shell a minute during that time. We had two short spells later. The shells were dropping on the support trench and Grenadier quarters. I believe in staying inside the dugout, because it is the splinters that do the harm

10

and you are alright if the shell does not pick on the dugout. The tendency is however to run out and move further up the trench and it requires a good deal of self control to stay in, but it seems to me that they might easily shift their line of fire and then you would get caught in a crowd. I think it must be the bang that upsets one's moral equilibrium.

(Heald, July 19th)

Robert Graves's view was that having been in the trenches five months he had passed his prime, and that an officer's usefulness gradually declined as neurasthenia set in, unless he had been given a few weeks rest in a technical camp or in hospital.[1]

Having the advantage of both guns and ammunition, the Germans firing over the Douve valley from the Messines Ridge could inflict such damage as they felt inclined upon their enemy who had little of either billetted in Neuve Eglise:

Apparently Thursday is the regular day for a bombardment of this place: anyway it came off all right & we had four men wounded in 'D' coy. one seriously. Our 2 majors nearly got blown up also. The roof of the baths was damaged, & for an hour or two things were rather lively. The shells were of large calibre sent up huge fountains of earth on explosion. The market square, about 200 yds. from this house is the chief 'theatre of operations'. It is also where our Brigadier lives; perhaps that accounts for it. I am due to take 2 platoons out tonight to dig support trenches.

(Hodgkin, February 25th)

After marching about three miles from the village with his working party, Hodgkin arrived at 7.30 p.m. at La Plus Douve Farm. They worked on No. 6 & 7 support trenches, low breastwork till 11.30 p.m. The way out from the farm to the trenches was mostly along a 'corduroy' road made up of sections of logs laid across and very uncomfortable to walk on. They got back very tired at 1.30 a.m and covered all over with mud of the very highest quality, the snipers were busy as always:

I had a look at the damage done by those shells yesterday, & found one unexploded in a field 6" × 2'6" long about. They say the Germans are being supplied with very poor ammunition just now. It certainly looks like it, as the shells which hurt our men also did not explode: the fuze & the stones thrown up on impact did all the damage.

---

[1]R. Graves, *Goodbye to All That*, p. 143.

The roof of the baths had every tile blown off, & the interior of the building was completely wrecked: an officer who was bathing at the time must have had the time of his life: his particular tub escaped damage but was filled with rubbish of all kinds. There is a gigantic hole in the square; this was the shell that nearly did for our Majors.

(Hodgkin, February 26th)

Bombardment with high explosives destroyed more houses on the following day, killing eight and wounding twelve of the East Surreys. One man had his head blown off and another his leg, their injuries were terrible and made every onlooker feel physically sick, hoping against hope they would never see the like again...

In the evening by way of contrast, the C.O., C. Johnson, Dixon and I played centime nap with the gratifying result that I won 3 fr.50. By the by, about 8 of the German shells failed to explode again. I forgot to mention that yesterday I met one Cope, a subaltern of the Devons (1st Battalion Devonshire Regiment), with whom I had been at Repton. He is heartily sick of it all.

(Hodgkin, February 27th)[1]

Two days later, it was Heald's turn to go up to the trenches. It was very cold that night and he considered them very poorly made. Previously McGowan had taken the opportunity of writing home by the light of a bright frosty moon. He had assembled in the village at Brigade Headquarters with four officers and eight N.C.O's plus seven students from the Artists Rifles (28th Bn. the London Regt.) stationed about six miles away who were undergoing a kind of O.T.C. training. Split up into two batches by an officer of the Brigade Staff they marched off with a water cart and supplies. Like the others they tramped through the muddy lanes past the ruined houses and farm buildings to the advanced H.Q. of the battalion. Divided further into three smaller groups they were then guided through the water logged field across the path of wood logs immediately behind the trenches:

As we approached we heard rifle fire, and had several times to stand rigid while a 'Very' light (sent from our own or the enemy's trenches) burnt out. Our guide informed us that if any shots did come past us we should dive to right or left for being a bright night the enemy's snipers might have this path under fire lengthways, in the hope of catching ration parties.

[1] Hodgkin's friend, Arthur Cope, had been at Repton School from 1906–10. Although wounded he survived the war, becoming an acting Lieutenant Colonel in 1918 and was awarded the D.S.O.

Preliminaries

We reached No. 3 trench first and here I reported myself and party to the Captain commanding the Coy. He kept my N.C.O. and student in his trench, and sent me under guidance of his Sgt. Major to Mr. S, the subaltern in charge of the platoon occupying No. 4 trench, some 50 yards to the left of No. 3. Mr. S. greeted me in a most friendly way, and we were soon chatting in front of a charcoal fire in a brazier outside his dug-out, after which I walked with him to note all points particularly his machine-gun emplacements. The trench was about 60 yards in length with about half-a-dozen traverses (built this way to curtail damage from enfilade fire) and is roughly 3'6" deep with sandbags placed on the parapet to provide a bullet-proof rest for the rifles. So many men and an N.C.O to each traverse. When obtainable, boards and boxes are placed on the ground to provide dry standing. Immediately behind the fire trench there are little dug-outs, or rain proof shelters for men to lie down in when not standing to arms. They are only about 18 inches high so are essentially just for lying. Latrine pails are placed by these dug-outs and these only must be used so sanitation is pretty fair. We next went to visit the "listening post" — two men 50 to 100 yards to the flank, and in front of the trench. They dig themselves in with their hand entrenching tool, and remain there until relieved to watch that no enemy makes towards our trenches undetected. This done we again sat down by the fire. What with the fire from our artillery guns behind us, occasional rifle shots, and the "Very" light it was like a glorified 5th of November. By the way "Very" lights are a sort of Roman Candle or sky rocket fired from a pistol to light the ground between the trenches when searching for "listening posts" or patrols. A fatigue party has just arrived with a supply of sandbags and men have been detailed to fill them. This provokes some "grousing", though it is really a fine job to keep them warm. The enemy's snipers can see nothing at night, and there is plenty of walking about behind the trenches as it is long odds against getting hit by a stray bullet. Mr. S. had just returned from a visit to the support trench behind and reports that the rations are on their way.

The rations arrived — hot tea, biscuits, tins of "Machonichee", cheese, bacon, cigarettes, matches for the men, some bread for the sergeant and a newspaper sent by a pal of his from the reserve coy. at Hd. Qrs. These have to last 24 hours. Shortly after an orderly came along with the officers' dinner including a share for me. Hot stew and hot cocoa carried in a hand hot water oven, also a packet of sandwiches each. The meal went down well, and after it, I crawled into S's dugout. (a comfortable shelter 6ft. by 4ft. and 2ft. high) lit my pipe, glanced at a current number of *Punch* and fell asleep, after hearing an orderly arrive with hot

13

tea for the men. They are well looked after by night, as no-one can come near by day. S. had gone over to No. 3 to have a conference with his captain. I was woken at 4.00 a.m., as an orderly arrived with our breakfast — hot porridge, and hot cocoa with more sandwiches. Just two nicely served meals each 24 hours. More hot tea arrived for the troops.

Just before dawn the "listening posts" are withdrawn, and the men ordered to unfix bayonets and clean rifles. After a brief walk around S. retires to his dugout, leaving his sergeant in charge. It is now quite light and essential to keep heads down below the parapet, for the German snipers are expert shots. I tried out my periscope and find it works well.

At noon word comes from No. 3 for all men to stand-to-arms, and extra ammunition is distributed. This means an attack is possible but nothing further happens except for some heavy rifle fire on our left, and considerable artillery fire overhead, mostly from our guns firing behind the enemy's front line. I could see shrapnel shells bursting in the air, and lyddite shells breaking off the tops of trees. You cannot actually see the shells because of their speed, but follow them by sound.

5.00 p.m. Well I'm waiting for darkness to set in and an orderly to arrive to guide me back to our village. Although it has been a most interesting 24 hours I shall be glad to get back to our billets and shall not be pining for the time when we take our turn in manning the trenches, but the job is not as bad as I expected now the trenches have been improved. Four days in and four days out is the usual duty.

(McGowan, February 26th)

Once it was realised that the armies were digging for seige warfare, periscopes of all shapes and sizes were showered on the men by concerned relations and friends. But according to a prisoner taken from the 8th Bavarian Reserve Regiment (opposing the 14th Brigade) those Germans had never heard of a periscope. After the first battle of Ypres, the prisoner informed them that their regiment had remained at Wytschaete while receiving a lot of new drafts. The last levy came from the Landwehr Ersatz Reserve recruits of the 1915 class, who were apt to shoot wildly and suffered from frost bitten feet, rheumatism and sickness. Their regiment did not have cooked meals brought up to them, as the field cookers never came nearer than Oosttaverne and Messines village on the ridge; but their rations were plentiful, having their own coffee and bacon cooked in the trenches accompanied by the customary brown rye bread.

Their boots were good and clogs were issued to put over them as protection. Each company always manned the same trench which was connected by telephone both to the headquarters and to the one next door, all their trenches were shockingly wet and required continuous baling out. The hard work of trench digging and drainage was carried out by pioneers who constructed also the thick barbed wire stake entanglements four or five rows deep. At dusk, each company sent two men to crawl just outside the barbed wire to act as a listening patrol. This wasn't considered especially dangerous, as in any case they were relieved hourly. No regular system of sniping was in vogue, the sights of the rifles, fired through loopholes of steel plates or wooden box pattern, were always aligned on the top of the opposite parapet. Their men fired only when ordered to, when they could really hear or see something, and not as often as the British. Although the prisoner's company had had no machine guns since the fighting in Metz in August, other companies usually had one or two in the trenches, well dug in and with good cover. Generally they employed the Belgians to mend the road, but did not let them work in or anywhere near the trenches. The Germans had commandeered all the Belgian cattle and foodstuffs, but the prisoner had not heard of any sequestration of copper or brass articles which it was rumoured that the Germans had looted from the Belgian churches.[1] They had heard nothing of the naval battles in the North Sea. On February 23rd life was no more palatable to this informative soldier than to the British. He said that several others would probably surrender too, but for the fact they had all been warned that the British shot all single prisoners captured.

By the end of February 1915, the High Command had despatched as many as forty-eight Territorial battalions to reinforce the British sector of the Western Front. This was in spite of the fact that many of these civilian soldiers lacked proper skills and were very short of weapons and ammunition. In the House of Commons on December 21st, 1914, there was dismay when Lloyd George stated: 'What we stint in material, we squander in life; that is the one great lesson in munitions'. Captain H. Fitzherbert Wright, R.F.A., Member of Parliament for Leominster, when serving at the Front in 1915, with the 4th Midland (Howitzer) Brigade wrote to Lloyd George on May 29th, 1915: 'We are starved to death for want of shells, we are outclassed in guns, number and quality... having little or no ammunition. In our division there are two machine guns per battalion, the Germans have sixteen. Our hand grenades hand made, and truly "hand"'.[2] In 1914 the British unprepared for a war of such magnitude had only four heavy guns per

---

[1] It was reported in the British Press that the Germans had collected Belgian brass and copper kitchen utensils and had removed the brass doors of Antwerp railway station. *Illustrated War News*, Vol. II, part 31, p .28
[2] *War Memoirs of David Lloyd George.* Vol. I, p. 210

division, some of which had been almost outdated in South Africa while the German's strength in the field numbered about two thousand heavy pieces giving their one hundred and four divisions nearly twenty heavy guns each.

Following a visit of *The Times* correspondent, Colonel C. à Court Repington, to Sir John French's H.Q. at St. Omer, there was an article published on May 14th about the scarcity of shells. A week later the headlines of the Northcliffe press blazoned: 'The Shells Scandal, Lord Kitchener's Tragic Blunder' in the *Daily Mail*. Public outrage at this criticsm of a national idol was such that copies of the offending *Daily Mail* were ceremonially burnt outside the Stock Exchange.

The first winter of the war proved long and hard, it extended well into March when snow was still falling. Battalion Headquarters was battered with ceaseless streams of orders and miscellaneous information from G.H.Q. Heald kept by him a little brown notebook entitled 'Notes from the Front, collated by the General Staff'; it included a memo from an 'Artillery Officer attached to G.H.Q.':

> The shooting of the German artillery can only be described as "uncanny", parties of troops... have to make constant changes of their position or incur the penalty of having a dozen of the large shells dropped right into them without warning. The German infantry cannot touch ours and their shooting is deplorable. They seem to depend entirely on their machine guns which are the very devil and magnificently handled.

On March 3rd Hodgkin with 2 platoons carried large white floor boards & sheets of corrugated iron up to No. 1 fire trench, 130 yds. from the Germans, in brilliant moonlight:

> This took us a considerable time, as we were fired on to some extent. As on the previous occasion, I was much pleased to find that my feet reached a certain degree of coldness & remain there for an indefinite period without becoming painful: this with Lotus boots fairly big, & one pair of wool socks.

> Nothing could have been quieter than this 24 hours 'fighting': it was only enlivened by the usual snipers, & 'grandma' our new 9.2 gun, which was being fired for the first time dropped colossal shells about 200 yds. in front of our trenches. We came out about 7.00 p.m. on the 2nd, & most of today had been occupied in censoring men's letters. It's odd, but no kind of cigarette is the very least use to them except the famous "Woodbine". The Gov't cigarettes they despise utterly. Tonight

16

Preliminaries

I again go with a working party, beginning at 12.0 midnight. Our precious sleep is sadly curtailed by this war.

The above working party was carried out in a sort of light hail of unaimed rifle fire. One man of the DCLI just in front of us was wounded. We were lucky enough to escape altogether. Got back at 5.30 a.m. & went to bed in broad daylight.

Was awakened by one on our batteries of 4.7 guns firing heavily.[1] Later on the Germans shelled the village & hurt a few more men, besides killing a woman. The main street is full of house wreckage. One has no peace at all in this place: the regulars say they prefer being in the trenches & I almost believe it.

(Hodgkin, March 3rd)

On March 4th a notice appeared in battalion orders that two men of other regiments had been shot for desertion. Hodgkin said it was 'pour encourager les autres' but thought it rather horrible. In January and February that year further soldiers had been executed and it was official policy to publicise widely these events. Although medically, shell shock was starting to be treated in 1915 it was not widely recognised. Furthermore, it was unusual for a man under sentence of death to have a medical report. Citations of cowardice, which were made public on parade caused a great deal of revulsion and resentment among all ranks.

Lance Corporal Bolton wrote that the men were worked so hard that some of them fell asleep on sentry duty:

After this, C and D coys were formed up to listen to 4 court martials of our Regiment. They were all for sleeping at their post. The first to be read out was that of L/Cpl Wilson, one of my old Coy. of Devonport. His crime was not so serious as he was in support at the time he was caught, the others were serious and they were on sentry in the firing line and they were sentenced to death but the sentence was not carried out, the good work of the Regiment saving them.

(Bolton, July 1st)

Some punishments eventually became notorious, on January 25th, 1917 Hodgkin kept a sketch of the so called 'Crucifixion' 'so much talked of in the

---

[1] By 1915 the 4.7 gun on travelling carriage was obsolete, and deemed unreliable. It was kept in use because of munition shortages.

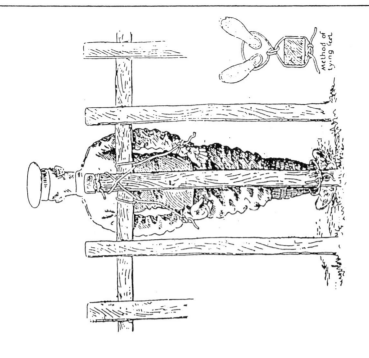

So called "Crucifixion".

Any further communication on this subject should be addressed to:—

The Secretary,
War Office,
London, S.W.,

and the following number quoted

105/Gen. No./2331. (A.G. 3.)

War Office,
London, S.W.

12th January, 1917.

Sir,

I am commanded by the Army Council to inform you that they have had under consideration the question of the method of carrying out Field Punishment No. 1, with special reference to paragraphs 2 (b) and 2 (c) of the Rules for Field Punishment (Manual of Military Law, page 721), and they have decided that, with a view to standardizing the method in accordance with which a soldier may be attached to a fixed object, the following instructions will, in future, be strictly adhered to:—

With reference to paragraph 2 (b), the soldier must be attached so as to be standing firmly on his feet, which if tied, must not be more than twelve inches apart, and it must be possible for him to move each foot at least three inches. If he is tied round the body there must be no restriction of his breathing. If his arms or wrists are tied, there must be six inches of play between them and the fixed object. His arms must hang either by the side of his body or behind his back.

With reference to paragraph 2 (c), irons should be used when available, but straps or ropes may be used in lieu of them when necessary. Any straps or ropes used for this purpose must be of sufficient width that they inflict no bodily harm, and leave no permanent mark on the offender.

An illustration of a method of attachment which complies with these regulations is given overleaf.

I have the honour to be,

Sir,

Your obedient Servant.

R. J. Wade

Daily Press'. As part of Field Punishment No. 1, an army order stated that the feet were not to be tied so tightly that they could not move and that breathing should not be obstructed by the ropes or other means with which they were tied.

Eventually Neuve Eglise became unbearable for its inhabitants and a huge mob of people trekked out from the village. On March 5th Hodgkin, having ventured into the dangerous area to have a bath in a large wooden tub had a lucky escape as two German shells had landed on the double doored brick building which served as the hospital. The latter was completely destroyed and several more were killed and wounded.

> One of our CSMs, Warnock, had a miraculous escape. A shell came in & burst in the same room with him, killing an RAMC Major & wrecking the place, but leaving him only scratched by a nail. A pioneer of D Coy. Daffern, who was in hospital, was badly cut about the face. Bde. H.Q. was damaged & the Brigadier's bedroom demolished. I saw another house vanish completely in a gigantic cloud of brickdust. The Church I believe was also damaged. These shells make a horrible whistling noise while arriving. As usual a larger proportion of them failed to explode, which is very lucky for us.

> While all this was going on, the men were being collected at the prearranged rendezvous in a field, where they proceeded to play football. We came back for lunch only to have to turn out again about teatime. After about an hour or so we came back again. This sort of thing is a great nuisance, but the men seem very cheerful about it all.

> We hear that a 15" gun has arrived & is due to fire at noon tomorrow: in consequence this is to be known as 'Grandma' and the 9.2" is therefore degraded to 'Mother'. the 2.6" guns down the road are 'The Heavenly Twins'.
>
> (Hodgkin, March 5th)

In spite of it all, life was not wholly devoid of humour:

> Tonight the C.O., the Adjutant and Dixon have gone out fearsomely caparaisoned to look for spies in a suspected barn, the mess seems of the opinion that it is a 'Chasse à oise sauvage'. One of our Coy. billets, the "Lion d'Or restaurant" is owned by a very pro-German old man who ridicules the men when they vacate their billets on account of shell fire. He should be locked up. In any case he nearly got a black eye from one

of our sgts today and I hardly wonder at it. *Later,* the spy hunters have returned empty handed.

(Hodgkin, March 5th)

No doubt those at Battalion H.Q. acting on an Army order of Feb. 19th considered it essential that constant vigilance be maintained against the enemy's spies, and the following notice was displayed:

Any stranger, be he an officer, soldier, or civilian, who makes enquiries as to his position, distribution, movement, relief or organisation of the troops, or concerning the site and armament of batteries must be regarded as a suspicious character, and prompt action taken.

The same holds good of suspected communication with the enemy's lines. Any officer or man who observes anything in the nature of signalling must consider it his duty to investigate the matter personally & on the spot. Subsequent reports are of no value.

Where three allied nations are working together in comparative ignorance of each other's language & customs, hostile agents are afforded exceptional chances of acquiring information.

Every person wearing the uniform of a British staff officer, and every officer with a motor car should carry, & is liable to produce on demand, a pass valid only for the current month. Priests, chaplains, gendarmes, & Red Cross assistants have no right to question troops, & by doing so render themselves liable to arrest.

Anyone who permits a suspected person to escape is guilty of Neglect of Duty. This responsibility must be constantly impressed on all members of every unit, especially of Supply Trains, Ammunition Columns & Field Ambulances.

A mistake made through excess of zeal in arresting suspects can do little harm & is quite excusable; an opportunity missed through timidity in taking action is unpardonable, & may endanger the security of the Force. A spy in the hand is worth any number in the bush.

Accurate and heavy German shelling of Neuve Eglise at this stage was so intense that the Cheshires were ordered to evacuate all billets during daylight. Rumour had it that a spy signalled the enemy with the hands of the church clock and accordingly the C.O. once again organised a spy hunt but to no avail. In spite of severely curtailed rest by day, the dark nights were spent in perpetual vigilance against attack and the fortification of their dilapidated waterlogged trenches. While crawling up forward in the bitter cold on March 9th, Heald's platoon came under heavy fire after the enemy had lit up the sky with flares. Luckily there were no casualties, but they had to lie flat in the open with the zip of the bullets sounding in their ears, and then to disperse across the undulating country to avoid the burning haystacks all around them. They were stiff with cold and soaked through.

When the men were forced out of Neuve Eglise on March 7th, Hodgkin felt sure they would have to stay out in the open fields in the rain, but by a brilliant flash of genius he managed to spot a farm which could accommodate the company, and accordingly

Roof of a barn roost at the farm. Note the artistry of the birds!

moved them into it at once. 'Here we found the good people had killed the ancestral pig the previous day so they at once set about cooking us pork chops: this with excellent coffee and bread made us a jolly good lunch'. At midday, regular as clockwork the Germans shelled the town but not much damage was done as a battery of 4.7 guns by La Plus Douve Farm shut them up. The 4.7s on 'Caterpillar Wheels' fairly leapt into the air when they were fired and required a lot of pulley hauling after each shot. Hodgkin then perpetrated a sketch of the farm: The farm hen fascinated him, as also the little man apparently offering it a bun.

On returning to the village after dark the atmosphere was getting jumpy:

> Spy mania is beginning to catch on here: it is rumoured that 10 were caught the day before yesterday; & 2 men with fixed bayonets were seen on the Church Tower, presumably expecting to find the spies on top of the steeple. The C.O. still prowls mysteriously in gum boots o'nights, with Dixon as interpreter. Various dogs are suspected of carrying messages to & fro': one of our sentries suffered a crushing defeat in this connection: a big yellow dog with a clanking chain came along a road in the pitchy darkness: the sentry had had orders to 'coax' any dogs coming along & then search them: this man however tried to coax it with a

21

bayonet, whereupon the dog flew at him & then made off at once, leaving the sentry paralysed with, I presume, fear & mortification.

Same performance was repeated today as yesterday. The pig was not yet all consumed so we dined sumptuously once more. It did not rain much, but was very cold. In the evening I was told to go off to one of those loathsome carrying parties to the fire trenches. The night was as black as pitch, and at the Headquarters farm, confusion & language struggles with each other of supremacy. I never saw such a mix-up in my life. We got back at times varying from 2 a.m. to 8.30. a.m. Gumboots when marched in, make one's feet very sore.

(Hodgkin, March 7th)

The pig lasted them for three days before their next twenty four hour tour of No. 1 trench.

Our guide, a very pronounced Cockney of the E. Surreys kept us waiting for about ½ hour about 50 yds from the trench: this was a most disconcerting performance, as if the enemy had cared to send a few flares we might easily have been spiflicated. When our men were fixed up in their places, I was casually accosted by an officer who had just come in from patrolling out in front of the trench, & had found a German trench mortar bomb. It turned out that it was one Geary with whom I had been at Keble for 3 years. He told me that Hallowes, of the same college, was doctor to the Devons, so that the College is fairly well represented in the Brigade. I shared Geary's dugout with him which was the same as that I occupied on the 23rd, so that there was not much room. The platoon that went into the trench was given a section of its own, & did quite well. The brigade has received orders "to make life hideous to the Germans by day & night". Consequently a terrific fire was opened about 8.00 p.m. while we were still on our way to H.Q. farm. At the same time a field battery opened fire just behind us, & we could see the shell flying through the air all red hot, just like fire flies. Several people disbelieve this statement, but the whole coy saw it, so there can be no mistake. Whether the shell is actually glowing, or whether it is purely an atmospheric affect I do not know. Shortly after a farm caught fire near the battery, probably from burning pieces of wood. It blazed magnificently, & lit up the whole place. But to return to our trench. All was quiet when we arrived & remained so till about midday on the 11th. The Germans then started shelling with shrapnel & high explosive, & 2 of our men got scratched. This was rather unpleasant while it lasted: but at dusk they opened a very rapid fire, to which we replied with gusto, &

for about a quarter of an hour one could not hear oneself speak or think. Nobody was hit at all during this performance, but a vast amount of ammunition was expended. Things quietened down altogether after this, & we were relieved about 10.30 p.m. by the D.C.L.I. The smell of No. 1. trench is perfectly beastly, exactly like a very foul hen run: I had the smell of it still when I got back to billets. I should like all those good people who inveigh against anti-typhoid innoculation in England to spend a week with us. I rather think they would alter their opinions; or die in the attempt. We were all very tired when we got back to billets at 2.00 a.m.

(Hodgkin, March 10th)

After leaving Keble, 2nd Lieutenant Benjamin Geary had been a schoolmaster at the Forest School, Walthamstow. He was also an international Rugby player. Commissioned into the 4th (Extra Reserve) East Surrey's in 1914, only five and a half weeks after meeting Hodgkin, on the night of April 20th/21st he was caught up in the middle of the most ferocious fighting at Ypres on the notorious Hill '60'. Hanging on against impossible odds he wrote: 'Our trench was fast filling up with wounded and dead and eventually you could hardly see the ground.... At one time I discovered I was the only officer untouched on that part of the hill, and was the only one who lasted the whole time from 5 p.m. until early dawn'. As day broke on April 21st, Geary was severely wounded in the head, which later cost him the sight of an eye. Photographed after being decorated with the Victoria Cross his serious dark face with clipped moustache portrayed the suffering he had undergone.[1]

Rumours had proliferated in England belittling typhoid innoculations; people were influenced by the fact that the immunisation of the solidiers in South Africa had not proved entirely satisfactory. In 1914 the Army injected only those who consented to it (when the exact dosage was better known). Apart from the objections to innoculations, and arguments to keep a pure blood pure, consumption of alcohol was frowned on. 'Drink is doing us more damage in the war than all the German submarines put together', stated Lloyd George solemnly at a conference of trade union representatives on March 17th. Persuaded of this view, King George V wrote to the Chancellor of the Exchequer that if it was thought advisable, he himself would set an example and give up all alcoholic liquor, and on April 6th the King issued orders against its consumption in the Royal Household. Lord Bertie of Thame, British Ambassador in Paris observed on April 9th: "It will be an excellent result if the King's prohibition of 'drink' in his palaces brings about

---

[1] *Illustrated War News*, part 63, October 20th, 1915, p. 45

more moderation amongst the working classes", but he considered that there would be much discontent, and that if public houses were to be closed employers of labour should be under the obligation to issue a limited amount of drink to those of their workmen who apply for it, the cost to be deducted from their wages.[1]

Although this disapprobation was mainly directed against the munition workers who, it was thought, were slacking because of drunkenness it naturally caused a great deal of general annoyance to the troops. Some churchmen too denounced drunkenness and labelled it as being unpatriotic.

The evangelical Bishop F.J. Chavasse of Liverpool (1846 – 1928) preached a sermon in April 1915 before the Lord Mayor and Corporation of London when he spoke of the shameless callousness of men ready to rise and drink themselves drunk, while their own kith and kin were facing death, wounds and hardships in the trenches. On March 12th, Hodgkin wrote 'Today the rum ration stops under orders from Corps H.Q.! We all think the teetotal brigade in the House of Commons must have won a victory'.

Feeling sick and out of sorts Hodgkin once more trekked on up to the line. Heald joined him later and was sent out that evening from No. 2 trench in front of 'Gabion' Farm on an officer's reconnoitring patrol. As if playing in a macabre game Heald with his platoon dashed up the slope to the enemy barbed wire and brought back a German scarf they found hanging there. One of the men, Private Anderson was wounded in the head and bled profusely. 'Gabions', kinds of cylindrical baskets filled with earth and stones were sometimes placed in front of buildings for defence purposes, probably they fortified this farmhouse. Four days later Heald was sent out once more to 'no man's land' from the same trench to lie in wait for enemy patrols. Their stay was in vain, there was no activity except for a German marksman lying in wait who shot and killed one of his platoon, Private F.E. Jones.

Outbursts of shelling continued inexorably in this 'quiet sector'. Eventually a shell fell into the parish church at the corner of the village square but miraculously the priest found it unexploded on the steps of the altar. Night after routine night there were fatigues up to the trenches; in order to create some diversion on March 15th an inter platoon football league was organised but before long the play degenerated into 'kick and run' as the men were not in very good condition. On March 17th, the whole of 'D' Company filed up to No. 5 trench by Big Bull Cottage with the East Surreys on both sides. At first all was quiet except for sporadic sniping:

> Nothing happened till about 11.30. Then the Germans started off with their beastly "whizz-bangs", small high explosive shells: they dropped 6

---

[1] *The Diary of Lord Bertie of Thame.* I p. 142

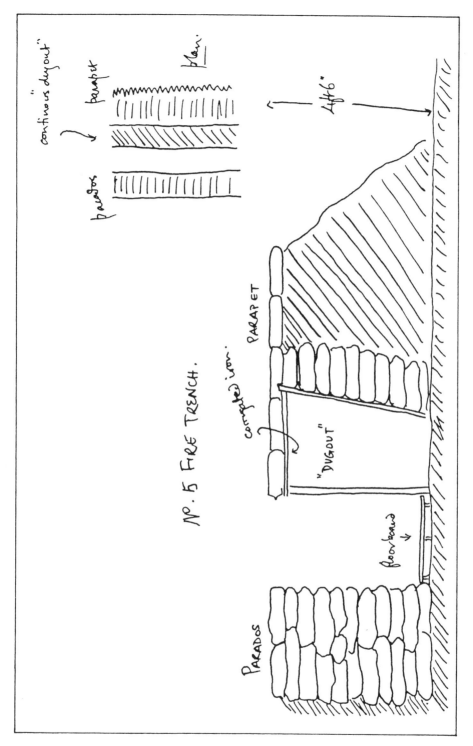

No. 5. Fire Trench at Neuve Eglise

or 7 just in front of my dugout & covered us all with earth. They then switched off to the left a bit: the last shell but one burst on the parapet, wounded C. Johnson in the backside, smashed up 2 men's shoulders, four — mere scalp wounds. Dixon had just left this dugout & came back to find the place where he had been lying simply riddled with bits of shell. This was most deplorable, & as luck would have it the shells ceased & enabled us to make the wounded as comfortable as possible; they had of course to remain where they were till dark, when the stretcher bearers took them away.

19th

We heard that Johnson was all right but had 14 wounds, all harmless, the scalp wounded ones were all right, but the others bad.[1] There was no firing today, but there was a fall of 3 or 4 inches of snow. This made the trench very messy & wet. Sniping as usual: the Germans are capital shots. There was a loophole in the trench right through the parapet about 4″ square. This was kept closed on our side with a bully beef tin. Later on we found this tin shot right through. I did a bit of shooting on my own account but could not mark any of the shots.

We were relieved by A coy about 9.0 p.m.

We got back to find that the C.O. had not only moved some of our billets but had also been round collecting the men's dirty washing & had called in all the footballs & boxing gloves. There was also a revie parade at 6.15 a.m. presumably to annoy the platoon commanders: if this was so it succeeded admirably!

We have now been in trenches 4 days out of 8 & have made 3 journeys over it: I think we deserve a rest now.

(Hodgkin, March 18th, 19th)

Just over one month's training was spent at Neuve Eglise, at the end of which the battalion was ordered to march north to take over a section of the line near Kemmel. It was an even more unsavoury place than the Douve valley. The Battalion Headquarters was located in a farm behind Rossignol Wood, and in order to reach the trenches in front of the Petit Bois Wood, the road there was subject to cross fire at the right angle turn. A portion of the 'supports' were billeted in 'Support Barn' dangerously situated near the

---

[1] *2nd Lieut C. Johnson was severely wounded in the back and leg.*

Preliminaries

One of the few occasions when the German positions were overlooked. Taken from the slopes of Mount Kemmel looking east, May 1986.

The Bandstand at Kemmel in May 1986

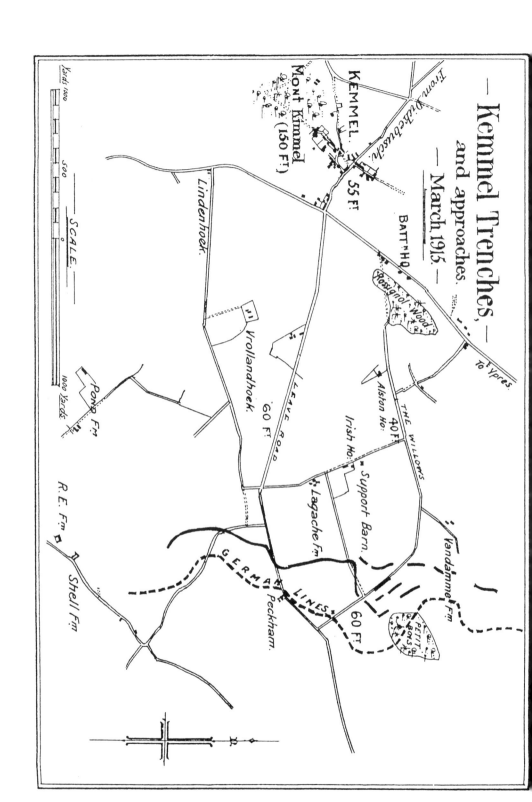

Kemmel Trenches,
and approaches.
— March 1915. —

Yards 100   500   SCALE   1000 Yards

From Dickebusch

KEMMEL.   55 F.T

Mont Kimmel
(150 F.T)

BATT.N H.Q.

Rossignol Wood

To Ypres

Lindenhoek.

Vrollandhoek.

Pond F.m

Alston Ho:

THE WILLOWS

40 F.T

Irish Ho:

Support Barn.

LEAVE ROAD

60 F.T

Lagache F.m

Vandamme F.m

PETIT
BOIS

R.E. F.m

Shell F.m

Peckham.

GERMAN LINES

60 F.T

N

enemy lines. Like Neuve Eglise the little village at the foot of Mount Kemmel presented a bleak scene in the March weather as it too had suffered badly from shell fire. Heald who went there on March 25th, noted its neat village green where he saw to one side of it a circular bandstand, its roof surmounted by a pinnacle supported by slender columns. Wistfully he thought how pretty it would be in Summer. But no respite was granted after their march from Neuve Eglise. Hodgkin's company was ordered to proceed to the new trenches without delay and found them filthy. The day was spent in cleaning them up and getting their bearings:

> At night we were relieved by C. coy, who arrived very late when the moon was up & got 5 men wounded in consequence while relieving J8 trench. Ellington took 2 platoons back to HQ farm, & I had the other 2 in the support farm about ½ mile back from the trenches. This is a ramshackle old place that has been shelled at some time or other, & is very filthy. There is a line of narrow trench dug for use in case shells arrive during the day time. No lights must show at night & no smoke by day, so that the cooking problem becomes rather difficult. It resolves itself into preparing a drink of hot tea just before dawn in biscuit tins which mostly leak, & living on cold rations for the rest of the time.
>
> (Hodgkin, March 24th)

Amid mounting tensions on March 25th, Heald in reserve was detailed to a carrying party that night. They distributed stores to most of the new trenches which were very isolated and the approaches dangerous. They found wounded men in J2 a very advanced trench, and took a stretcher party in and got the lot out safely; afterwards they were commended by the Colonel, after returning to their billets at Locre around 5.30 a.m. The next day there was a further carrying party:

> When we got to our support trench J10, told that enemy were breaking through J3 and ordered to reinforce same. Fixed bayonets and charged across. Found enemy had only made attack with hand grenades. Got back safely. Very luckily had no casualties. For our promptness I and No. 6 were specially commended by the General. No. 6 Platoon very proud of itself.
>
> (Heald, March 25th)

Meanwhile, Hodgkin who was manning J10 with 'C' Company was observing these proceedings with much apprehension. Only forty yards from the enemy having little or no wire in front of them, the unconnected trenches J3L and J3R were dangerously exposed to a continuous glacis of bullets:

29

In the evening, about 9.00 p.m. we had a regular field day: we heard several grenades go off in J3 followed by a message from Dixon saying that the Germans had got into the trench, & demanding immediate help. This stirred us up no end. It so happened that at the moment there were 2 platoons just behind J10 who had come up carrying material. Ellington at once ordered a section of these go to and reinforce J3: his order was misunderstood by Heald, who fixed bayonets & charged wildly with a whole platoon down to J3. How they got there without casualties is a miracle. Meanwhile in J10 we had been distributing ammunition. Both I and Ellington dressed ourselves in gumboots, a British warm, & a revolver, which sounds rather a ridiculous garb to fight Germans with. All the firing died down in about 10 mins & the RHA sent a few shells just skimming the parapet of J3 which burst over the Germans. All that really happened was that a few Germans had crawled up & thrown hand grenades. We had no casualties, but I think a German was accounted for. We sandbagged the dangerous side of the support barn, which made the rooms very small but safe. The night of the 26th was quiet, & was again spent in cleaning up the place. No shelling at all took place in the daytime. On the way down to headquarters a man was hit in the back by a "spare" & killed, & 2 men of our coy. who were on a carrying party to J3 were shot dead. Thus in four days D. coy had had 5 killed & a few wounded: bad luck, but as long as J3 had to be held it seems inevitable. We marched to Locre the same night for a 4 day rest & got into billets about 1.00 a.m. The people here are I believe pro German: at any rate they are very disobliging. This does not pay them at all as our men won't stand that sort of thing at all. Attended Church in the convent in the evening: medium sermon. I have taken over Coy Mess President. Also had a look at 'Grandma' our 15″ gun: it's enormous & has a whole train of gigantic motor traction engines, some to pull, & some to push it along.

(Hodgkin, March 28th)

In spite of the disobliging inhabitants, Bolton thought Locre rather a beautiful place. He particularly liked the grand old church and resonant bell. On the following day Hodgkin walked some four miles to Bailleul and was very glad to eat lunch from a china plate and not to have to turn it over and eat the second course on the back of it. He enjoyed a bath in the lunatic asylum a most palatial place with real white enamelled baths and as much hot water from a real tap as he wanted: 'Truly they do the lunatics well'.

As it was their turn for the trenches, there was general packing up and then back to the support barn which 'A' Company had left perfectly filthy. They worked till dawn on the dug-outs. During this time Heald who had found it difficult to find his way around the trench network, crawled into J3R and tried to get across to J3L on his own. But the place was strewn outside with dead though the enemy made no sign. Eventually not having located J3L he crawled back to safety bringing with him five pairs of field glasses. Still in J3 R the next day he had his periscope shot away immediately it was raised over the parapet. He found crawling very fatiguing and the trenches rotten. It was impossible to raise their heads, there were no entanglements in front, altogether the Germans had the upper hand and the enemy snipers fired with deadly accuracy. McGowan who relieved them tried to make light of it all when writing to his parents:

Belgium. Thursday, April 1st 1915
My dear Mother & Dad,

It's a simply glorious day here today, bright and warm, and the birds are whistling across the fields. I'm sitting with my back against a 4ft. bullet proof parapet, less than 50 yards from the German trenches. That is to say I and my platoon are manning the notorious No. 3 trench of this sector. I should explain that each trench throughout the length of the British line bears a decent index. Each sector is lettered and the trenches in each sector numbered from 1 upwards. I do not name the letter because of the information I've given you previously about the supports behind this sector. The trench although probably one of the worst in the line is not really so bad, once you get here, but the getting here is certainly a bit of a problem for the ground is perfectly open without cover of any kind. To try and get in standing up, stooping or even kneeling down, is just asking for trouble with a bright full moon such as it was last night. We all wormed our way from the support trench lying flat on our stomachs and it took us every bit of an hour to cover 150 yards, but did not even attract the enemy's fire let alone have anyone hit. We were all very sore when we got in, but if you take it in the right spirit, that sort of thing is quite a sporting game in which you may consider yourself beaten if you so much as let the enemy see you. One or two men might get through alright with a series of short rushes, but this is impossible with a large party. We are to man this trench for 48 hours instead of 24 hours and then we shall retire in support at Head Quarters farm for the other 48 hours of our 4 days. I preferred to do this. A wriggle such as we had last night followed by a similar wriggle to get out again is not worth a mere 24 hours. My platoon sergeant and about a third of the platoon are manning the left-hand half of this trench which is separated from this half by about 80 yards of open ground. I must crawl there and back at dusk before the moon gets up to see how

things are with them. My servant who follows me about like a faithful
dog will come with me. The trench periscope is exceptionally useful in a
trench such as this for by day you dare not show a hair of your head
above the parapet. One of my sergeants last night got a bullet through
his hat but fortunately it didn't even touch his scalp, and another man
was temporarily stunned by a bullet that just missed his ear. Although
things were rather lively through the night while we were busy trying to
improve the trench a bit, it's been very quiet today and the men not
actually on the lookout are stretched out on the floor sleeping peacefully.
I'm wondering if there will be a truce over Easter, similar to that at
Christmas time.

The Artillery of both sides have just started sending over our heads their
messages of love. Its just like a game of tit for tat. Our artillery sent one
towards their supports, they replied with two aimed in the direction of
our supports. They'll keep this up for a bit and then stop for tea.

On Christmas Day 1914 there had been many reported incidents along the
Western Front of an unofficial truce when both Germans and English joined
together in parties singing Christmas hymns swapping hats and exchanging
gifts of wine and cigars. Many of the overtures originated from the German
side where the troops placed lighted Christmas trees along the trench
parapets. Both sides helped each other to bury their dead with burial services
held in two languages. News of this Christian goodwill was received by the
public in both countries with surprise and consternation and fraternisation
was afterwards expressly forbidden, never to occur again: 'Even if Easter Day
is respected by reduction of firing on both sides to minimum, troops must
remain in trenches as usual and there must be no attempt to fraternise; please
let J3 know at once and other trenches if possible'. (Instructions to 5th Bn.
Cheshires from Brigade H.Q. April 2nd, 1915)

Friday, 5.00 p.m. April 2nd.
Well there hasn't exactly been a truce, for there has been intermittent
rifle and artillery fire all day, but things have certainly been quieter than
yesterday, and it's as well for a shrapnel shell that burst just behind
No. 2 trench about this time yesterday, unfortunately it disabled some of
our company who were manning that trench.

I myself was as near being hit yesterday as I wish to be. After writing
you I had a sketch to make of this trench and was looking through my
periscope to get a view of an old trench on the enemy's side of our

Sites of J2 and J3 trenches by the road, in May 1986

parapet, when a bullet actually cut through the curl on my forehead (I hadn't a hat on) taking some of the hair with it. I can tell you it gave me a headache for the rest of the night and I shall be careful not to try for too sharp an angle with periscope again, but I rather fancy the bullet must have cut through the top sandbag where it was only layer thick.

Well we should be relieved tonight about 8.00 p.m. and I shall not be sorry for it is a bit of a strain being so close to the enemy and very liable to surprise attacks under advance conditions. None of we officers can see why they persist in holding this particular trench, for we could keep a watch on the enemy as well or better 100 yards further back and advance from there when required, as easily as from here. We are told it is held for purely sentimental reasons because it was taken from the Germans a few months back (December) by some Scottish regiment at great cost.

(McGowan, April 2nd)

Hodgkin related that he had been told by two officers of the Royal Scots Fusiliers that the previous Autumn, that particular sector of the line had been the centre of an attack. Both the Gordons and the Royal Scots had penetrated

33

the Petit Bois Wood in the German line about five hundred yards in front of the Support Barn, and would have held it except that the Gordons had to give way and on their left the French had also failed. Only trench J3 a few yards away was retained, it was therefore a matter of honour to hold it.

With the arrival of Holy Week, the Bishop of London, the Rt. Rev A.F. Winnington-Ingram visited the Front on a mission, bringing with him 'The Bishop's Souvenir' consisting of ten thousand booklets of Good Friday and Easter Day thoughts written by himself. Believing the nation to be engaged in a great crusade, tantamount to a holy war, Winnington-Ingram who was swept away by patriotic fervour had a great instinct for drama. In a speech displaying fervent eloquence and some self advertisement he described the planes flying over one of his open air services during that week as guardian angels watching over a target of four thousand men with a Bishop in the middle. 'The army wd. love Ingram' declared Bishop Wand who had wished to make him Chaplain General in the Boer War. Before 1914, undergraduates drawn by Ingram's personality had flocked to listen to the sermons of the handsome Bishop who preached at St. Mary's Oxford. At a great patriotic service on July 25th 1915 he preached an address to three thousand Territorial troops on the steps of St. Paul's, positioning himself by a stack of drums. But on Easter Saturday, April 3rd, Winnington-Ingram's style did not appeal to Heald who was present at one of the Bishop's services. Never happy with dramatic displays he described the Bishop as 'Rather too theatrical, no voice, not impressive.'[1] Hodgkin was given no opportunity of attending a service. There was no sign of a truce although it was Easter Sunday, and the snipers continued to waste their ammunition:

About noon the message on the other side was received & our guns fired a couple of rounds, apparently without fuzes, to emphasize it. This message proved wholly unnecessary as the enemy shelled us for 2 hours with heavy high explosive. They dropped all round J10 and smashed in part of the parapet of J11, destroying a lot of rifles & equipment. These howitzers are beastly things. I went outside, sunning myself at the back of the trench when I heard the first one coming, & I had time to get right into my dugout, 30 or 40 yards away before it dropped, making a terrific crash & shaking all the ground around, & throwing up fountains of mud. They kept on coming closer & closer, the nearest finally dropping a very few yards from our dugout. Everybody was in a thorough good funk during this performance. The one comic touch was when the C. S. M. who had his mouth wide open as usual, got it filled

[1]On arriving at Charing Cross after being wounded, Siegfried Sassoon was handed a leaflet by the Bishop of London earnestly advising him to lead a clean life and attend Holy Communion. S. Sassoon, *Memoirs of an Infantry Officer*, p. 171.

up with mud & earth, to his intense and voluble annoyance. The result of some 3 or 4 dozen shots was one NCO, Cpl. Burgess lightly wounded in the knee. Rather an expensive performance for the Germans. We were relieved about 10.0 pm by the 2nd Royal Scots Fusiliers & got home to Locre about 2.0 am, exceedingly cross. We billeted in a school, where the Nuns as usual did everything they possibly could for us.

(Hodgkin, April 3rd)

After a mere thirteen days near Kemmel they were ordered north once more to a small hamlet near Dickebusch for a few days rest, where following a wet and muddy march the battalion was crowded into billets fifty men to a hut. Owing to the intricate nature of the country with its maze of trenches and small woods, it was clear to them that the useless and confused nature of the fighting was producing no tangible results.

Both Heald and Hodgkin out on a spree walked the five miles or so into the nearby town of Poperinghe where they found a 'ripping café serving excellent chocolate and ate as many sticky cakes as possible'. Heald had also enjoyed a good lunch and Hodgkin had a hair cut and shampoo. Later they staggered home about 7.30 p.m. and were for some reason at once offered roast beef. While the rain, wind and mud prevailed outside, illuminated by two or three candles, several officers in field kits ended their meal smoking fat cigars. As a centre for recreation, Poperinghe with its crowded narrow streets and gothic churches disappointed none. It was a welcome focus for thousands of troops who strolled around there allured by its magical brightly lit shops where they could wander to their hearts content. There was even a Post Office, and well stocked book shops.

Dickebusch was only a staging post. At noon on April 6th 'A' and 'B' companies marched off towards Ypres, where 'A' company took over a trench from the 1st Battalion the Cheshire Regiment to the south of the city known as '27' close to the Ypres Commines canal by Triangular Wood. This trench, merely a sandbagged breastwork was located a scant sixty to one hundred yards from the enemy who were situated on the slope above. An earlier battle had left its grim legacy of a number of decomposed bodies lightly buried underfoot. On the way, Heald with 'B' Company detailed to be in support, stopped to make tea, and was surprised to find their dug-outs in the tall wooded sides of the canal bank to be absolutely sheltered, the quietest place they had been in, where it was possible to stroll about by day and reach the trench in safety. But Hodgkin who had left Dickebusch on April 7th at 7.30 p.m. with 'C' Company:

Had a perfectly beastly march which was begun in fours, owing to some fad of HQs about march discipline. This formation having with much

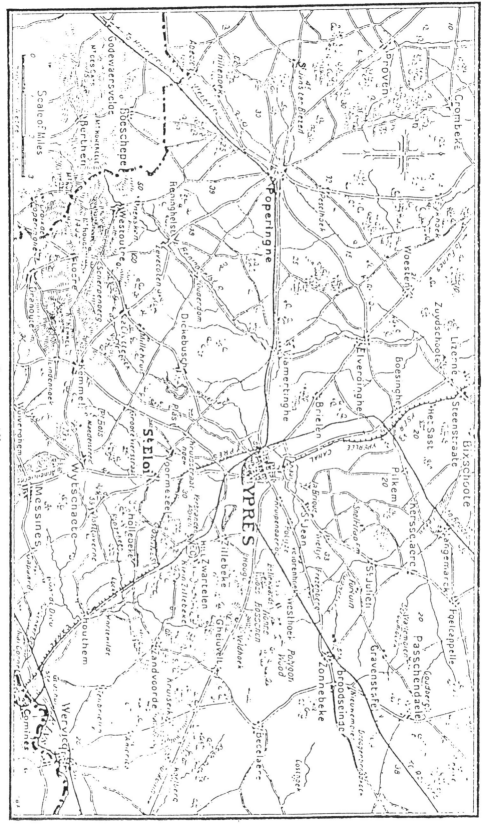

Country round Ypres.

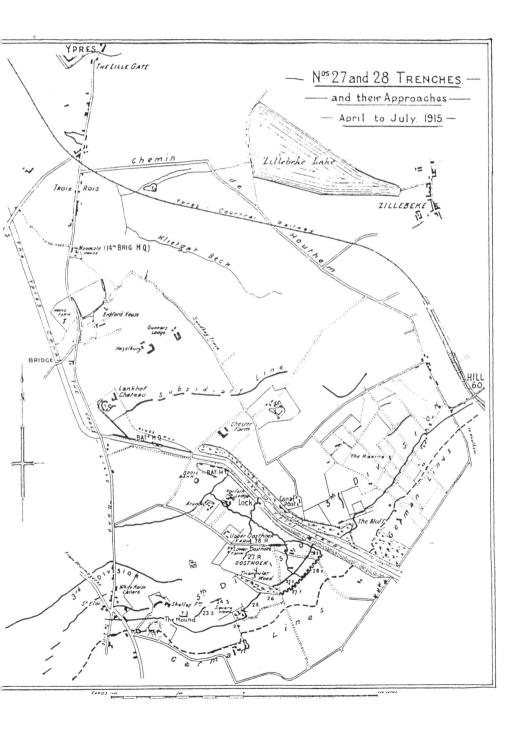

pain & cursing (Marlborough's army, you remember, swore terribly in Flanders) been found impossible owing to the state of the roads, we progressed more easily in file & finally took up our quarters in the Cavalry barracks at YPRES. The building has suffered comparatively little from shell fire, although yesterday a shell dropped into a room in an adjoining house & killed or wounded 50 men. Anyway there were a certain number of iron bedsteads which were very handy after a few sandbags & our field kits had been laid on them. By the time that we were ready for bed it was 1.0 am.

(Hodgkin, April 8th)

In Marlborough's day however, it was the custom for any campaign to finish at the end of the Autumn, when the armies retreated into their winter quarters, and the officers despatched to the comforts of home.

During the first weeks of April, deferring to the wishes of General Joffre, Sir John French, then sixty-two years old, took over nearly five miles of extra front occupied by the French. Sir John, a cavalry officer had commanded the B.E.F. since the beginning of the war. Short and of stocky build he was known for his irritable temper and swings of mood and though he understood a little French there were difficulties in language communications between the generals. Many of the trenches left behind in this sector were not only dangerous but in a wretched condition, and owing to the French removing their anti-aircraft guns there were increased attacks from the air. Cooped up within a salient, inferior in guns and severely rationed with ammunition, the British forces were in many places overlooked by the attacking Germans on higher ground sometimes only 50 yards away.

CHAPTER 2

YPRES 1915

Before the battle of 'Second Ypres' intensified, the city still appeared a lively place with fine ramparts. In frivolous mood, Hodgkin negotiated for a French '75' unexploded (but emptied) shell which had caught his eye in a shop window. After twenty minutes of hard bargaining in loud voices, Hodgkin, not satisfied with the price made to leave, but subsequently the Belgian shopkeeper having demanded 60 francs was eventually beaten down to 25. Agreement reached however, the owner obviously seemed pleased with the transaction: 'shall I wrap it up for you? It will look like a bottle of wine and what will the Commandant say if he sees you in the street?' Hodgkin well delighted, felt as if he had gained a glorious victory. All the while the shopkeeper's wife stood by watching mildly amused by the whole performance. Ellington standing outside in the passage split his sides with laughter. Was the objection to the bottle of wine or to the shell? Hodgkin does not say.

Meanwhile Heald found circumstances neither enjoyable nor amusing. In terrible weather he had been on carrying fatigues to the trenches, the men were very tired and the mud was awful. Afterwards there were the wounded to carry away over three miles along the canal bank, past the ruined Lankhof Chateau by the side of the dreary stretch of road leading through the Lille gate to Ypres, where they billetted in the Cavalry Barracks. Next day visiting the once glorious medieval Cathedral and Cloth Hall, like everyone who saw them Heald was saddened at the desolate scene. Miraculously though there was still a good dinner to be found in a nearby restaurant. Lt. Col. W.A. Murray (of the 1st Warwickshire Battery R.H.A., 5th Division), wrote of Ypres to his sister Claudine on April 4th. 'The tommies call it by a name which reminded me of napkins... All the beautiful wall paintings are destroyed by water and in the Grande Place a pile of dead horses are burning'[1]. Living in Armathwaite, north Cumberland he judged Ypres (or 'wipers' as it was known) to be the same size as the nearby small town of Hexham in Northumberland.

Hodgkin perhaps buoyed up his triumphant shopping expedition moved up to the dugout on the canal bank on April 12th and found the spot 'idyllic':

> The banks are very high on both sides, & there are pine trees on top.
> The dugouts are on the w.side & are of the usual 'half-dugout, half-
> sandbag' style. The canal is dry & full of large frogs & bullrushes, but

[1]Ms diaries of Lt. Col W.A. Murray, Imperial War Museum.

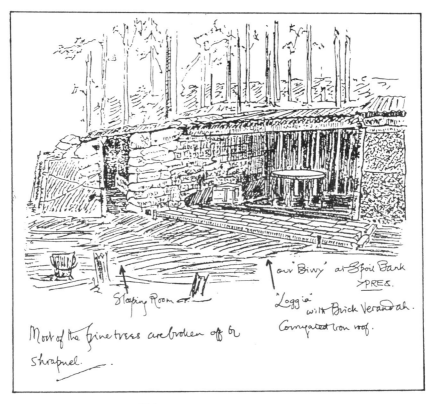

Most of the pine trees are broken off by shrapnel.

Sleeping Room

our 'Bivy' at Spoil Bank
>PRES.

'Loggia' with Brick Verandah.
Corrugated Iron roof.

we manage to get sufficient water to wash with. The bank is terraced & the dugouts hold from 8 to 12 men each. There are no smells here, only pine & the whole place, were it not for 2 graves, would seem like a holiday camp. We worked all day improving our homes: it is strange, but every place we have come to so far seems to have been utterly neglected by the troops that previously occupied. The dugouts here for instance were in a most ramshackle condition & all without exception have had to be rebuilt. On the other side of the canal bank, there are more dugouts which are occasionally visited by shrapnel. An aeroplane dropped a bomb not far from us today.

(Hodgkin, April 12th)

As so often happens in spring, the weather suddenly turned and April 13th became warm and sunny. For once there was no shelling, and Hodgkin's company creeping warily up to No. 27 fire trench at 11 p.m. found the way fairly safe except for the odd 'spare', the last hundred yards running through a fairly deep communication trench. As they got nearer 27, there was an all pervading acrid smell of death, which even chloride of lime could not eradicate.

They found the place indescribably filthy and full of far too many half buried corpses to be at all pleasant:

> The scene of desolation outside the trench is appalling; the ground is covered with tins, refuse of all kinds, smashed rifles, equipment, cartridges, one unexploded shell, barbed wire & graves in all directions. Standing with one's back to the enemy & looking N. towards the town of YPRES one sees the village of ST. ELOI on the extreme left, a heap of absolute ruins, the trees all stripped & broken off and beams of farmhouses sticking up in all directions; the German trench runs right round the front of the village & is in full view. Further to the right, on a green field that ought to be full of black & white cattle, there are 14 unburied soldiers lying where they fell: it is impossible to bury them as the ground is quite open. Following round, one sees next a fine communication trench leading to the rear, & on the right of this our own support trench. Behind this are the high canal banks where our dugouts are, & on the extreme right is all that remained of a pine wood: shrapnel has stripped the trees till there is literally nothing remaining except the battered stumps. This wood is I think the most extraordinary sight of all. The whole view is backed by the towers of YPRES. It is not easy to see what is in front of the trench as it is almost certain death to look over the parapet for more than 2 seconds, & the view from a periscope is very limited. The Germans are about 150 yds. away & slighty above us. Today they put a few small shells into our support trench, but did no damage. They began very quietly & continued so until about 11.30 p.m. Then without any warning the Germans began to bombard St. Eloi for about 20 mins. the village must have been a complete hell: shrapnel 'high explosives of all sizes were bursting continuously & the smoke soon developed into a thick fog, through which could dimly be seen the star shells sent up from both sides. Some of the support trenches & a road also received a few shells. We of course stood to arms at once. The smoke gradually crept up with the wind and soon we also were enveloped in the fog & smell of burnt explosive. Everyone was I think rather expecting an attack, but there was hardly any rifle fire on the part of the enemy. Anyway nobody got much sleep during the night.
>
> (Hodgkin, April 14th)

During the spring of that year, persistent intelligence reports of enemy gas containers concentrated in the enemy lines had not been credited by the French commanders. As luck would have it, the Germans ready to make a gas attack on March 10th had been frustrated by unfavourable wind; but they had already prepared themselves with over twenty thousand tulle mouth protectors (to be soaked in suitable liquid) which had been manufactured in Ghent. No British officer really believed the gas reports either, although on March 24th General Plumer commanding V Corps passed on the warnings for what they were worth. Photographs of respirators against poisonous fumes from high explosives had already been published by the *Illustrated War News* on March 24; there were two pictures of a sergeant modelling one, having a safety muzzle with a small valve in the upper part. But no general protection had been issued against chlorine gas to the luckless army in Flanders, and no special advance medical preparations were ordered. As late as April 11th a German deserter with a crude respirator had given himself up to the French 11th Division, and related how tubes with asphyxiating gases had been placed in batteries of twenty tubes for every forty metres along the front, but the French had summarily dismissed even this news.

A little to the east of the Ypres Commines canal lay Hill 60, an artificial mound on the other side of the railway cutting comprising an area of about two hundred and fifty square yards where the Germans were entrenched on the upper slopes. To the southwest of it, April 16th was quiet and Heald having relieved Hodgkin in 27 was enjoying a good day's sniping. He was trying out a new rifle with periscopic sights which could be fired over the parapet without putting his head up. Having observed an enemy dug out through his loophole he fired at it through their loophole. To make sure of good results, he landed a huge high explosive bomb from his trench mortar right into the middle of the dug out and blew it to bits. But at 2 a.m. the next morning they heard terrific firing to the left and the whole line simultaneously started to fire rapid for about a quarter of an hour. Standing by, Heald wrote:

> We had been warned to expect an attack by asphyxiating gases.
> However, it was a false alarm. That afternoon we were told that at Ypres
> some mines under the German trenches would be fired, followed by
> artillery fire and an attack would be made by a brigade on our left and
> we were ordered to occupy the enemy's attention to prevent him sending
> reinforcements and to hold our own trench at all costs if counter-
> attacked. So we made all ready. At 7 p.m. prompt the mines were fired.
> We saw mountains of earth and debris rise up into the sky. The
> explosion was terrific. Simultaneously our guns opened and rained shells.
> It was hell let loose over there. It seemed one mass of bursting shells
> with terrific rifle fire added in. We in our trench opened rapid fire but
> got very little reply. We subsequently heard that the West Kents had
> taken the enemy's trenches on Hill 60 in three minutes and found only

one German officer and 13 men left. About 200 yards of trench had been blown up. Our men dug themselves in and repelled the counter-attack which came in about two hours. We lost rather heavily in repelling the counter-attack but only five men when attacking.

In our trench we were reinforced about 2 a.m. by 'A' company and got back safely. Another attack was organised by the same brigade to capture the trenches to the right and left of the position taken and timed to start at 6 p.m. There was the same hell let loose and we heard that we had successfully captured two more trenches. These we have held in spite of heavy shell fire. Had to fetch rations from road, four shells burst overhead, but luckily did not touch us.

(Heald, April 17th)

Expecting news of a divisional attack on the left, all transport was forbidden on the Ypres/Lille road. Hodgkin, who spent April 17th transforming the canal dugouts into shelters in preparation for the inevitable counter attack wrote: 'So well did the men work that I had 20 of them completed in time, 15 ft. by 3 ft. by 6 ft. deep'. Behind them for the space of half an hour a battery fired 40 rounds per half minute. 'The bombardment continued throughout the whole night: we think of the atrocious nature of the whole proceeding apart from the waste of good metal'. As 'whoofers' were dropping close to their bivouacs they sheltered in the trenches for five hours, emerging frozen stiff with cold. The next day Hodgkin went to see the parson at church:

He, poor fellow, had spent the night & morning after in the dressing station, seeing all the horror of the affair, without any of the excitement. I'm not sure the RAMC don't have as hard a time as the infantry after all, especially the stretcher bearers. There was a good deal of gun fire today, & we spent some intervals in our trenches. I was hit a good thump on the chest by a piece of a 'crump' (a big high explosive). This makes the second time.
As I write this, they had just begun the bombardment again (9.0 p.m). I do hope we shan't have to spend the night in our muddy little holes!

(Hodgkin, April 19th)

At midnight they received orders to be prepared to move at a moment's notice, which had the effect merely to make them turn over on the other side and sleep more soundly. Chancing their luck, Captains W.A.V. Churton and Ellington together with Hodgkin ventured into Ypres for tea at 'In den Hemel' where Hodgkin met one Henry Birrel Anthony of the 1st Monmouth

Regiment (T.F.) with whom he had been at Repton. Only eighteen days later on May 8th, Birrel Anthony, a solicitor in civilian life, was killed after this chance encounter with his school friend. The weather grew warmer and with it came the flies that increased in hordes swarming on decomposed corpses. No. 27 proved to be an easy target for enfilade fire and Private Nicholas was shot through the head.

Beginning on April 21st, a gigantic bombardment made Ypres practically uninhabitable and the deafening noise of the shells resembled runaway tramcars riding over bumpy rails. Sleeping in the open fields, Arthur Gregg of the 1st Battalion the Cheshires, found there was no such thing as shell proof covered billets, and was sent to search for quarters in the casemates made out of the old city ramparts. Even though most of the terrified citizens had fled, the place was never entirely deserted as smoke curling upwards from the chimneys of a few damaged houses indicated signs of life. Inside he came upon a few aged Belgians with long beards and wearing small peaked caps huddled over their stoves in a dazed condition. Gregg found some of the shops worth a closer inspection, and he descended some cellar steps of a large café well known a month before. Inside were to be seen racks of every kind of wine and rows of untouched bottles of champagne. One room was strewn around with ladies clothing including numbers of hats. Selecting one of wonderful purple velvet, decorated with a large feather, Gregg fancied he looked rather smart in it.[1]

At midnight on April 21st Hodgkin returned to the dugouts at 'Spoil Bank' by the canal:

> The names of places round here are quaint. Thus we have Chester House, Bedford House, Spoil Bank, all of which have been christened by the various regiments that have been quartered there. Our own dugout I have christened 'Ye Olde Cheshire Cheese'.

> The Germans have either been dropping bombs from aeroplanes, or firing shells containing poisonous gases. 1) about 4.30 pm. I smelt a very strong smell of chlorine, as did several others: so much so that it gave me a temporary sore throat. 2) Later on, about 6.30 pm, all the men in the neighbourhood were suddenly afflicted with an intolerable smarting of the eyes. Two men who arrived late from Ypres said that they had the same experience as soon as they got on to the Lille Road. A man had picked up here a piece of bomb smelling very strongly indeed of H.28. The eye smarting affair smelt very like mustard seed... However, we cannot I think legitimately complain, as I think the French are also using

---

[1]Letters from Arthur Gregg, Crookenden, pp 37–48. Arthur Gregg was killed in 1917 with the R.F.C.

these diabolical contrivances. Yesterday I heard that 15 E. Surrey
Officers have been killed and wounded. The casualties during the taking
and holding of Hill 60 on the 17th are 1200.

(Hodgkin, April 22nd)

Lance Corporal Bolton who had marched along the railway to Hill 60
wrote: 'Here we see some of the most gastly sites (sic) possible to see and it
was nothing but a continual stream of Stretcher Bearers with very bad cases'.
At the Field Dressing station at the foot of the hill he noted: 'Some terrible
sites (sic) beyond earthly aid', but added: 'I did not see one man of the
Surreys anyway effected by the sites (sic)'. After the German bombardment of
the Hill the Surreys started singing 'Here we are again'. Most of Bolton's
platoon had been buried by sandbags for there was hardly one part of their
trench left intact after the bombardment.

Ultimately over one hundred officers and three thousand men became
casualties lost on the hill by the Fifth Division, the surface became a rubbish
heap, pitted with holes and craters, in which lay the bodies of the dead and
dying. Those few who remained fought on until finally overwhelmed by
enemy gas and high explosives:

> The Germans took Hill 60. They opened with a terrible bombardment,
> then let loose their gas and our infantry had to clear out. So all those
> ghastly days with their enormous losses had been of no avail and now we
> have to attack again this afternoon and I suppose there will be another
> horrible battle and all the time we are tied for want of ammunition.

(Murray, May 5th)

Heavy fighting and the shelling of Ypres continued on April 23rd,
intensifying all week. In case of retreat, Hodgkin was ordered back to the
trenches to reconnoitre a cross country path, the walk did him no end of
good, as he was feeling dismal. The men who had also got very touchy were
firing off at the least provocation. Lt. A.H. Cowap observing them said: 'If
those damned fools in their trenches all happened to let off 'verey' lights at
once, that constitutes a signal for rapid fire, should that coincide with those
from the Germans, then pandemonium would be let loose and millions of
pounds would be fired off into space'.

> We had a horrible experience here today: we noticed a lyddite shell burst
> just in front of our support trench & could not make it out at all. Then
> we had 2 or 3 that only just missed our own parapet. We made signs
> with the flag that is provided to tell our gunners that they are firing
> short, but without effect: the telephone could not get on to the Battery:

it is always out of order in an emergency. The next shell burst just behind us, & the following one came right through our parados, killed one man outright & wounded eight others, none however seriously, except perhaps Sgt. Allan who got a nasty cut behind the ear & whose lower leg may or may not have broken. The shell was 4.7″ as far as we could make out: it is a miracle that it did not do more damage. After this the battery mercifully shut up, & we heard later on that it had been dropping shells promiscuously behind our lines. Our men were all very shaken, & well might they be; to be shelled by one's own guns does not inspire confidence.

Tonight Ypres is blazing furiously: the fire is behind the Cloth Hall which is silhouetted against the flames in all its nakedness. A pine wood or something is blazing further to right & the whole sky is lit up. Meanwhile shells, very high up, are for ever whistling towards the city. Otherwise the night is quiet.

(Hodgkin, April 24th)

And so the days continued with more frightfulness, when it was light their billets became too hot, thus forcing them into the open fields. By night Heald found the fatigues increasingly dangerous as the bullets pouring down on them at random, like hailstones, fell from the shrapnel shells bursting over the countryside. On April 25th, the turmoil having temporarily abated to their left, they were sent to so-called 'rest' at Spoil Bank near Battalion Headquarters, thankful to leave the area where latterly they had been up to the trenches eight days out of nine. Curiously enough, only within roughly half a mile from the enemy, Heald stripped off his filthy clothes and enjoyed a bath behind a rock in the canal. After sleeping till the late afternoon he felt quite restored. Back to the stench of 27 three days later, the Germans enfiladed the trench with high explosive, two were killed and eighteen wounded:

Our journey back from the trenches to YPRES was enlivened by 2 high explosive shells which dropped on the rear of our coy on the road, hurting 2 men only, & hurling one across the road into the ditch. A very lucky escape for all concerned. We got to bed about 8.00 a.m. in an open field.
Later on we constructed turf huts, very nice, but very stuffy. This is now the 8th day that the Germans have shelled the city without stopping. We saw some of the 17″ shells arrive: the affect is terrific. Another pinnacle has been shot off the Cloth Hall. A big battle is raging N.E. of the town, but we get no news of its progress. The weather is

46

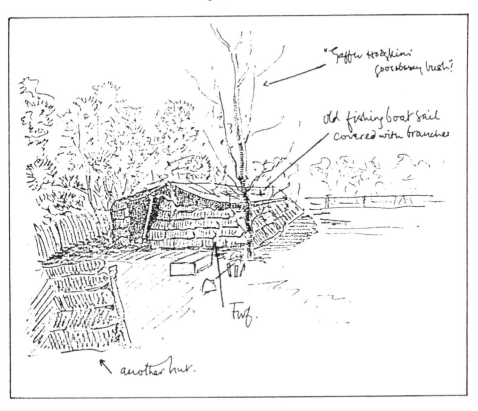

delightful, and were it not that one cannot get any sleep for the noise, the nightlife would be delightful. We have a new Adj. Capt. Bengough, & the C.O. is now busy showing off to him, & making the life of everybody a perfect burden to them. Bairstow & O. Johnson have just been down to ROUEN to fetch various drafts up for the other regts. they took them to ARMENTIÈRES, where they said the trenches are veritable health-resorts, paved with bricks: it is very bad form to shoot there, & there is a pianola in full swing at Battn. H.Q. Here I have had to break off to take what little cover a ditch affords from a few heavy high explosives that have just dropped about 100 yds. away. I fear the battle is not going very well for us.

(Hodgkin, April 28th)

Progressively as the mounting casualties drained away their strength, tensions mounted, and fatigue always the enemy of reasonable men took command. Even the need for adequate rest remained unrecognised. In the eighteenth century, Marlborough old and ailing as he became, used to tramp the fields of Flanders to ascertain for himself whether his men were not strained beyond the limits of their endurance. In 27 Heald was shelled again, three more of his company were killed and about ten wounded. Before returning to Ypres and their bivouacs, he blew up his trench mortar while firing it, but luckily no one was hurt as he had been careful to get everyone out of the way. As soon as they reached the bivouac, another fatigue was ordered up forward directly. Heald was worn out: 'New adjutant fairly making things hum. He and Col. give men no rest at all.' After a further fatigue the following night when Privates W. Cole, T. Feeney and S. Thomas were killed, Heald wrote: 'C.O. is an absolute coward and dare not go to the trenches, also does not know his own mind. A wash out.'

It was May 1st. Hodgkin found the surroundings an odd place to spend May Day in and wished he was near Magdalen Tower (though he had never attended the sunrise service when at Oxford):

Went down to a couple of farms just behind our reserve trenches to get sandbags & other articles wherewith to adorn the aforesaid loggia: got a wooden tub for a bath & some stone pots for water. Then proceeded to make a cockyolly bird to go in a birdcage I found. Here he is: he was made out of a turnip with cardboard wings & wire legs. His tail was the turnip root. In the evening the men organised an impromptu concert until the noise of the guns drowned it.
(Hodgkin, May 1st)

The 'Cockyolly bird' was an important character in 'The Tale of the Tootleoo' a book written for children by Eleanor and Bernard Darwin. Heald delighted in the story and later cut a cockyolly bird in topiary which he cherished for many years in his garden.[1]

Positioned in the trenches a little to the south west of Hill 60, the battalion had escaped the brunt of the gas attacks swirling forward in banks of deadly greenish clouds annihilating those fighting so desperately on Hill 60. But they were close enough to witness the horrifying casualties which affected most of those lying down in the bottom of their trenches, where the chlorine gas had settled. Taking their advantage, the Germans opened rapid rifle fire all along the line, while after 7.30 that evening, enemy shell fire fell on the approaches to the trenches by the railway cutting to prevent reinforcements. Hodgkin saw eighty dead lying out at the back of the Field Ambulance Station on May 6th and said that as many died the day before. He pronounced the mouth pads hastily provided by the government as useless although supposed it was all that could be done about the matter. If there were no pads, the troops had been ordered to hold wetted handkerchiefs or cloths attached with plaster to their mouths and when water was unavailable sometimes whisky or urine was used instead. As no proper respirators had been issued some divisions had straight away set about improvising some rude kind of protection. Accordingly, various officers were despatched to Paris to buy up muslin, flannel, gauze and elastic which were made up by seamstresses in the small towns of Bailleul and Hazebrouck and in some of the front line villages. When McGowan wrote to his parents on May 26th, he told them:

Several of our battn. helped to bring the cases to hospital and to bury the dead (in one case as many as 24 in one grave). Many of the poor fellows staggered back in a half suffocated condition almost to where our ½ battn. out of the trenches was at rest (that is to say almost 3 units) only to fall when they got there, while those that lived were in agony foaming at the mouth and gasping for breath & little could be done for them except to give them a glass of water. I believe this path up to the trenches was literally strewn with dead, in fact only last week when on duty in that part of the line, while taking a short cut across the fields, we came across three unburied bodies — no pleasant sight, for the intense bleaching power of the Chlorine effects (sic) clothes & buttons as well as the skin. It was truly a diabolical act, but thank God it will not happen to anything like the same extent again for the whole army is now prepared, were it not, I would not have given you even the few details

---

[1] Charles Kingsley *Two Years Ago,* (2 vols) London, 1881, p.7. in a chapter 'The Cruise of the Water Witch', wrote of 'charming little cockyoly birds'. (thought to be yellow hammers.)

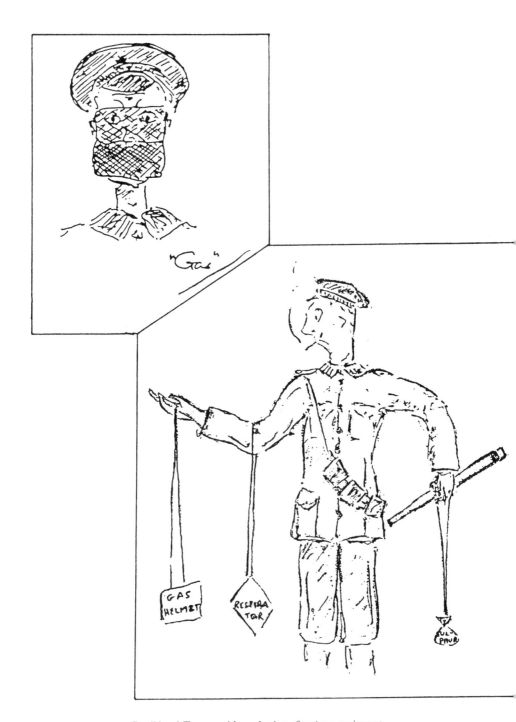

Bewildered Tommy with a selection of anti-gas equipment...

50

that I have, & you can rest assured that if the necessary precautions are
taken there is now little fear from an attack by gas.

(McGowan, May 26th)

The Dutchman Louis Raemaeker first published his horrifying pictorial
indictments in the form of cartoons in the *Amsterdam Telegraf*. In December
1915 there was an exhibition of his war cartoons at the Fine Art Galleries in
Bond Street where crowds thronged to see the collection for twenty weeks
before it toured the major British cities.[1]

Reassuring though McGowan may have seemed, the new type of gas mask
issued to them, made of a black mesh bag containing cotton waste, and soaked
in lime water with a veil to cover the eyes was also useless, even though
frequent parades were ordered to practise the doubting men in wearing them.
These models were then superseded by the 'smoke helmet' consisting of a bag
of impregnated flannel with celluloid eye pieces. In addition, the troops were
issued with vermoral sprayers (such as were used in the cherry orchards in
Kent) to disperse the pockets of greenish yellow gas persisting in the bottoms
of the trenches. McGowan wrote home:

> I understand that we are now to use gas too, but not one that will cause
> diabolical torture; it will merely send the opposing troops to sleep
> peacefully & enable us to take them prisoners. It's far better than they
> deserve, but then we are a civilised nation & could hardly bring
> ourselves to act like the incarnate fiends opposed to us.
>
> (McGowan, May 26th)

(In retaliation, gas was used by the allies in September 1915.)

By May 22nd the 'smoke helmets' had been issued to all ranks, but
Hodgkin who thought them doubtless most efficacious against chlorine said
they were more trouble and worry in the matter of returns than they were
worth in camp and trench.

In the following year when Hodgkin became an adviser on Chemical
Warfare at 3rd Army H.Q., they practised on themselves the efficiency of the
standard gas masks. He noted down the effects of the concentrations used: –

(i)	Pure phosgene	1 in 250,000)	no discomfort was
(ii)	" "	" " 5,000)	felt at all by any
(iii)	.....chlorine.....	250,000)	of 10 NCO.s or
(iv)	--------	50,000)	myself.
(v)	--------	2,000)	

(Hodgkin, September 2nd 1916)

---

[1] *Raemaeker's Cartoon History*, pp. 142, 144

SLOW ASPHYXIATION

THESE men were lying, struggling for breath and blue in the face. On examining the blood with the spectroscope and by other means, I ascertained that the blueness was not due to the presence of any abnormal pigment. There was nothing to account for the blueness (cyanosis) and struggle for air but the one fact that they were suffering from acute bronchitis, such as is caused by inhalation of an irritant gas. Their statements were that when in the trenches they had been overwhelmed by the irritant gas produced in front of the German trenches and carried towards them by a gentle breeze.

Official Investigation by
Dr. J. S. Haldane, F.R.S.

52

THE GAS FIEND

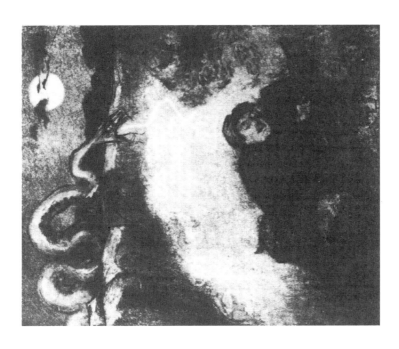

A T some time between 4 and 5 P.M. [April 22] the Germans started operations by releasing gases, with the result that a cloud of poisonous vapour rolled swiftly before the wind from their trenches towards those of the French west of Langemarck, held by a portion of the French Colonial Division. Allowing sufficient time for the fumes to take full effect on the troops facing them, the Germans charged forward over the practically unresisting enemy in their immediate front, and, penetrating through the gap thus created, pressed on silently and swiftly to the south and west.

OFFICIAL EYEWITNESS.
April 27, 1915.

We shall not allow these wonderful weapons, which German intelligence invented, to grow rusty.

The Cologne Gazette

Germany was a signatory to the declaration at the Hague Conference of 1899, and an article in that Declaration ran as follows : "The contracting Powers agree to abstain from the use of projectiles the sole object of which is the diffusion of asphyxiating or deleterious gases."

The first few days of May were spent in repairing smashed barbed wire entanglements and installing telephone wires above the communication trenches while at night there were the eternal carrying fatigues. Hodgkin viewed the superfluous nature of these activities with some impatience:

Up to Spoil Bank at night, carrying barbed wire entanglements, & also rations for the whole battalion, after the former had been left at Bde Hqrs. This does not sound very dreadful, but the Platoon commanders have very lurid views on it. To add to our enjoyment 2 Platoons had afterwards to go and help garrison No. 28 trench at 3 minutes notice. The C.O. is going off his head: we have 2 or 3 officers out here to look after 10 men on a carrying party. He apparently does not consider the Platoon commanders fit for their jobs. After all of which it is ordained that we stand to arms at 2.30 & carry bricks to pave the CO's apartments.

(Hodgkin, May 7th)

However, in spite of these irritations two days later he noted: 'We all had a half glass of wine tonight and I became very frivolous. I horrified the men with my attempts to play a penny whistle: my masterpiece is 'We shan't be home till morning'. There was a saying around, that if you didn't possess a sense of humour why join the trenches?

But there was no time to make proper repairs to No. 28 trench newly allotted to the battalion on May 8th. Having a lot of dead ground in front it was disconnected at that time with 27, a soggy marsh lying between them and it reached right down to the canal bank. Early on May 10th, 2nd Lieut B.S. Walker, a tall kindly man, Heald's loved childhood friend with whom he had volunteered in the previous August, was shot through the head. Hodgkin related it as:

A black letter day. I was standing in No. 28 taking in the sunshine at 5.30 a.m. with Walker and Hartley when a bullet came through the top of the parapet and killed Walker. It is an awful shame and we shall miss him dreadfully. We had only just taken over the trench and on examination we found that practically the whole of the parapet is unsafe at the top.

Regiments that leave their trenches in this condition ought to be told off for it in public.

(Hodgkin, May 10th)

54

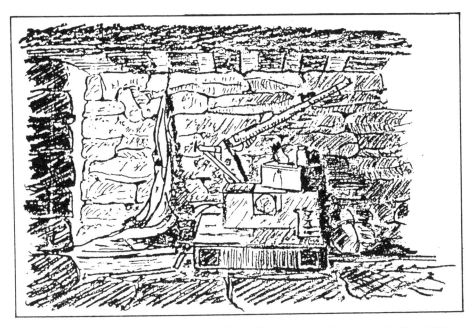

The door of our dugout in No. 27 trench. YPRES (showing part of "sniperscope".) May 7 1915

View over the pond from the road at Spoil Bank on the south side of the former Ypres/Commines Canal looking south east, taken in May 1985. The trees on the left are on the southern side of the canal. The first line of poplars are in the approximate position of Trenches 27 and 28. The poplars on the crest mark the German positions.

Ypres 1915

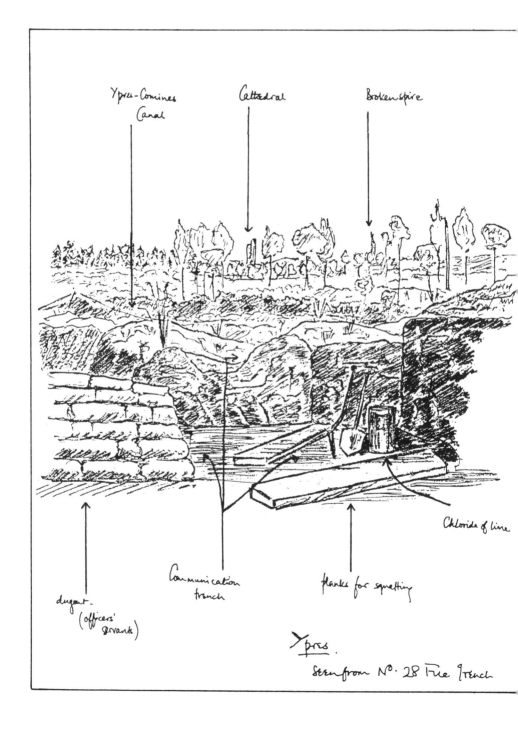

Ypres-Comines Canal

Cathedral

Broken spire

dugout (officers' servants)

Communication trench

planks for squatting

Chloride of lime

Ypres.

Seen from Nº. 28 Fire Trench

Heald who had been woken up with the news in his dugout at Spoil Bank described it as:

> The worst day of my life. Upset me frightfully. Luckily I managed to
> get into the wood by myself. It does seem hard that poor Basil should be
> taken. I shall never meet a better man as long as I live. He was hit in
> the head whilst chatting to the officers in front of their dugout. Suppose
> his head must have been too high though some say the bullet came
> through the parapet. He knew nothing about it. He is very much missed
> by the battalion. Went up to the trenches at night to see Hartley and got
> Basil's things. We put him in the dressing station for the night.
>
> (Heald, May 10th)

Before they left England in 1915, the 5th Battalion had a marching song composed by its subalterns, the first two lines were as follows:

> 'The Earl of Chester came to me and shook me by the hand,
> He said the Fifth Battalion was the finest in the land ...'

Walker had set this simple ditty to music with a lively tune, and now that universally loved man was dead.

The weather was glorious, and after four weeks of dodging shells and bullets either in the trenches or support dugouts the battalion was relieved and all marched to their bivouacs about four miles away in the fields. McGowan told his parents that they should have been thoroughly happy camping out in the open air but for one deep sorrow: 'It seems that poor Walker's wound was very serious and from the first there was no hope for him and he died within an hour of being hit. He was a great favourite with all officers and the men of his company'.

Heald had been entrusted with the honour of carrying Walker's body to the rear:

> We put him on a stretcher with a blanket over him and carried him
> down by night. Ypres was burning fiercely and lit up the whole country
> and Hill 60 was being attacked. Amidst all this, we took to our old bivis
> and laid him in a tent with a sentry over him for the night. I made a
> cross of wild white daisies and put it on him., The battalion was lined
> up in two long lines and we carried him to his last resting place between
> them.
>
> (Heald, May 11th)

There was not a great deal of ceremony but it was a solemn and impressive procession that left the camp for the field hospital cemetery a mile away at

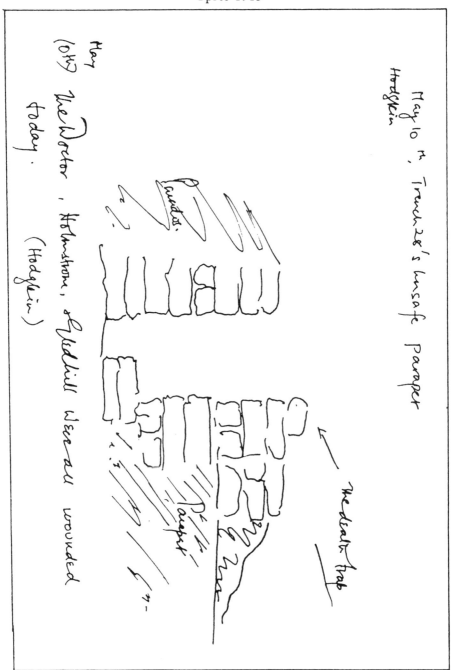

Site of Walker's death, May 16th 1915.

3 o' clock. The long files of soldiers saluted as the bodies passed (Private J.W. Hayes who was killed on the Tuesday evening being buried at the same time). On the way they passed an encampment of Indian soldiers and of a Scottish regiment, all of whom paid their respects as the procession carrying the litters passed by. In his sorrow Heald wrote: 'His grave lies in a small cemetery on the second road to the left off the Vlamertynghi Road from Ypres. About 900 yards down. It is a quiet spot amid beautiful green fields and trees. May his body lie there in peace.' Walker's grave now lies in the same cemetery, an undisturbed and beautifully preserved plot. J.W. Hayes of Northwich, Cheshire, lies beside him. Having been in Flanders only for a short time, the battalion was still a well knit group and it is obvious that the death of such a popular officer

Walker's grave in May 1986.

was deeply moving. At that point in the war, it seems that such a funeral was still possible, and was in contrast to the unceremonious burials (if any) after the later battles.

McGowan impressed by this solemnity, attended a voluntary service in the field held later that evening by the chaplain, as preparation for Ascension Day communion:

> His beautiful address to us did much to turn our sorrow into joy. He is a splendid man. He took his text from the opening verses of the 14th Chapt. of St. John & among other beautiful things said we who knew from experience what a truly happy home was, could form some faint picture of what our future home in heaven would be, whereas those who had not had that earthly privilege could look forward to that happiness

which would be theirs some day. Next morning communion was held in the Colonel's tent at 9 a.m. There was quite a good attendance, for it is three weeks ago since we had the privilege of attending Divine Service.

(McGowan, May 12th).

In 1915, the British Army wore only their caps, but steel helmets known as 'Adrians' were adopted by the French Army later that year and the British soon followed this example. The reduction in casualties from head wounds especially from shrapnel was immediate. Though not especially newsworthy in the turmoil of the Ypres battle, since the middle of February upwards of two hundred and fifty casualties killed, wounded and sick had ebbed away the strength of the battalion, in a steady haemorrhage. Overshadowed by simultaneous events taking place to the north and east of the salient and the campaign in the Dardanelles, the tale of the heroic stands on Hill 60 in April and May did not receive full coverage by all the papers. In any case, war correspondent reports were rigorously censored, and photographers banned from the front line, where only the accredited war artists depicted selections of chosen scenes. John Buchan, a war correspondent for *The Times* in 1915 was struck by the sudden green countryside so close to the fire zone. He compared its peaceful fields where the cattle grazed, to Oxfordshire, and noted the girls in the scattered hamlets making lace in the sunshine outside their red tiled houses. Then all at once came the festering odour of latrines, the incinerators and the dead corpses of humans and animals. The peace shattered by shells, bullets and the roaring guns.

Replacements from England arrived to replace the battalion casualties. One of these was P.B. Bass who was straightaway detailed to McGowan's company. To Bass, McGowan, steady and always looking on the bright side would have been a reassuring companion:

It really is a grand healthy life here were it not for the too close proximity of shot & shell I can eat almost anything, anytime, and plenty of it. Most of the men are at work digging etc. by day & a few at night on work that must be done under cover of darkness, while a certain number are kept on sentry work.

I should imagine such jobs as these were quite common in the South African war but then I expect there would be days together when they never heard a shot fired, to say nothing of shells.

De Palingbeek (near Hill 60) how a nature reserve has been made of the filled in canal. This is the view from the German positions of Trenches 27 and 28 occupied by the 5th Cheshires. As usual the Germans occupied the high ground. Photographed May 1985

I try to get 3 hrs. sleep between 9 p.m. & midnight & Bass between 12 p.m. & 3 a.m. & both us again sleep (if things are quiet) between 5 a.m. & 10 a.m. Last night I was disturbed about 6 times in all, telephone messages, stores receipts etc. & once by the Mach. Gun Officer of the — who was passing on his way back from the trenches to listen to some news he's just recd. wind of. (1) the sinking of the Lusitania. If that is a fact (can hardly yet believe it) surely the Americans will no longer remain impassive spectators, but will throw in their weight with us & help to crush quickly those barbarians. (2) A great trench victory — an advance of 1½ miles over a 15 mile front. That too seems almost too dramatic to be authentic. (3) Another British advance near Neuve Chapelle. If this is so things ought to be a bit quiet here abouts. Oh I received the parcel the first night here & very acceptable it was. Thanks to it, & some of the grub I had left out of the last, Bass & I have had some excellent meals out here in the open. The crab by the way was delicious. Not the least bit thirst provoking, quite the reverse in

61

fact. We are going to have some of the Huns' beans tonight along with our usual Irish Stew, which my servant has made for us each evening while here. Its my own recipe and consists of Maconachie (I described what that was some time ago I think) Bacon, Bully beef, an Oxo cube & potatoes of which there is a plentiful supply in a ruined farm close by. I hope the Colonel & Adjutant don't disturb us in the middle of it this evening as they have done the last two days. However, when I showed them round they seemed quite pleased with the work done. The 5th Cheshires have got a splendid name in the Division for digging work & possibly we've that to thank for the fact that altho so near to the very heavy fighting the trenches we've been told off to occupy have all along been comparatively quiet.

Yesterday *30* of our reinforcements arrived. They could be swallowed up by one company and hardly noticed. I've not been troubled again by the toothache thank you but I will see the dentist at the first opportunity. I broke my inhaler & spilt the oil a week or two ago. It's difficult to carry glass things about with one.

Thanks all the same but I shall not need the goggles I think, the gags they've now issued us with have a bit of cotton mesh with which to cover the eyes. Don't put yourself out to get the cocoa tablets for I drink tea more now I've got the 'unico' & now the hot weather's arrived. Thanks for chocolate, a bit of that is always welcome.

Well I must get this to the post or it will have to wait another day. This isn't as interesting a letter as I'd like to have written, but one must be careful.

(McGowan, May 10th)

On the day following Walker's funeral the weather deteriorated suddenly, transforming their camp into a sea of mud. Hodgkin wrote caustically:

Battalion parade in the morning presumably to ensure that the men should get thoroughly wet and remain so. It's rather hard lines when they are sleeping in a tent about 6 ft × 11 ft. and 3ft. 6ins. high and have no means of drying their clothes, result a big sick list in the morning.

(Hodgkin, May 11th)

Becoming perturbed, the M.O. said the men were so worn out they would catch anything. Several cases of measles were reported and they were visited by the D.A.D.M.S. who rode over from Reninghelst and sent a hundred men away for a rest on May 18th.

Heald had a deft touch when firing off the trench mortar, so was elated when he and 2nd Lt. S.P. Gamon were appointed grenadier officers to train a section of fifty men:

> Our duties are to make life hideous for the Germans in the trenches with rifle grenades, trench mortars etc. and when we attack, to lead the battalion and beat the enemy out of their trenches.
>
> (Heald, May 13th)

Even though it became too wet to do much training, they were given a new trench howitzer fired by a gun cotton charge which seemed to produce accurate results. But after a week it was removed and they had to make do once more with their old weapon.

McGowan, newly designated as Sapper Officer, didn't know much about the work beyond the fact that he had to leave his platoon and take charge of twenty four battalion Sappers; but he was fortunate that he was given a very good sergeant from his old platoon who had been a rock miner. He wrote home:

> Captain Hartley is jolly sorry to lose me but possibly it is only a temporary change and when I have turned the sappers into a properly organised squad I may be able to leave them in charge of an N.C.O.

Early one morning after tramping back from the line they passed close to a couple of their batteries belching forth towards the German lines trying to silence the guns continuously shelling Ypres:

> They've evidently been using incendiary bombs of late for whenever one looks in that dirn. by day one sees a thick cloud of smoke rapidly rising heavenwards & by night a dull red glow which must be visible for miles round. On the way here this morning at one point we could distinguish five separate conflagrations. We cannot fathom the reason for such persistency on their part. If their object was to move all troops out of the vicinity they did that 2 or 3 weeks ago. It's probably nothing but wanton destruction so dear to their bestial natures, & as a matter of fact we like to see such a large amt. of precious ammunition spent involving very little loss of life & damage only to property already rendered useless except to art lovers & historians.
>
> (McGowan, May 12th)

Subalterns of the Foot

It was impossible to keep squalor at bay and the discomfort of feeling dirty and verminous added to the general insalubrity:

> There are five families of rats in the roof of my dugout which is 2 feet above my head in bed, & the little rats practise back somersaults continuously through the night, for they have discerned that my face is soft landing when they fall. It's wonderful how many things militate against one's comfort in this world.
>
> (Murray, May 14th)

They resorted to sending their laundry home as the postal service up to the front line was reliable and efficient. Letters took on an average four days and McGowan's letters often mentioned parcels received and sent:

> You might let me have the clean clothes as soon as possible, but I expect I shall get them this week, then I can change. I'm glad when I can send you anything for you are very good to me.
>
> (McGowan, May 12th)

Lace making being a local activity, McGowan had spent some time (in spite of language difficulties) negotiating with a French demoiselle for a nice handkerchief and pin cushion cover for his stepmother. Food, eagerly anticipated was the most prized commodity of all, even crumbly cakes arrived without disintegrating too badly as did cooked chickens and ducks, puddings and Edinburgh Rock.

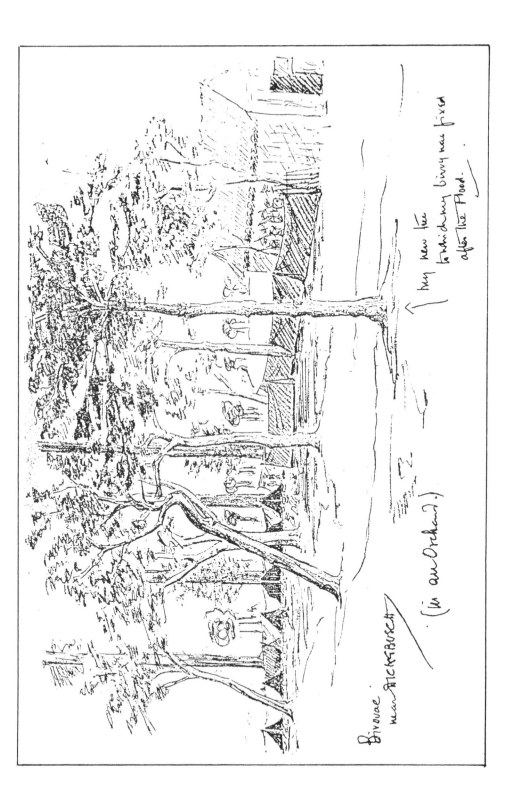

Bivouac near PICKFABURCH

(in an Orchard.)

They here the branching binery was fixed after the Flood.

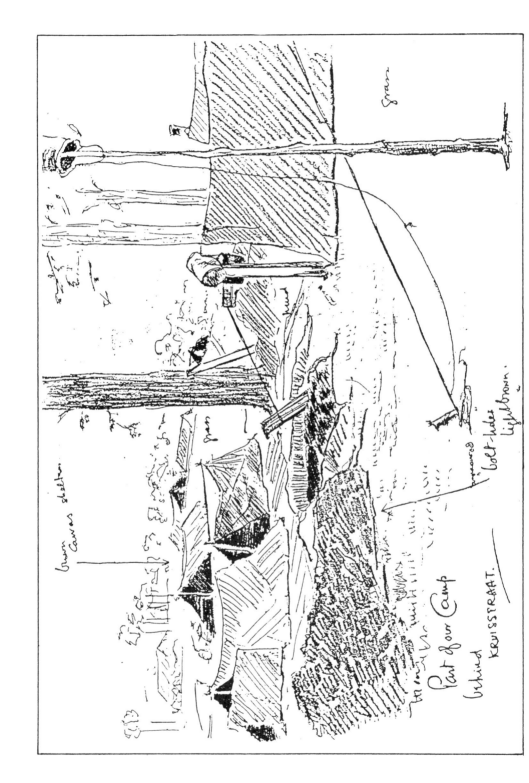

Part of our Camp
behind
KRUISSTRAAT.

CHAPTER 3

AFTERMATH

Need for rest was becoming imperative, for some sort of low fever had broken out and the men having a strange nightly rise of high temperatures fell out wholesale on working parties. From the start, McGowan thought that their physique had never been of the best, now their depleted energies were entirely used up with fatigue and nerve strain. It was not the custom to pay much individual attention to the health of private soldiers, if a man became a liability in the ranks there he stayed until he became a casualty. 'One or two of the officers are affected, but of course we do not get such trying times as do the men, at all events when 'off duty' and are better able to look after our bodily health'. (McGowan, May 17th) Eventually they retreated to a camp under canvas behind Kruisstraat. But not much respite was allowed and when McGowan was ordered to take the sappers with 'D' Company on May 23rd five miles across country for a hot bath, even his equable temperament was shaken:

> Why march tired troops 10 miles for a hot bath when there is a pool close by deep enough to swim in and a sun shining hot enough to make toast. And why it was necessary for 5 officers to accompany 80 men when two would have been quite sufficient is another puzzle it's no use trying to solve. Our's not to reason why etc. However it wasn't such a bad walk & while the men were bathing four of us sat under a pear tree archway in the garden of one of the shops there & partook of a little light refreshment. It was a splendid kitchen garden with peas, beans, potatoes, beetroot etc. all neatly laid out like many a kitchen garden one sees attached to gentlemen's houses in England.

> We left the camp at noon & did not return until 4.30 p.m. when it pleased the powers that be (Colonel & Adj) to hold a check kit inspection. Immed. after this office hours were held (which I now attend each day as I am now in charge of a separate detachment of men) so about 6 o'clock I was able to sit down in peace & eat, but not for long for an orderly soon came along with orders for work. This was quite an unpleasant surprise for the orders for the night's working parties had been issued as usual about 5.30 p.m. & I quite thought I had escaped & could settle down for a quiet rest after the long march, but it seems a special telepd. message came through for as many men as poss. to carry mining stores to one of the fire trenches where they are busy sapping towards the German lines & so I had to start off straightaway with 80

men & a junior officer. It was every bit of 4 mls. across the field to the off-loading place, where we had to wait ¾ hr for the transport to arrive, unload the waggon & distribute the load among the men, who were by this time reduced to 72 (8 having fallen out sick despite the fact that I warned every man before we started that any man falling out & getting 'medicine & duty' on his sick report, would be brought before the Commanding Officer the next day for slackness — (scrimshanking as we call it out here). The stores then had to be carried best part of two miles from the off-loading place to the fire trench. While waiting for the transport I had a chat with the Brigade Major & he told me that our Battn. was to go back for a rest tomorrow (Sunday) evening so I was particularly anxious to avoid casualties of any kind, nevertheless one man was hit (fortunately a nice flesh wound through the upper part of leg & it so happened we were quite close to a field dressing station when it happened so I expect he'll be on his way to England now).

After delivering the goods to a mining engineer officer & his staff (whom I hear are all mining specialists recently sent out & commanding much higher pay that the ordinary R.E. soldier) we made our way back as quickly as possible, for there was a big thunder storm raging over the German lines & although I didn't care how much damage or inconvenience it caused them I'd no wish to get my men hurt or wet through. The lightening was very vivid & the thunder altho' fairly distant quite drowned the noise of the artillery which has been comparatively quiet in this part of late. However, we were not caught & got back quite dry & very tired about 2 a.m. that day.

(McGowan, May 23rd)

Eventually on May 23rd they were evacuated for one week's rest at Boeschepe:

The march was rather a hectic performance: the whole of the Officers' Mess Cart was taken up with the C.O.'s baggage, & he had the grace to declare that he didn't care a damn what happened to the Companys' mess boxes, & much more in a similar strain. This will give a hint as to the relations existing between him and the other officers. It is a great pity, as the efficiency of the battalion is very greatly affected by it. However, the battalion attended by several ambulance waggons, finally arrived by many routes, the companies moving independently, at Boeschepe, about 1.30 a.m. on the 24th.

(Hodgkin, May 24th)

Aftermath

McGowan's legs ached so much after the endless marching that he did not sleep as soundly as usual but was up in good time to attend divine service conducted by the chaplain:

> The service was quite voluntary but there was a large attendance of Cheshires & detachments of R.E.'s & artillery-men encamped close to us. There was of course no organ or other instrumental music & the chaplain who leads in the hymn-singing is invariably out of tune & doesn't know it but the volume grows with each verse & we generally managed to drown him before the end of the third verse, & altho' he cannot sing he preaches magnificently so we always have an enjoyable & helpful service.

> The ordinary service was followed by Holy Communion in the officers mess tent, & there was again quite a good attendance of both officers & men. To look upon the small altar of cedar-wood — the silver vessels set out upon a white linen cloth & the white robes of the chaplain (who always exchanges his military tunic for cassock & surplice at communion service) it is difficult to believe that one is so near to the battle field.
>
> (McGowan, May 23rd)

Most of the afternoon was spent in cleaning up the camp site for the next unit, but as the grenadiers and sappers brought up the rear of the procession, neither McGowan nor Heald were involved in the general hassle of the earlier evacuation. The specialist sections had been ordered to load up the wagons with stores and didn't exactly hurry over the job in the hope that the Colonel and Adjutant would have left by the time they returned. But no such luck as they had waited for them, and it was a case of 'no smoking' and 'no noise' all the way although they were marching right away from the firing line. About half way along, horse drawn ambulance carts were waiting to pick up the sick who struggled to keep up, loaded down by their full kits. McGowan's sappers were billeted a mile from the village in the barn of a nearby farm, and adjutant or no adjutant nothing would have made him trudge back to H.Q. that night. While negotiating with the farmer for drinking water for his party, McGowan 'parleyed' with him to let him sleep on some chairs in his kitchen till morning. Feeling in luck, he rolled into the farmer's bed at 5 a.m. after the man had got up to work, McGowan waking at 9 a.m. found that the good lady of the house had cooked him breakfast for which she only asked half a franc. Gratefully McGowan rewarded her three times over.

Boeschepe was a delightful spot, from the top of a neighbouring hill you could almost see the sea. Surrounding the village the chocolate brown fields were criss crossed with a forest of long bare hop poles, their strings stretching out between them with orderly precision. Except for the distant rumbles of the big guns, the green trees and hedgerows of early June remained undisturbed by the lacerations of war. It was peaceful, the sun shone and Heald having slept out of doors, sunbathed 'in the altogether' before he bathed and dressed. McGowan who had not been missed at H.Q. in the village strolled around in bright moonlight, pipe in mouth, having found himself a decent bed sitting room in a cottage close by to the farm. He fed well, as his batman cooked with local eggs, butter and milk to eke out the dull army rations:

4 p.m. Tuesday May 25th:

Another glorious summer day in which I've done nothing thus far but inspect the rifles of my men & held my own office hrs. convicting one man to 72 hours C.B. for general slackness on parade — not a very terrible punishment but just sufficient to remind him & the others that although we are here for a rest, the country is still at war & discipline must be maintained.

My otherwise most comfortable sleep last night was disturbed about dawn by the persistent energies of a little stranger (or possibly the plural of that ilk) but I quickly checked his enthusiasm by the application of a little disinfectant powder that forms a part of my war-kit.

The colonel & Adjutant have just passed on horseback & called me out to advise me that 'Bn. Office Hrs.' will be held at 6 p.m. each evening. They both seemed quite cheery & as yet have not devised any new tortures to inflict upon us, so I'm hoping that they really intend to allow us a genuine rest. Of course I've no idea how long we are to remain here, but I expect we shall wait until properly reinforced.

I suppose you will have received my p.c. posted yesterday but, before I close this letter let me thank you once again for the parcel received on Sat. & the letter received on Sunday both of which were very welcome. It's very good of you to take so much trouble over the watch. You both quite spoil me in your eagerness to satisfy my every want.

(McGowan's parents had commented on another very detailed diary sent home by a friend from another part of the line)

Aftermath

...Of course it may be he has been in the thick of it — still been able to keep a detailed diary but from what we heard from one of our officers who conducted a draft of men to Armentières about a month ago things have been very quiet at that part of the line for along time & the officers are living in dug-outs furnished like houses, in fact he actually saw & heard a piano playing in a dug-out not a mile from the firing-line. One of his remarks when he came back was 'The officers there might very easily have their wives staying with them & bid them goodbye when leaving for the trenches with no nore compunction than they did at home when leaving for the office each morning.' Of course it's easy enough to keep a decent diary when in a place like this, but not so in trenches with an active enemy less that 50 yds away or even when in reserve if shells are dropping less than 100 yds away & you are out with working parties every night.

About one and a half miles away, Hodgkin found billets with some nice homely people:

We slept on a stone floor, & during the night a slug committed suicide on my waterproof sheet. Incidentally, I had arranged myself all unwittingly bang in front of the door giving access to the room where is accommodated the enormous patriarchal family, with the result that all the morning, people were gingerly stepping over my head: so much so that I had to cover it up in self-defence.

Pigs are voracious animals, notoriously so: but I never saw one try to devour a set of web equipment before today: nor jump a barricade when chased.

Ellington goes to hospital tommorrow: he has had a kind of low fever for some days.

(Hodgkin, May 24th)

Heald and Gamon, sent to billets near their grenadiers had a great welcome from some engineers living on a train which had been fitted up ingeniously on a nearby railway. Both of them were plied with whisky and soda and the engineers played a selection of their records on the gramophone while listening to stories of the trenches. Heald did not remember a more enjoyable day. He had not tasted a whisky since leaving England and was delighted to hear some music. When the invitation was repeated for the following day, it was accepted with alacrity.

71

But May 26th became a day of wrath. The C.O. kicked up a fearful row because Heald and Gamon were not carrying on training their grenadiers and had left their bombs behind. Gamon who had misunderstood the situation had inadvertently returned the bombs to store before leaving Boeschepe. Hodgkin waxed indignant as 'Gamon was then sent off with 50 innocent men and a transport wagon to Kruisstraat to get the bombs; this means a march of 23 miles in addition to this he and his men will miss their dinner'. As Heald said: 'One man would have done. An instance of his petty spite because he had given no order re our stores. Gamon had dinner with the Brigade Major and told him all about it. I expect that Staff have sized up our C.O. pretty well and we are here for a rest too. They got back at 3 a.m. dead tired'. That night the officers seethed with wrath. Hodgkin quoted from battalion orders issued on May 26th which he considered showed how dirty linen could be washed in public to the best advantage:

'Discipline:

When the Commanding Officer first visits Companies and Detachments each day the whole Company or Detachment is to be called to attention by the first Officer, N.C.O. or man that sees him. The senior officer or N.C.O. present is then to be informed at once that the Commanding Officer is present. The Senior Officer or N.C.O. is then immediately to report himself to the Commanding Officer and await instructions.

The procedure which obtains at present shows great laxity of discipline in some Companies and Detachments. Officers and Non-Commissioned Officers have been observed to deliberately move away on the approach of the Commanding Officer and cases have also been noticed of their remaining in the background until their presence has been demanded'.

For four consecutive nights Hodgkin who had been consistently running a temperature of 101° was despatched to the convalescent hospital on Mont Noir to the east of Kemmel. Grinding through the mire of a narrow lane, all the sick had to turn out in order to jack the motor ambulance out of the mud. Frequently acting as chauffeurs many civilian drivers from England had presented their cars to the Automobile Association and the Motor Union of Great Britain to be converted into ambulances, even on occasions driving them bravely up to the advanced dressing stations and first aid posts, often under fire and as near the front as possible. Stretchers for the wounded and sick were laid on shelves or on rather primitive springs inside the vehicles, which did not effectively cushion the jolts.

An Old Fleming in the frontier
Examined at MONT NOIR.

The hospital which belonged to a Belgian merchant at that time stranded in German territory, turned out to be a magnificent red brick château with cream corner stones. At the gates there was a small lodge from which a grand avenue of beech trees lead up to the front entrance. Inside the château a finely paved entrance hall opened on to a large lounge furnished with comfortable easy chairs and settees; there was a piano and a multitude of books and magazines. Through some folding glass doors there were in succession a games room, a writing room and finally the dining room all handsomely decorated. The dining room had a wide balcony with panoramic views of the densely wooded grounds and the large roughly cut lawn which stretched down towards the flat countryside to the south. Altogether twenty six cases of sick or slightly wounded officers could convalesce there in utmost luxury.

On arrival, Hodgkin found the next door bed occupied by Captain G.H. Woolley, the first Territorial to have won the Victoria Cross and in consequence felt much reflected glory. With nostalgia the two room mates turned to the subject of their old Oxford days and mulled over a score of mutual friends. Before enlisting in the Queen's Victoria Rifles, Geoffrey

Woolley had been at Queen's College, subsequently like Benjamin Geary gaining his Victoria Cross on Hill 60. The son of a clergyman, Woolley also took holy orders after the war and was an assistant master and chaplain of Harrow School from 1927-1939.

On Tuesdays and Fridays there was usually a convoy to bathe at the asylum at Bailleul, and Hodgkin recovering somewhat joined it on June 9th. He enjoyed turning on the abundant hot water and luxuriating in plentiful towels:

> Meanwhile the Padre raids the shops for new crockery for the hospital; he refused to buy certain delectable plates inscribed with a riddle the answer being written underneath. It seemed to the rest of us that this would considerably add to the enjoyment of our meals.
>
> (Hodgkin, May 28th).

All at once, when a lot of senior officers arrived at the hospital, the atmosphere quickly became sedate, but Hodgkin managed to hitch a joy ride to nearby Hazebrouck to buy some collars: 'It was not at all a bad little place'. At one end of its cobbled street lay the church, the clock tower surmounted by a finely pointed spire.

While Hodgkin was convalescing, Heald resumed training his grenadiers. He found a billet in a small cottage with a flower patch of colourful annuals in the front garden which was railed in to keep out the hens, who clucked around and scratched up the rest around the fence. At one side, a dog trotted along in a huge revolving wheel that worked a churn in the house. Other dogs resembling mastiffs, usually three together were used by the country folk for drawing small carts. The sheep were milked with quite good results and altogether he felt happy there. Numerous windmills could be seen dotted around the hills on one side of Boeschepe, but as spy mania still prevailed, the sails were kept set in a fixed position as it was suspected their rotations were manipulated for signalling to the enemy.

On the last day of May, the battalion was ordered back to their old bivouacs at Spoil Bank behind trenches 27 and 28 by the canal. The grenadiers led the march thus escaping the dust kicked up on the dirty road by the rest of the column. On hearing of their impending departure, Heald and his grenadiers had taken good care to let off their stores of explosives so as not to have to carry them back. They achieved some beautiful anti aircraft gun effects with one trench mortar, timing the bombs to burst high in the air. On the whole, Heald felt that his men had now become quite promising at bombing along a trench and were ready to do the enemy down.

A maze of newly constructed alleys greeted them on return which found their way from Headquarters to 27 and 28 about half a mile away, McGowan who embarked on a tour of inspection with the Colonel and Adjutant took all of three hours to complete the circuit. On each subsequent day McGowan and his sappers laboured away at shifting mountains of earth to improve the drainage of the labyrinth. Eventually before knocking off one evening, tired as they were, the men's interest became aroused at the results when McGowan ordered them to open all the dams they had made in the draining ditches. Gathering strength on the way the water like a young Niagara poured down towards the canal.

About fifty yards behind 27 and 28, commodious and palatial dug outs had been excavated in the communication trenches connected to the supports. In one of these, not a hundred yards from the enemy, McGowan came upon Heald reclining on a spring mattress of rolled up wire netting, held up by stakes driven firmly into the ground. Here the grenadier officers rested during the day. The room was furnished with a stout round oak table big enough for six that had been looted from goodness knows where, two chairs, some shelves and various pictures completed the scene. Heald was in a happy frame of mind, he thought his quarters luxurious and was looking forward to quite a decent time. He had organised his grenadiers into snipers and had under him for instruction as well a fine platoon of Kings Royal Rifles. McGowan jokingly asked him where the bathroom was, to which Heald in all seriousness told him it was under construction, a bit to the rear where a drainage well was within easy reach:

> This trench warfare is a marvellous business, I used to think it sufficient cause for wonderment that here in the support dugouts we were able to have a cold bath each morning, but after visiting our fire and support trenches, I've come to the conclusion they have the acme of comfort...
>
> Of course no doubt people at home would say, our time would be far better spent in taking more pains to drive the Germans back, but it must be remembered that they are just as strongly fortified, if not more so, (in fact we have heard of a case of a captured trench which revealed dug-outs containing suites of furniture, walls covered with leather, glass doors fitted & electric light laid on). Such fortifications as these can only be taken by the aid of plenty of artillery fire & supporting troops which we apparently are still a bit short of, but when the time is ripe for an advance I've no doubt we shall leave our comfortable trench-houses readily enough & leave the enemy's behind us too, if possible, but in the meantime, partly for amusement, we believe in making our present residence as comfortable as possible one for another for as long as we shall need them. Of course these particular trenches are now some of the best in the neighbourhood, for instance, those we spent three weeks in at

our last place were none so nice, nor for that matter were these in the Winter & early Spring.

(McGowan, June 4th)

To say the least of it, the grenadiers were not at all that popular with the others, their unstable weapons being liable at any moment to backfire alarmingly in their own trenches. For some reason when those in 28 couldn't use their trench mortar, Heald tried his luck with it using some of his own bombs. The first one was rotten but the next two exploded in the enemy trench fairly knocking it out. As a result he won several francs from the sergeant major who bet they couldn't get within twenty yards of their target.

About fifty yards from the Germans' trench, 28 remaining as dangerously exposed as ever took its further toll of death. On June 3rd, 2nd Lt. Drummond Fraser who had only recently arrived from England on April 30th was fatally wounded. This time only a small group could be spared to carry the body to the little churchyard at Kruisstraat on the Ypres Kemmel road, and McGowan was required elsewhere:

It is very sad especially for his parents but to my mind not so sad as Walker's death, for at the time he was hit he was out with a working party putting out wire entanglements in front of our trenches, extremely useful and necessary work, and he was certainly 'killed in action', although it will probably be reported officially 'died of wounds' for he was shot through the chest and dead within 24 hours.

(McGowan, June 4th)

Heald was having a lively time in 27 and 28 but in spite of the chancy nature of his existence, temperamentally the skirmishing tactics suited his sporting instincts. But he never cared for being cold, and he resented having to send home his lined 'Burberry' when their kit was summarily reduced to thirty-five pounds:

Good day's sniping but was not so fortunate with bombs. Germans have at last knocked down the last two church spires in Ypres. Swines! German snipers are wonderful shots. Knocked the foresight off one of our sniper scopes at 300 yards. Managed to repair it though. Have found some good positions for snipers loopholes. K.T.R's have gone out and Cheshires in again. Germans keep on sending up red lights, don't know what they mean. Trench mortared them hard all night. Brigade Major asked us to fire, so we did and blew out their parapet.

(Heald, June 4th)

76

For this they got shelled the following morning, killing one and one being
wounded.

> Was on parapet at night putting in a loophole when we looked up and
> saw a bomb dropping on us. (You can see them by the sparks) we dived
> full length round a corner and it blew out the parapet. It saved us a lot
> of work but rather trying. They blew another hole about ten yards away
> so we put another loophole in that. We bombed them until they shut up.
>
> They rifle grenaded us so we replied with trench mortar. Unfortunately
> it blew up. Faulty bomb. No one hurt. I always take proper precautions
> to clear every one out. Enemy had all their own way. Managed to pitch
> a rifle grenade on their parapet.
>
> (Heald, June 5th)

Mysteriously the following day three men were hit, dropping dead
simultaneously. The breastwork being very flimsy, Heald thought the
Germans had fired continuously at one spot eventually making a hole, the
bullets smacking loudly into the parapet with whip like precision. That night
he crawled over the top of the parapet to spot a place for an advanced
listening post. Having made a hole in the ground where his men could camp
out, he started to dig a trench which he finished in the pouring rain on the
following night. The weather grew thundery and he started to feel done up
and disinclined to do much; in addition they were shelled heavily again,
causing four casualties in the two trenches. He developed a bad sore throat
and suffered badly from want of sleep. In spite of his malaise he set up a fixed
rifle on one of the parapets which snicked away at the enemy's sandbags at
intervals throughout the night. With teutonic predictability the Germans
began to shell their trenches as regular as clockwork and Heald thought it was
a nice baptism of fire for the two platoons of the D.C.L.I. [Kitchener's] who
had arrived for instruction; but Hodgkin felt it must be annoying for the
'New Army' to be taught by the 'damned Territorials'. Although Heald's
throat worsened it appeared to make him even more tenacious in his desire to
do down the enemy, a feeling that had strengthened increasingly since
Walker's death:

> Have established two 'listening posts' outside our trench about 200 yards
> in front and made four of my grenadiers occupy them at night to watch
> for hostile parties creeping up and bombing our trench. Some of my
> men don't like it a bit. They are very nervous but will soon get used to
> it. They are under cover and really in no danger if they keep awake. I
> shall not allow any shirking as I think it does them good to learn to

depend a bit on themselves. I and my sergeant and corporal crept out up to within 40 yards of the German trench to investigate a sap head which we thought they were mining from. We found nothing at all so we chucked four bombs in and doubled back safely.

(Heald, June 15th)

Hodgkin didn't think that the patrols and raids, so much encouraged at Brigade H.Q. would have much success in capturing any unwary Germans as in his opinion the opposite trench was garrisoned only by 'a caretaker and his wife neither of whom wandered about much at night'.

Feeling cold and shaky, fearing an onset of fever, Heald dosed himself with quinine and covered in a blanket lay shivering in his dug-out all day listening to sporadic shelling outside. Recovering somewhat, he was told by the Brigade to go on a raid and get a German prisoner to ascertain who exactly was opposite. He thought of devising a trap to set in an old communication trench they suspected the enemy of using, the whole shattered area having British and German trenches winding about in every direction. In order to entice the enemy in they put up a flag thinking to dare him to come and get it, but in so doing Heald's platoon had rather a hot time as there were several bursts of rapid. He didn't think the Germans could manage to get the flag without their lot spotting it so giving the listening posts special instructions to shoot, he positioned a new trench mortar to warm up the evening. By June 17th the Germans had not fallen for the bait and like Hodgkin, Heald didn't think there were many opposite, but for good measure he gave the enemy trenches a good doing, getting no reply. They returned about 2.30 a.m. to their bivouacs in a peaceful orchard near Dickebusch. He still felt very off colour.

Hodgkin, who had heard distinct knocking directly under their trench, surmised they were probably being mined. He thought the 'caretaker and his wife' had been exceedingly industrious as the shaft must have been at least two hundred yards long. Another officer confirmed it as he heard a man sawing wood underground; in fact the whole mining business set them so much on the detective trade that they could all have sworn that the Germans had laid a chlorine fuze in the floor of their dug-out. After a hurried investigation their fantasies collapsed when they found that it was only the man attending to the latrines with chloride of lime. On the night of June 16th they had two men shot and wounded on patrol, having failed to find a gap in their own wire through which they could return. Very foolishly the men had crawled up towards trench 27 where 'A' company opened rapid fire with keen promptness. Night patrolling in that wilderness was a perpetual tangle, creeping round a hole or stretch of wired posts, it was at times impossible to discern which was German line or their own, and distance in pitch darkness was a matter only for conjecture. It was thus fortunate that only two of the patrols merely suffered flesh wounds, though one man was hit six times, lucky to escape with his life.

For over two weeks now McGowan had been labouring away in the communication trenches, and with the deterioration in the weather, the water welled and stagnated underneath the floorboards and slats. On June 11th and 12th he had received two long interesting letters from his parents and three days later he snatched an odd hour to reply in the afternoon:

> It is nice to receive such letters. I was just going up with the Colonel & Adjt. at noon today to inspect the comm. trenches we have been working on when the enemy started to be 'frightful' with shells & while waiting in the C.O's dug-out for them to calm down, I began to read your letter through again. The Adjt. jokingly remarked 'My word that's a fine long letter. I never get letters like that'.

> Dad's suggestion about a land torpedo for breaking through the enemy's entanglement is quite a sound one, but the torpedo would have to be launched at night from a special stand above the level of our parapet so as to clear our own entanglements & the rough ground between us. The French have, I believe, an aerial torpedo used for some such work, but it has not I think the strong metal flanges. They also, I believe, have something in the nature of a large grappling iron with strong rope attached which is thown out & then drawn back dragging the enemys's entanglements with it. Whether this is propelled outwards by explosive force I don't know, but such an arrangement might well be arranged. This, if effective, would be very useful to employ if we expected to be attacked & were not ready to attack ourselves for we could thus steal the enemy's wire to shield us.

> I too always carefully study the casualty lists whenever I get hold of a paper, always hoping never to see what I look for. I'm glad to see that so far the 6th M/crs have suffered comparitively (sic) little compared to the 7th & 8th M/crs. for despite the fact that I shall be very glad when it is all over I don't in the least regret coming out, & although every hour has its risks (some more so than others) there's a certain fascination & the satisfaction that we are all doing our share. How glad I am I came out with a commission. I know I should not have been half so happy as a private or even as an N.C.O. That is why I like my new job for I'm even more my own boss than I was when a platoon commander. I often think what a sacrifice those of our aristocracy and the upper middle classes who are serving in the ranks out here, have made, especially

where they have not others of their kind with them. Not that I'm saying anything against the ordinary British Tommy, far from it for they are almost without exception a fine lot especially those who have been any length of time in the firing line. Their common risks makes them all brothers in the truest sense of the word & more cheerful companions you couldn't wish for.

(McGowan, June 15th)

How could Heald have guessed on that day that just over twenty years later he would be called to raise again and command the 6th Battalion the Manchester Regiment in preparation for his second war against Germany?

It was a long cold business slogging up with the stores from Dickebusch, a distance of between three or four miles often not returning until four in the morning. But resting on June 20th, it being a Sunday, Hodgkin listened to the new parson's discourse from the privacy and comfort of his fleabag. Later on that evening he relaxed over a 'Kipling Evening' with Heald and Lieut. E.J. Bairstow.

At long last they heard rumours of leave starting up, and delighted though he was, Heald who was still feverish gave vent to his feelings: 'Oh our C.O. I shall be pleased when our battalion reaches its dismembering strength and I will get as far from our C.O. as possible. He's futile'. He felt aggrieved that the Colonel couldn't leave his tired men alone in the daytime, when on fatigues all night and had started up platoon drill and camp inspection, in addition to their nocturnal marches. Heald's temperature continued to rise and he felt it a further misfortune when he was told off to dine and play cards with the C.O. The next day he saw the Doctor who sent him forthwith to hospital at Reninghelst ten miles away. It took about three hours to get there uncomfortably bumping about in the front of a one horse unsprung ambulance. Feeling very cold and done up he slept that night on a stretcher on the floor. By contrast on the following day, he was sent by a Daimler motor ambulance to Mont Noir and was put to bed in a comfortable room with a fine view. The Doctor in charge was a fine Harley Street man who told one of the orderlies to massage Heald's aching legs and back that afforded him much relief. Feeling somewhat better, a fool of an orderly gave him some diluted carbolic acid to drink in mistake for water, and although that didn't seem to do much harm, Heald suffered a relapse of fever with a high temperature which the Doctor suspected might be typhoid. This was a false alarm and Heald starting to recover, soon longed to be off a diet of eternal bread and milk.

Deviating for once from the well worn track to 27 and 28, Hodgkin carried mining stores across the canal to a wood close to Hill 60. Now the graveyard of thousands, the pock marked mound only showed occasional manifestations of death by a few rudimentary wooden crosses crookedly protruding at random from the mire. Intersected by lines of old trenches and jagged tree stumps, flights of crumbling brick steps could be seen leading nowhere. The arch of the brick bridge over the Ypres Courtrai railway cutting remained mostly intact, but now it served no useful purpose. There were still plenty of bullets about in the wood but as their guide put it: 'Owing to the ground you either gits shot in the 'ead or the foot so it don't matter much'. After their return about midnight the Germans who were shelling somewhere near Vlamertinghe woke them roughly by sending a heavy shell shaking and hurtling directly over their bivouac.

Ellington having left for a few days leave, Hodgkin remained in sole charge of 'C' Company in reserve. He considered superfluous the endless drills by day closely following the inevitable nightly fatigues when the whole line suddenly became alive with hollowed eyed men dragging up supplies. Hodgkin's boredom was punctuated by random publications of propaganda miscellanies from the foreign press selected by the 2nd Army Corps. On June 26th he copied down a telegram from the Kaiser to his sister, the Queen of Greece which had been published by a Greek newspaper:

> Our offensive is advancing successfully on all fronts. On the East front the Russians have lost, since the beginning of the war, more than 700,000 men, including 70,000 officers. On the Western front the French have had certain small successes at various spots, but with such great sacrifices that it would suit us perfectly if they gained a large number of similar successes. Our final victory is certain. Woe to those who still dare to draw the sword against me! My compliments to Tino.
>
> William.

('Tino' was King Constantine of Greece, the Emperor's brother-in-law) On the same day, Hodgkin noted a further communiqué from the Dutch Press:

> The Emperor of Austria has published the following Army Order: Full of pain & indignation, I order that the 27th Regt. of Infantry be struck out of my army on account of cowardice & treachery in the presence of the enemy. The Regtl. Colours will be handed in and placed in the Military Museum. The history of the regiment now ends, as it is for ever 'tainted'. (The 27th Regt. was a Czech Regt. from Bohemia.)

Seldom failing to observe the humourous angles of army activities, Hodgkin described Brigadier General Maude's farewell to the battalion on June 26th on his promotion to Major General:

He said all the usual nice things, & the C.O. in the excitement of the moment dismissed the parade with fixed bayonets! General Maude then shook hands with all the officers & was cheered by the men.

(Hodgkin, June 26th)

In the same vein, Hodgkin noted in a further communiqué, an application for leave from the wife of one stretcher bearer Meier of the 3rd Bavarian Regiment manning the opposing lines:

'Sir,
I have the honour to request that a suitable period of furlough be granted to my husband, stretcher bearer Meier, so far as the exigencies of the Service will permit, in order that he may see his son, born last January, and also that he may contribute further to the fruitfulness of the nation at this time when so many men's lives have been lost.

I have the honour to be Sir,

Your obedient servant,
Hildegarde Meier.'

It seemed that stretcher bearer Meier was an industrious and persevering worker and therefore recommended for leave. The G.O.C. 3rd Bavarian Division in granting him fourteen days only made proviso that: 'A report should be rendered in due course to this office'. (Hodgkin, June 24th)

On June 27th as the sultry spell finally broke, the winds blew and the rains descended in torrents with great fury:

I was calmly sitting in my bivvy enjoying the futile efforts of the subalterns of C. Coy to stem the torrent that was entering their somewhat amorphous dwelling (known either as the Labyrinth or the Pagoda) at all points, when my attention was suddenly drawn to the peculiar behaviour of several of my tins of tobacco, which had suddenly taken unto themselves legs & were swimming gaily around the tent. This unusual occurrence was quickly followed by a rush of water, & within 3 minutes every mortal thing I had was soaked through & the waters covered the face of the earth. It was now time to parade for a carrying party, so I left my servant to struggle in the downpour & rescue what he could.

Went up to 15th Bde at ZILLEBEKE carrying stores, & returned to find my bivvy removed to the most eligible site in the orchard.

(Hodgkin, June 27th)

After two hours drill the following day Hodgkin wrote: 'At the C.O.'s office hours he confided in us that when in the trenches he never forgot the height of the parapet, "No not for a moment". We also had observed this.' That night, all the subalterns of 'B' Company with whom Hodgkin dined played childish and amusing games and indulged in much frivolity.

Returning once more to relieve the Devons in 27 and 28 the skirmishing sporadically continued:

> The Germans had a joy day with whizzbangs on our reserve trench: Moyan got a cut on the nose as the only result, & when bandaged up created a sensation by setting fire to his dressings with a cigarette, luckily he did not damage himself further. Various exalted personages visited us all at once today: to wit, our new brigadier (Col. Compton of the Somerset LI), the Bde Major, a Major & a Capt. from the V. Divn. our C.O., the Adjutant & a parson.

> I made myself a capital bed out of 2 poles & some wire netting.
> (Hodgkin, June 29th)

Before dawn at 'stand to' on July 3rd, young 2nd Lieut. H.F. Davies, who had enlisted with Heald, manned the fire step in 27 with loaded rifle to inspect their barbed wire entanglements over the parapet. Always on the alert, a German sniper fired, severing the artery in Davies's shoulder. In the haemorrhage of blood his life seeped away so that death came shortly afterwards. This made a loss of two officers to 'C' Company in two days. Besides the whizzbangs flying around, they caught a whiff of the eye smarting gas smelling of the crushed mustard seed they had first sensed at Spoilbank in April. It became evident that gas shells were exploding somewhere in their rear. There was further excitement when:

> Hignett had been firing regularly at a certain place in the German parapet for some time, when finally a shot of his was followed by an explosion & column of smoke in the German trench. We are hoping that he blew up their store of infernal machines or sausage magazine or something of the kind. At any rate they seemed to let it rankle in their mind, & got rather peevish about it in the afternoon, when they sat down systematically to shell our trench with whizzbangs. They had a special aversion to our main communication trench, so we cleared the adjoining traverses & let them waste their ammunition. In due course our gunners sent some of the 'bags of peas' across to Fritz, & then each side made life thoroughly hideous to the helpless but necessary

infantryman. There was a lull while, presumably, the Gunners had tea, and then they began again. A man shaken up a bit & about a dozen sandbags burst was our total casualty list, but I think the Germans got one or two in the neck, at least as far as we could see. Right at the end of this 'artillery duel' we got a message from the Adjutant to the effect that the Gunners particularly wanted to know the effect of their fire: so Ellington sallied forth with the periscope just as dinner was brought in. It is almost needless to say that the guns stopped firing instantly, & the only effect observed was that Ellington's temper got hot to the detriment of his dinner which was cooled in proportion.

(Hodgkin, July 4th)

Having rested at Mont Noir for eleven days, Heald began to recover with the luxury of good food, rest and walks in the grounds amongst the beautiful trees around the chateau. Two concerts had been organised by the R.A.M.C. which revealed a surprising amount of talent and he enjoyed the freedom of meeting and talking with new found friends. Impressed by his good orderly who had been at Dulwich College, Heald thought the lad cared for him very well, even to cleaning his boots. At the end of his sojourn, like Hodgkin he was taken off to have a bath at Bailleul, as there seemed to be no proper bathing facilities at the château. But on returning to the battalion he was unreservedly glad to see all his friends once more, and to find that as the C.O. had departed on leave the same day, they would have some peace. Indeed, for a few days everything on the front was quiet, Hodgkin was granted five days leave shortly after, and travelled via Bailleul and Boulogne, eventually reaching Victoria at 5.00 a.m. on July 12th.

Still working away with his sappers, McGowan writing home on July 10th tried to allay his parents' constant fears for his safety:

I will I assure you not needlessly expose myself to danger. Apart from personal thought, trained officers are too valuable here to be lost as was Davies. Both Capt. Hartley & the Colonel were vexed as well as sorry about it.

Sunday noon

I wasn't able to finish this in time for post yesterday as I went along with Cowap, the Machine Gun Officer to pick up a little information on how to load & fire a machine gun. It's an instrument I think every officer in the battn. should not be a stranger to, for in an attack it's worth 50 men but cannot be used by an absolute novice.

Aftermath

We were relieved on Thurs night & got back to bivouacs early Friday morning. We are not, as we heard at first, to be turfed out of our own trenches for I understand we are to go back there again in little short of a week. Why the early relief I don't know unless it was because there is a lot of defence work to be done & they thought the Cheshires would be more use to the Brigade generally, out of the trenches. At all events we are providing something like 500 men for work up near the firing line each night, but I as a specialist have got off with a two hours task each night loading wagons close by the camp. I was able to finish one & almost a second, of those advanced dug-outs we were working on before leaving the firing-line. They are regular strong-holds with brickfloors & roofs capable of resisting small shells. The Colonel was quite pleased with the work done & said so, which is unusual for him as he is generally more prone to find fault with, than to praise constructions of that nature, being a bit of an engineer himself.

From the English papers it would appear that the Germans are massing large bodies of troops on this front, preparatory to another thrust towards Calais. Things are very quiet here at night at present & it may be the calm before the storm, but we too are working hard to prepare for them if they do try it on & if only our guns are plentifully supplied, with food we ought to be well equal to the task of holding them if not of pushing them back.

Contrary to expectations we received a draft of 100 men last week, which makes it better for all concerned, but we still need some 300 to 400 more men & about 8 officers to bring us up to full strength.

On Friday an English aeroplane was brought down by shell fire while flying just over our heads & fell not ½ ml away for we passed the shattered machine when going to the baths that afternoon. Evidently the pilot was hit & lost control of his machine (It's unusual for there to be only one man in a plane as a rule there is one pilot & one observer who is also a competent pilot) & he poor chap was killed instantaneously & the machine hopelessly shattered. That is the first plane I've seen brought down all the time I've been out for usually the shooting is pretty wide off the mark.

The Germans have been putting pretty heavy shells into the village just across a few fields from this camp, but it's surprising how few of them do serious damage even to property & the inhabitants take it very calmly.

As soon as it begins they just walk out into the fields till they've had their fling & then return probably to find all the windows of their houses smashed if the house itself has not been hit. I suppose they only stop because they are doing profitable business here. I know if I was in their place I'd pack up my few valuables & retire westwards if I had to turn gypsy.

The weather has turned quite cold, grey & windy these last few days, quite a change after the intense heat of last week.

Well I trust you are both keeping well & happy & not worrying yourselves too much for you must remember that God will just as surely guard over me & keep me unharmed when exposed to many perils as when in comparative safety at home if we seek his guidance.

(McGowan, July 10th)

Even though they were back in the bivouacs, practically the whole battalion was out every night working on fatigues. Crossing over the banks of the canal by Battalion H.Q., Heald walked along the other side to inspect a new trench being dug in front of the notorious and battered 'Bluff' ridge about thirty feet high by the canal just over fifty yards from the enemy towards Hill 60.

For some time there had been a crescendo of rumours of an impending move south. But for a week before this materialised, the battalion suffered some heavy casualties although no major battle was in progress. It was a beastly journey up to 27 and 28 during the week of July 17th, the heavy rain relentlessly poured down in torrents and enemy shells screamed down at times at the rate of one every minute. On July 18th Heald noted:

Our artillery very active. We got shelled and I had one man rather badly hit. We trench mortared them and the gunners sent a few football bombs over trench and we met a ration party coming in. It caused an awful mixup. Couldn't move backwards or forwards. Thought we should have to wait till daylight. Eventually we squeezed past. It was said that the Manchesters thought that the "gas" had come. Caused by the language used, no doubt. We got back absolutely wet through and done. The journey there and back being about twelve miles and on skates most of the way. The mud on the hard surface below being very slippery. My servant had a very hot cup of cocoa ready when I got back which was fine and I could get into a blanket. The men had to go wet.

(Heald, July 18th)

The following day as expected they had it very hot with eight casualties (one later dying of his wounds) in 27 and about twenty-five, two killed, in 28. When in the evening of July 19th 28 had a dose of the really heavy stuff, Hodgkin who at 7.30 p.m. happened to be watching five shells richochet off the top of 27 got rather badly wounded in the back by a piece of 'Woolly Bear' (6 inch, H.E. shrapnel). Heald who was not far away wrote: 'Captain Hodgkin very characteristically got the time fuse of the shell that hit him and took it with him'. Although at times in great pain, Hodgkin managed to record: 'Being carried on a stretcher is not so bad if the bearers do not go too fast: a train is passable, by a motor ambulance is awful'. His journey home wound round Dickebush to Bailleul, eventually arriving at Treport No. 3 General Hospital near Dieppe where his binoculars were stolen from his kit. Here he remained five days before travelling to Newcastle-upon-Tyne on July 25th. Although he returned to the western front in December 1915 he never rejoined his battalion to fight with them in action.

About midnight on July 19th, McGowan, who was returning from doing repairs to some support trenches with his sappers, passed by his old platoon who were struggling up forward carrying heavy rolls of barbed wire. As the group had degenerated into a disorganised rabble with no officer to lead them, McGowan sent his sappers on ahead, and turned back to help the Sergeant disentangle the platoon in the pitch dark. It was exceedingly slippery after the heavy rains and in the effort McGowan pitched headlong into a recently made 'Jack Johnson' pit five foot deep. Fired from 15 cm guns, man high 'Jack Johnson' shells (so called after a famous American boxer) that plunged several feet into the scarred earth, excavated wide cavities in the ground like so many craters on the moon. Their delayed action fuses burst with heavy explosions that spewed forth towering volumes of dense black smoke high into the air. Leaving the platoon to its own motley resources, McGowan hobbled back as best he could in the darkness and just managed to unlace his boot, having a badly sprained ankle.

Muttering about a three week job, the doctor sent McGowan off on a stretcher to the loading station. A motor ambulance conveyed him to the Field Dressing Station and eventually he arrived at the Mont Noir Convalescent Hospital, happy that his servant had rescued his field kit from the transport lines. McGowan was not pleased to be away from the battalion when they were about to make their big move and felt disappointed about his mishap. They were expecting a new draft of eight officers with two hundred men and so was particularly anxious that he wouldn't find his job as Sapper Officer permanently in someone else's hands when he rejoined. But optimistically he felt on the whole he was on the best side of the Colonel so would be probably be reinstated alright. He told his parents that before his accident, the chaplain Captain C.M. Chavasse, son of the Bishop of Liverpool (consecrated Bishop of Rochester in 1940), had visited their dug-outs to celebrate Holy Communion. 'He preached a splendid sermon, and it was a most enjoyable service altogether & within ½ a mile of the enemy at that. Funny warfare is it not?'

Having made his mark with the Doctor, an orderly carried McGowan piggy-back to what probably was used as a servant's bedroom on the second floor of the château. It was well ventilated, spotlessly clean and tastefully decorated with cream coloured paper and paintwork:

Another orderly brought up all my kit & asked me would I like a cup of tea brought up & in 5 mins. it was there with biscuits. After a wash & a change into my clean togs I carefully hobbled down to lunch. This establishment accommodates 26 cases when full (& it generally is) the other 6 officers were in bed — 20 officers of different ranks & regiments sat down at the same big table to a very nicely cooked lunch with orderlies who 'waited' in the approved style. After lunch I secured an easy chair on the balcony & sat reading there in the sun all afternoon & away in the distance could see the burst of German shells in the French lines. Most of the others were out as it is bath-day at the Lunatic Asylum & a motor-ambulance conveys those requiring a hot bath there each Tues. & Frid. I was of course too lame to attempt it. A few others were attempting a game of Badminton on the lawn, but the wind was too fresh for it. At 5 p.m. afternoon tea with nice cakes was served both in the lounge & on the balcony. At 6.30 p.m. I went to my bedroom again as at that time the Doctor goes his duty round & he wished to see my foot & when he saw it he remarked that it was 'some' sprain & said I had better keep to my bed for a day or two. He thought I had burst a small blood-vessel & hence the rather abnormal swelling. I wasn't overpleased at the thought of confinement to bed, for altho' a day or two in bed when the body is ill is more or less alright, it's a different thing for a restless chap like me when I'm otherwise feeling quite fit & make's me wish it was a sprained arm (left) so that I might spend my time walking around this beautiful part of the country. However, I had my foot bandaged with thermogene-wool & got into a pair of pyjamas they kindly provided me with. At 7.30 one of the orderlies brought me up my dinner, or rather the first instalment of it — some very nice soup followed by salmon & salad, followed by veal cutlet, kidney beans & potatoes, followed by trifle (with) followed by a cup of coffee; but before I got my dinner the orderly brought along & fixed up by my bedside a magnificient gramophone with plentiful supply of good records, so that I could provide music with my meal & so prevent indigestion by heavy thought over meals. This is quite a new experience for me for I've never been used to such luxury. It's a funny war isn't it with its up & downs, or rather its downs & ups — down in a J.J. hole and then up at Mont Noir ...

You will I expect think that the army have no business to provide such luxuries for us as this, but when I explain that the average stay of an officer here is less than a week & the majority are cases of nerve strain after a stiff time in the firing-line you will I think agree that good food & other luxuries are not out of place, in fact the medicine to work the speedy cure. The only thing needed to make it a perfect paradise is a staff of pretty nurses, but they don't grant us that, the R.A.M.C. men do everything — cooking, cleaning & medical duty & do it all very well indeed.

Well my bedroom mate has just had his foot massaged & it's 11 p.m. so time for invalids to go to sleep so I'll close with fondest love & best wishes.

(McGowan, July 21st)

At last on July 23rd the others received their orders to move southwards, but before leaving they had been awakened early with the ground shaking violently by an explosion of a huge mine that blew up a section of German trench opposite St. Eloi. Fearing a further British assault on the crater, the enemy promptly peppered the trenches with small shells which appeared as numerous as rain drops spattering up a dusty road. As the enemy artillery slowly worked its way towards them, those manning 27 and 28 were thankful to retreat at last in safety.

'It does no good being depressed. I believe in taking everything as it comes and making the best of it.' Murray too, had heard on July 20th that the division was going right way down south. 'It will be very interesting & I shall be glad to get back to France, I hate Belgium... they say a man is as old as he feels, & a woman is as old as she looks. I am glad it isn't the other way on as I should be 103'.

During their ten mile march to Reninghelst, the rain mercifully stopped, allowing the ground to dry out at the new camp site. It would have been awful to have had to pitch the tents in mud on arrival as the men were completely worn out:

We rested all day and march at night about ten more miles to a place called Ecke, where this battalion was to rest before entraining for our new position. It was a lovely moonlight night and we quite enjoyed it though rather tired. Were billeted in a farm. The farmer's wife had some eggs and coffee ready for us officers. A Belgian would never have done that.

(Heald, July 25th)

It was Heald's turn at last for leave and getting a lift with a group in a motor lorry to the station, he had a comfortable journey home via Boulogne with a smooth crossing. His first call in London at 3 a.m. was at the Turkish Baths in Jermyn Street, where he later slept and ate breakfast. On the day following his arrival north, his first thought was to see Walker's people and to play a little golf. Leave anticipated so eagerly, but comprising only three days at home was an unnerving business. Wherever they went they carried the war with them. Trench life which followed its slimy mud infested trail across Belgium and France belonged alone to its victims, while those at home observing the wan staring faces and mud caked garments could only dimly guess at the realities. Unwittingly they had become a race apart.

On his return through London, Heald was anxious to look in on Johnson whose wounded leg shattered in March had necessitated an amputation. But in spite of it Heald was relieved to find him very cheery, and even thought he was having quite a good time. At the end of July, the 5th Division was removed from the Ypres salient. It had not been the men's fault that the 2nd Army had been unsuccessful in breaking the deadlock, even though the British defending their positions had flung sixteen divisions into the line to the German's eleven and a half. Besides being woefully short of guns and ammunition the tactics of the battles were impossibly weak, worsened by gas attacks and the fact that there was a lack of proper communications, language difficulties and unification of command between Belgians British and French. Eventually utter exhaustion closed the main fighting, British casualties being over fifty-nine thousand, those of the Germans being more than thirty-four thousand.

CHAPTER 4

SOUTH TO SUZANNE

Up to the Summer of 1915, the inhabitants of the rural villages around the valley of the Somme had not seen the tramping columns of khaki clad 'tommies' whistling their familiar tunes. They gave their British allies a great welcome.

Weary after the usual tedious journey from England, Heald had been told to join the battalion at Corbie:

> I and two other officers of our brigade on leave overslept ourselves in the train and did not get out when it reached Amiens, but for the train stopping for two hours would have been taken to Paris. As it was we missed our connection on to Maricourt where we should have gone to. It turned out very luckily after all because we spent most of the day at Amiens and got an A.S.C. car on. My battalion had not arrived when I got to our billets. So I could have stayed longer in Amiens. We are billeted in farmhouses about 15 miles from the firing line at present. The battalion turned up at 8 p.m.
>
> (Heald, August 1st)

Next evening he rode back into Amiens on horseback with two of the others. In the fading light the peasants were tilling the fields, working on the harvest and he saw several carpenters attending to some red tiled cottage roofs. Heald had never been much of a rider at home, that part of Lancashire was above all golfing country, and there was no 'hunting set' as in Cheshire, but he got the hang of it fairly quickly, although he was stiff from swimming in the river that morning. They enjoyed a good dinner, not far from the renowned cathedral with its miraculous oak choir stalls decorated with more than four thousand carved figures. Having been occupied by the enemy for only twelve days in 1914, Amiens was a city almost undamaged by war.

It was a misfortune that the strains so evident between the C.O. and his officers should continue, the atmosphere was not a happy one, but it seemed to them that Col. Groves was either ignorant of it or did not think it mattered. Although Hodgkin was no longer around to voice his opinion, every so often there were sudden eruptions from Heald and the others:

> A day of frightfulness by the C.O. and Adjutant. Drilled all morning and because the C.O. found some faults with one of the platoons all afternoon too. Finally lecture by C.O. and Adjutant to subalterns in the course of which the C.O. told us (practically) that we should run away

91

when a crisis came. I know who would be the first to run and that would be our C.O. Every soldier in the battalion knows it too, which is very unfortunate from a disciplinary point of view. I am perfectly certain that any of our subs. would die sooner that run, but that is our C.O.'s way to insult his subalterns, and the silly man thinks he is regarded as the 'Father of the Battalion'.

(Heald, August 3rd)

Another trying day. We were to be inspected by the Army General in the afternoon, so all morning was spent in getting everything clean. Of course, an order altering the position of various articles of equipment came just before starting. We stood for two hours at the inspection. At night we marched eleven miles to billets nearer the firing line so the men were very tired having worn full pack for about ten hours that day.

(Heald, August 4th)

After McGowan had left Mont Noir, he had started his journey by train from Hazebrouck where he dined at the Hotel du Nord:

The town was full of soldiers for a new division of Kitchener's army had arrived there that afternoon & were staying in the town overnight. The train left at 8.30 p.m. for Calais & arrived there at 11.30 p.m. There was a train on almost straight away but as there was no particular hurry in my case I thought I'd spend the night in bed rather than in the train. Moreover I didn't at all like the idea of making a long journey through new country during hrs. of darkness.

The R.T.O told me all the hotels were very full, but showed me the side door of one quite close to the station. I knocked up the watchman & 'after parleying' with him for some minutes succeeded in obtaining a screened off bed in the second floor corridor & slept more or less well, but got up & had breakfast early (the bill for bed & breakfast was by the way only 3fr. 75c) so that I could have a stroll round before departing, but I was very disappointed with the place. It's a decidedly dirty, scattered & unbeautiful town. I have some postcards but they flatter the place very much indeed.

I got into the southern train leaving just before 10 a.m. There were a large number of French officers travelling down in uniforms of all colours — bright blue, dark blue, khaki, red & black, grey & sundry other combinations of colours & most of them wearing medals (metal ones & not ribbons such as our officers & men wear). The dining-car

92

South to Suzanne

Somme River and Marshes, May 1986.

was not joined through to the first-class corridor as is usual on English trains, but you had to book your seat for a certain time & then transfer yourself from the carriage to the dining car when the train stopped at a station about that time & reverse the procedure when you had finished the meal which was very good but of course after the French style Hors d'oeuvre, fish, hot meat, cold meat & salad, cheese, fruit & coffee.

Altho' I'd plenty of reading matter with me I didn't use it, for I was too interested in the scenery. Such rich country after the comparative bareness of Flanders. As we neared A- there were a large number of Indian troops encamped along the line, & another thing that interested me very much was the weird types of telephone poles in use in this part of the country.[1]

I had hoped to spend a few hrs. in A- for I very much wanted to see the cathedral, but unfortunately the last train for Corbie left about ¼ hr after I got in.

As it happens I might very well have spent the night there but of course I didn't know that the battn. was comparatively near the railhead & I didn't have to report to the Divn. or the Brigade but just direct to the battn.

The Colonel seemed pleased enough to see me back again & I've still got the sappers to look after so that's all right & I expect there'll be plenty of work for us to do when we take these trenches over from the French.

(McGowan, August 7th)

---

[1]A = Amiens

93

Their new location was in a sheltered wooded area on the banks of the Somme, where the small village of Suzanne was one of the most picturesque places along the valley. At this point the river made two large loops with panoramic views on each of its high outer sides. Between these outer boundaries, the wide meandering Somme divided itself into streamlets, the ground between them remaining soggy and lush with tall grass. A canal cut through the centre. The area was thick with overhanging trees and dense undergrowth, and there were aquatic birds in profusion bobbing in and out of the patches of water lilies lying on the surface of calm patches of water. Fisherman's and hunter's paths stretched through the grass causeways into No Man's Land in the green centre of the marsh. Straining to listen for every alien sound over the noise of the water pouring loudly through the small sluices, it was eerie to prowl in solitude along these paths with the sun's rays playing fitful tricks among the rustling leaves.

Although McGowan's ankle was almost well, it failed him during the last four miles of the ten mile march from Ville Sur Ancre, and he finished up riding on one of the transport wagons. The road itself was quite good but the surface had become greasy after the recent rains. On arrival at Suzanne, they found that Battalion H.Q. was comfortably installed in an old sizeable red brick château with a pinnacled stepped central gable. This imposing building was set in a railed off park very close to the river. Several new officers had arrived to make up the depleted numbers, among them was Dr. John Costello, a very cheery medical officer who was a catholic Irishman. Apart from displaying a particular interest in sanitation, he proved himself to be an able and popular president of the mess. Heald, who had been invited to dine with some members of one of the French regiments before their departure had enjoyed several very good meals with them, so was happy to learn that his new mess augured so well.

McGowan climbed stiffly down from the transport wagon and succeeded in billeting his men in the outhouse of one of the farms that lay back off the main street. Having satisfied himself that the men were comfortably settled in the home-made bedsteads rigged up by their host, he got into his pyjamas and fleabag, sleeping till nearly noon on the floor of the farm kitchen:

At 3 p.m. I set off with the C.O. & Adjt. & several other officers to make a preliminary survey of the line (you cannot call them trenches) that we were to take over from the French that night. We had heard before arrival that this was a 'cushy' spot, but were not prepared for what we actually saw. The first section we visited we approached along a road whose surface had never so much as been disturbed by a shell, although the German trenches were plainly visible on the hillside about 1500 yards away. Then we struck into a wood & came across different

Vaux Sur Somme and Suzanne, 1915.

Château at Suzanne in 1986.

groups of French soldiers sitting in homemade summerhouses or lying beneath the trees playing cards or dominoes. Then we came to another good road which was competely hidden from the enemy by a rising slope well wooded & into this were built some of the finest dug-outs I've yet seen. There is an unlimited amount of timber about & they have made splendid use of it making roofs strong enough to resist anything but the very heavy shells, which are unknown in this part of the line. At one end of this road a river ran, in which some 20 or 30 French soldiers were having a thoroughly enjoyable bathe for the weather here lately has been exceedingly hot. I wondered when we were going to come to the trenches themselves but soon learnt that there were none, at least not garrisoned trenches. Owing to the natural surface of the country at this part, (a river & a marsh forming with surrounding hills a peculiar shaped basin) no large movement of troops in either dirn. is possible except by the flanks which are themselves well guarded & moreover it is not possible to entrench nearer to the enemy than we are now who are at the nearest point 500 yds. & at some points as much as 2000 yds. away. So the scheme adopted by the French has been to choose certain strong points, fortify them with intent to defend to the last if necessary & post sentries at different points around, to watch for enemy movements day & night & at night to send out frequent patrols towards the enemy for the same purposes. This of course takes comparatively (sic) few men & the remainder are free to do much as they like in a very nice place.

(McGowan, August 10th)

In the woods all around, clouds of flies and mosquitoes plagued the men working away on trenches and dug-outs. At one time, hundreds of tiny frogs hopped out of the marsh to inspect the digging, while after dark, nocturnal rats scurried in the undergrowth around their tents. In places the river was beautifully deep with ten feet or so of clear flowing water where no weeds lurked in the depths to entangle the divers. Compared with Flanders, it was a heaven of freshness for washing and drinking.

Heald and his grenadiers were ordered to 'B' Company, who were established in the wood on the heights above Vaux village opposite Suzanne on the doubled back loop of the river. The civil inhabitants still resided in the village and so far had not seen a shell. On the opposite side of the Somme the Germans occupied Curlu and for the present each army had tacitly agreed to live and let live. In the next few days, Heald reconnoitred their position and established connections to the left with the rest of the brigade. As they dared not show any smoke along the ridge, all their meals were cooked and carried up from the village below them; Heald soon became very bored with this rather uneventful life, he had caught a bad cold, and thought he preferred the trenches with their bit of excitement. He decided to go and dine with Hartley who was commanding 'C' Company in Vaux. By now, Hartley had been made Mayor of the village and having entire control of the small population was occupied with his own responsibilities. Across the road there was a strong barricade at one point where it had been decided by universal agreement that the inhabitants would all gather to die rather than give themselves up if the rest of the village were lost. There were plenty of eels in the river running by and an abundance of fruit on the trees, so they knew they would not starve if the rations failed.

After a few days, McGowan was accommodated in the château at Suzanne as billets elsewhere were scarce. He found it a mixed blessing being in such close proximity to the C.O. but was content to share a room with Dr. Costello where he could retire to read or write in privacy whenever possible; McGowan had received several letters and parcels from home, including cigarettes and tinned fruit, which he distributed round the H.Q. mess. In reply, he requested some cigs. and a fruit cake, together with envelopes and was very happy that a lace shawl he had sent home was so much appreciated.

He hoped that it would be used and not kept locked away among sundry less beautiful and less useful souvenirs:

> I've been at work again on communication trenches. There is one here leading from the village towards the firing line, that is 1½ ml. long, 8 ft deep — has in many places been cut through solid limestone rock so the French have done something during their long & quiet spell here. The drainage of this trench is not good, so I'm trying to remedy that fault. The French are also very clever at basketwork & use brushwood fascines for revetting trenches, a sort of skeleton breastwork of this brushwood and then fill it in with earth. They have also made all their own floorboards, tables, baskets & screens of this brushwood & we are trying to follow their example for it means a great saving in govt. stores & the cartage of same. Sandbags of which we used such a lot before, are almost an unknown article here.
>
> (McGowan, August 13th)

Some of the British gunners evidently thought it time to try out a little 'frightfulness' on the enemy as a reprisal on the first anniversary of the war. Misguidedly Vaux ridge received its first shelling wounding one of Heald's grenadiers! The following day, the battalion received a visit from Captain Chavasse who celebrated Holy Communion in the long picture gallery full of treasures in the château. Chavasse who was universally respected in the Brigade was decorated with the M.C. in 1917 and with the Croix de Guerre in 1918.

Still feeling rather bored, Heald heard of some experiments at Ribemont with a new kind of bomb and bicycled over the thirteen or so miles to investigate them. He was exceedingly disappointed with the trials and waxed scathing about the inventor of the bomb who obviously knew nothing of the latest methods. Fortunately, he met up with one of the Buffs officers (Kitchener's) who gave him dinner, they were jolly sorts and he enjoyed himself. Even the C.O. was quite genial on his return and stood him a whisky and soda in the mess.

During the following morning Vaux ridge got shelled once more. Heald and Hignett had a very narrow squeak, a shell screamed towards them and they thought their time had come. Bursting about twenty yards short, it exploded near a corporal of signalling standing by his dug-out, the unfortunate man being so badly wounded that he died shortly afterwards.

Leaving the ridge, Heald took a section of his bombers below to Vaux village to re-inforce 'C' Company. That evening, they were ordered to turn out the civil inhabitants from their homes as it was thought that some of them were spies. It was a pathetic duty and reluctantly obeyed.

A grassy causeway stretched from the village over the marshy ground for about two hundred yards towards the centre of the river. At the end lay 'Duck Post', where a small bridge provided the only access across the marsh, and the only exit on foot for any patrols into 'No Man's Land'. Stepping into a punt which lay conveniently moored among the water lilies on the sunny side of the causeway, Heald made a preliminary reconnaissance of the marsh.[1] Although it was August, the sun was not too hot and he took care always to keep on the alert as the noise of the rushing water cloaked every hostile sound. Having first spied out the land, later in the day he lead his section on foot to patrol the dense undergrowth. They did not chance on any Germans, but like schoolboys had good fun stalking each other amongst the leafy trees. That evening, in unorthodox fashion by dropping one of his bombs in the river, Heald managed to collect enough fish to supply the mess for dinner. A multitude of chub suddenly stunned by the explosion rose to the surface; they proved quite tasty but full of fine small bones.

Lt. Col. Murray whose gunners had been creating some of the 'frightfulness' on the opposite loop of the Somme was a keen fly fisherman back home in Cumberland. Chancing on a Frenchman who was having enormous success with a deadly ear of wheat as bait, Murray borrowed his rod and got three grayling. On August 22nd he told his father: 'I have been catching fish but not in the way you would approve of'. He, like Heald had got hold of a couple of bombs from the French, threw them in the river and got several bucketfuls. There was a mill nearby where a large grid was fixed below the sluice gates. When the grid was opened the water from the pool above rushed through it, leaving masses of eels and roach writhing high and dry on the grid. In the middle of a nearby pool about three hundred yards from the Germans, an allied shell proved a deadly weapon killing quantities of fish. A good humoured throng of French and English 'tommies' dived in and fought over a large pike in full view of the enemy who did not seem to mind.

A few days later the battalion patrol scouts were issued with new cloaks painted green all over with large yellow blotches, so that they became quite indistinguishable a few yards off in the dappled woods. Although the British camouflage service was first properly organised in January 1916, a few volunteers with certain trades such as scene painters connected with the threatre were assembled to work on camouflage at St. Omer. Concealment was no new art to the British Army, its own khaki uniform originally adopted in India to blend with the colour of the ground was made universal in 1898 more than twelve years before any other army adopted the idea.

---

[1] The author walked along the causeway in 1986. Nothing had changed, there was even a punt moored among the water lilies.

Donning their cloaks, Heald and a companion stole across the marsh and over the small bridge across the sluice at Duck Post. Creeping up to the German lines through the dense undergrowth, all they found were some broken pieces of wood laid across one of the paths to trap the enemy by a previous patrol. These were carefully replaced. Later that evening a German patrol consisting of two officers and six men came right past the Cheshire's listening post and up to their lines; their look-outs could easily have scuppered the enemy but had received orders not to fire. Heald was keenly disappointed that such a chance was ruined.

Patrolling the marsh became part of the daily routine and soon they were reinforced by a Captain Jones who had with him a section of Indian scouts (Pathans). Heald, whose right hand had become swollen and poisonous was sent off to an officer's convalescent post at Corbie, an important Third Army medical centre. Once hot fomentations had been applied, his hand recovered in a few days and he was glad to return. Although he managed some bridge with the other officers, he didn't care for the place much, as the feeding was poor in spite of there being plenty of fruit in the well stocked garden.

During his absence, the Germans had tried to capture one of their listening posts and in driving them off, the Cheshires had suffered one killed and another wounded. After the crescendo of the summer heat, tempestuous thunderstorms broke out and everyone became nervy, jumpy and irritable.

Resuming his patrol into the marsh, Heald took to the punt once more and landed on one of the soggy islets. He was careful not to disturb unwittingly the wild duck nesting on the drier ground whose sudden flight would betray his movements. In the centre of the islet there was a hut on which some English words were inscribed, but Heald wondered whether he was in German territory as the words were incorrect and written by a foreigner. All at once he heard the sounds of an exchange of shots between two opposing patrols in the woods and he turned away quickly to reach the skirmish. He did not succeed in catching up with the enemy as they as quickly vanished into the dense undergrowth.

It was a glorious morning on August 22nd, hot with a nice fresh breeze. After church parade in the château, followed by a bathe in the river, McGowan took a walk with Lt. Burnett the transport officer to inspect the horse lines:

> They were originally held by the French & are most picturesque, a state
> that transport lines are generally not. They have constructed a series of
> open air stalls of brushwood for the horses & a number of rustic huts for
> the men to sleep in, while the wagons are almost hidden from view, with
> large green thickets as a background. Good natural cover such as this, is

a great asset, as hostile aeroplanes in search of information can see little, except perhaps the well worn cart tracks.

We had quite a little excitement 'en route' for just as we were nearing our lines a mule, entirely unattended, trotted past us, off for a little jaunt on its own. Burnett with angry thoughts against the horse-line sentry, set off with me at his heels to retrieve the wandering one, after nearly half an hours strategical manouvering we got the beast only to find that it didn't belong to us, but to some artillery unit who had been calmly watching the chase, so poor Burnett had not even the satisfaction of venting his wrath on the sentry.

(McGowan, August 22nd)

On the whole McGowan felt life was good; it was so different from their previous experience with dreary spells in frequently shelled trenches and long unpleasant night fatigues. He was of course particularly well placed at the château with a bed to sleep on, nicely served meals and just enough work each day to make him appreciate his leisure time. He busied himself going round the other companies, viewing the enemy lines on the opposing heights and endeavouring to carve out dug-outs and trenches in the hard limestone and chalk.

On the eastern front that August, the Germans had occupied Poland, driving the Russians to east of Brest Litovsk. Through his field glasses, McGowan saw the Russian flag waving gently on the top of an opposite hill occupied by the Bavarians to celebrate the fall of Warsaw. Needless to say, the flag became a ready target for the more expert British sniper.

Having an experienced eye, McGowan praised the French soldiers who had managed to dig some of the communication trenches through the solid limestone rock. He thought it a great credit to them, as the regiment was composed of men between thirty-five and fifty years of age. Wickerwork had been used for revetting instead of sandbags, and in spite of the fact they had heard that French billets and trenches were kept in a filthy state, everything had been left perfectly clean and tidy. Altogether three companies of the Cheshires had taken over about a mile and a half of frontage along the river, but though he liked the area, McGowan thought it would soon be considered far too good for the 5th Cheshires, and some unit of Kitchener's army who had never yet seen a trench would move in instead. The Cheshires he thought would be moved to far more troublesome quarters.

Heald was kept constantly on the alert down by the river. Having helped to lay an ambush for the Germans, he left it while he went off to tea with the East Surreys. In the evening at 7.30. just as it was dark, their listening post heard the enemy coming, and having let them cross the bridge they fired rapidly:

> Directly we heard firing, I dashed up my bombers and the scout section under Bishop. We found one German badly wounded. We were proceeding to search the wood for the others when the Germans who had fled and had now come back with reinforcements to try and get their wounded man in, opened fire on us, we replied and drove them off. Unfortunately they shot Vernon, one of our officers, and a scout and killed them. The German was quite young and had red hair. He seemed very terrified. He belonged to the 12th Bavarian Corps. I managed to get one of his buttons.
>
> (Heald, August 30th)

Early next morning they went out and scoured the wood. They did not succeed in meeting any Germans, but found only the prisoner's cap and a grenade which he was evidently going to hurl at the listening post. They tried again to engage the enemy in the afternoon but to no avail.

My Dear Mother & Dad,

> Many thanks for your most interesting and helpful letter of the 26th inst. It was quite like an instructive little sermon not from the pulpit, but from the home whence many a help for my lasting good has originated & I thank God it has been so. That is a cheering little quotation from R.L.S.[1] Which particular essay or book is it from? I have a small edition of quotations from R.L.S but it is not in that.

> Thank you for the sprig of heather it looked very bonny. I've seen no heather out here yet.

> Don't expect me on leave again for at least a month but all being well I ought to be getting it about a month from now. We moved from our little township yesterday & I have left H.Q. Mess for the time being at all events. Fortunately I had held in reserve a few of the contents of my last parcel so had something with which to pay my footing into B Coy's mess which I have joined for the time being. I am sharing a dug-out in the wood with a S/Lt. Davies from Chester, one of the new subalterns who have recently joined us, but no relation to Capt. Davies.

---

[1] R.L.S. = Robert Louis Stevenson

Just before we arrived here yesterday 'C' Coy, just in front of us, had quite an exciting ¼ hr. One of our listening posts spotted a German patrol & fired on them. The noise of the firing caused our scouts & another patrol to advance to the scene of action. One German was wounded & taken prisoner but unfortunately one of our officers (S/Lt. Vernon recently joined) & a private were seriously wounded & died shortly afterwards.

We shall be relieved from this front line in a day or two & all retire back into the town for a short time but I don't expect I shall rejoin the Hd Qrs. mess as I fancy there will be a slight reorganisation as far as officers are concerned. You see three captains from the 2/5th Bn. recently joined us, which caused a little puzzlement to the Colonel for being Captains they could not well become platoon commanders which is a subalterns job, but on the other hand they were new to active service & hence not in a posn. to take command of or become second in command of a company, however the difficulty is being slowly overcome. Capt. Vernon is I believe not strong enough to stand the strain & will shortly be going back. Capt. Hatt-Cook has been given the job of town-major, which makes him responsible for military discipline, billeting of troops & the regulation of civilian traffic in & out of the town. The third, Capt. Bourne, is an engineer by profession & altho' the C.O., has said nothing definite I rather fancy he will take over my job at all events pro tem. In which case I shall either rejoin my company or be made signalling officer. I hope it's the latter but I rather think it will be the former, for with one thing and another we are again getting short of officers & as we've never yet had a signalling officer I doubt not the creation of the post will again be postponed...

One of the recent draft of subalterns, Almand by name, who is an expert chemist & an all round student went back on Sunday to join the Army Hd. Qrs. on chemical investigation work. That's the sort of job I'd like (in the telephone line I mean) something to exercise my brains a bit. I've seen quite enough of bloodshed. I'm afraid I'm not a born soldier, construction appeals to me more than destruction. However, I'm thankful that I've always been given strength to do what has been required of me out here & feel sure I shall receive the same help from above right thro', & I must remember that the whole policy of this war is a constructive one & that destruction is only a means to an end.

We've had some heavy rain & thunderstorms this week-end but it's fine again now & much cooler. On Sunday, despite the weather we are able to have our usual open-air church service, conducted by yet another chaplain, I forget his name but he is attached to the R.E.s & I think the most sincere of all I've listened to. That reminds me we had a French padre in to dine with us on Monday. He had on a most picturesque garb. All black, leggings, breeches & a coat with flowing skirt reaching to his feet. He was of Spanish blood, with a swarthy complexion & black hair, with a little black cocked hat, rode a black horse & wore a black bead chain & black cross round his neck, but despite his apparently gloomy exterior he was a most affable & jolly man.

Well it's bedtime so I'll retire to my fleabag with fondest love & best wishes from,

Your Affectionate Son
George

(McGowan, August 31st)

McGowan's earlier prognostications of a move proved all too correct. Heald noted on Sept 2nd that they spent the day showing round the 6th Liverpools who were shortly due to relieve them. All the officers were now billeted together at Suzanne and Heald once more went fishing with two bombs gathering up thirty five chub for the mess. A week later he returned to Vaux with his grenadiers who had been practising for a newly ordained bomb test to be held on September 10th in a specially constructed trench. Fifteen men including Heald managed to pass the test, and afterwards they were allowed to sport red grenadier tabs on their arms. The test at Vaux proved to be a fairly dangerous proceeding: 'The bits flew into Suzanne and we had deputations from all round requesting us to stop, but we had to carry on. No wonder bombers get the name of being frightful' (Heald, Sept 10th). After a C.O.'s inspection the grenadiers were complimented as being the best turned out on parade.

In the château, McGowan managed to snatch a few moments to write home sitting in his bedroom on a home-made stool at a home-made table:

Our C.O. is extremely fond of keeping everyone as occupied as possible at all times whether the work is really necessary or not, in fact we've almost got into the habit of feeling that if we are not working regimentally we must take our ease somewhere the C.O. is not likely to spot us. The lastest order is to the effect that all inspections must be carried out before breakfast & thus leave the day free for work. This is one disadvantage of being in a comparatively quiet spot. The C.O. is never so energetic where bullets & shells are plentiful.

Our big guns have been rather talkative of late & appear to be having quite the best of the argument, for we have not yet been seriously inconvenienced. I rather fancy the sort of understanding that was existing when the French were here still holds good — that is to say if we don't touch X they'll leave Y alone. Of course sooner or later the bond will be broken, but it's quite a sensible arrangement as things stand at present. Don't worry I'm quite enjoying my little self, but thanks to the C.O.'s little mania I find the days all too short to do all I wish to do at present quite like the old days before the war! I was up this morning at 6.30 a.m. & instead of washing from my bucket in the bedroom I went down for a swim in the river & at the same time fixed up a new diving board & exit ladder which one of my men made for me yesterday. At 7.30 a.m. I inspected my rifles, bayonets & gas helmets (a daily occurrence). At 8.0 breakfast of porridge, bacon & egg, folld. by marmalade (How's that for wartime?) By the way I'd like you to send me a tin of marmalade occasionally as they've stopped our ration of marmalade. It's either sent to the hospitals or retained by the A.S.C. for their own use & we in the front line get the less popular jams instead...

After lunch I surreptitiously stole off to my bedroom & enjoyed a quiet read on my bed for ¾ hr. I'd previously ordered my men to parade again for work at 2.30 p.m. & evidently that 5/- Ingersoll that I've given to my L/Cpl. (my Sgt. & Cpl. are both on the sick list in hospital at present unfortunately) is gaining, for when I turned up I found they'd already departed to their sundry jobs. That's an example of keeness if you like, though it was unintentional.

After visiting them & finding all correct I went reconnoitering along a reserve trench that was new to me & from the crest of it I got a magnificient view of the German lines, lying on the slopes of the hills on the other side of the valley & almost a mile away. Quite a good observation post in fact for our intelligence officers. It's strange warfare this — coming back I passed a French peasant busy cutting his corn, with his wife & little daughter helping him, all of them in full sight of the German trenches, while just behind them hidden in a thicket was one of our batteries that makes an ear splitting noise when it fires. Looking thro' my glasses I could see cattle grazing just behind the German trenches.

This reminds me of an amusing incident of a few days ago. Another party of French civilians were busy harvesting close to another of our batteries when a few German shells searching for this battery whistled over their heads & dropped perhaps 100 yds. behind them. They work on apparently unconcerned, evidently under the impression that as the shells were not meant for them they consequently would not hit them, until one dropped a little nearer than the others, then they stopped work & took shelter behind one of their own hayricks!

(McGowan, Sept. 8th)

The next day he was moved up to Vaux ridge and wrote by candlelight to the sound of rats scratching away behind the canvas draperies which covered the walls. He had got the men busy straight away erecting themselves a weather proof shelter, but had no material to make it bomb proof:

My word, we shall all be fit for the backwoods of Canada, or Australia when this business is over. In fact, shanty building out there it will be a picnic compared to this, for there will be no necessity then to limit the felling of trees, it won't matter there, if an aeroplane does spot human occupation & even if bullets do fly about occasionally there'll hardly be any necessity for protection against shell-fire...

I am quite enjoying being up here with 'B' Coy. for Capt. Churton the O.C. is an awfully decent chap & knows how to make the best of everything. We have quite a jolly mess together every evening & he is expecting a gramaphone any day now.

I've put in my application for leave today, but when I'll get it I cannot say. I'm apparently still in the Colonel's good books for one day last week he sent me in a grouse for my dinner with his compliments. As a matter of fact it was a pretty tactless thing to do to send anything in to a company mess for a subaltern but of course I thanked him profusely. He's not a bad chap taken all in all.

(McGowan, Sept 10th)

The fine hot weather extended well past mid-September while Heald and the others continued scouting in the marsh. They constructed a new path with eight bridges into the centre which enabled them to cut off the Germans when they came to attack the listening posts, but when Heald's patrol went out to make an ambush they found that the enemy had cut their telephone wire and discovered the trap. On the way home, they saw two German figures, but the light being too indistinct to get a decent shot they hesitated to disturb the silence of the shadowy wood. For the next six days, though they manned an ambush a little further back the Germans eluded them and Heald became sick of the tedious waiting. For two days they had been aware of guns thundering up north and wondered if there was a big scrap going on. Perhaps it was the long hoped for 'push' that would end the war.

Although Captain Jones with his scouts stayed out most nights, the keen eyed Pathans did no better than the others, and much though he liked Jones, Heald thought his own patrol put up a better show. On September 19th when Jones was recalled, Heald thought it because he had not been lucky enough to get a prisoner, but in reality there was a move afoot for the Cheshires to transfer to Maricourt. It was rumoured that there was every chance of their being in the 'push' starting on September 24th. (In Artois the First Army was engaged in the abortive battle of Loos to help the French where a great offensive commenced on the 25th).

Up in Vaux Wood, McGowan continued to enjoy the regular life, spending the evenings reminiscing on past battles over his meal and after dinner coffee:

> When I reached the dug-out tonight after a walk round with Hignett to see how a party were progressing with some barbed wire entanglements we are erecting to strengthen the defences of the wood, I found that either Davies's or my own batman had got our stove going. This stove was appropriated from one of the houses in our front line village now 'civilianless' & although a little overpowering now the nights are comparatively warm it will be jolly acceptable in the winter (I've vivid recollections of the temperature of undergound habitations in cold weather). It's a good little coal-burning stove with a tube chimney outlet thro' the roof of the dug-out. Yesterday two subalterns from other companies were temporarily transferred there to help with the work, of which there is quite a lot to be done by day & this necessitated three officers sleeping in one of the largest of our dug-outs.

> They say they are a bit cramped, but of course they have not spent 48 hrs. or longer in dug-outs such as we met with in the trenches when we first came out, where everything had to be accomplished in the lying posn. These dug-outs are palaces by comparison, with beds, tables, chairs & shelves not to mention a stove, walls lined with canvas, a hinged door with panes of glass, a window, a handsome flight of stairs leading down into it & a feeling of absolute security as regards the roof. Moreover these are for sleeping in only. We have a special rustic shelter for messing in, lighted at night by Japanese lanterns & shaded candles, & a 'Heath Robinson' bell to summon the waiter between the courses. Good cooking facilities in a specially constructed kitchen & plenty of crockery & cutlery which is a big step from eating 'Maconachie' out of a mess tin lid & drinking milkless, strong tea out of the other half of the mess tins.

The only thing I miss up here is the facility for bathing. In the wood occupied by one of our other companies they are able to get that luxury in addition to those we have. In fact they are always sorry when the day of relief comes round. I intend going round there one of these fine days, but am always kept so busy by day.

Undoubtedly, our recent shortage of heavy ammunition has been made good, for our guns continue to grow more & more active & provoke comparatively little reply from the Germans. I expect a large number of their guns are still across on the Eastern front & I shouldn't be at all surprised if they don't very shortly get a nasty shock along the Western front. There has been a continuous & heavy bombardment going on some distance North of us for some days now. By the way leave is stopped again but only temporarily I'm told, so I'm still hoping to be back with you again sometime this month. I wonder if I'll see a Zeppo? which reminds me that as we read in the paper of the latest raid, we were rather pleased to see that Norwich was one of the places visited. That is I believe where a large number of the home service-ites are stationed. It really does make us wild when we see the rapid promotion made at home while with us there has not been a single promotion in the battn. since we left England.

While eating an apple yesterday, I broke one of my front teeth, which has spoilt my beauty & turned all my f's into v's. I've seen the Doctor today & sent in a application to see the Army dentist at first convenient opportunity. My word the Doctor isn't half enjoying himself these days. Casualties are few & far between & there's not much sickness, so he gets a pretty slack time of it. He's taken up quarters in a little cottage in the front line village; the window of his room looks right on the German lines but nevertheless at the bottom of his garden he keeps a little punt & spends most of his day fishing, or endeavouring to shoot wild duck with a Remington rifle belonging to Bass.

(McGowan, Sept. 13th)

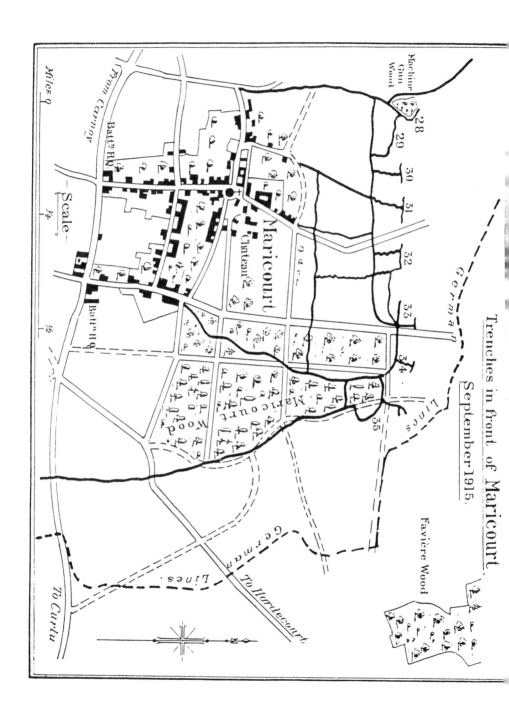

Trenches in Front of Maricourt.
September 1915.

Machine
Gun
Wood

28
29
30
31
32
33
34
35

German   Lines

Maricourt
Château

Maricourt Wood

Favière Wood

From Carnoy

Batt. HQ.

Miles 0

Scale
¼   ½

Batt. HQ.

German   Lines

To Curlu

To Hardecourt

N

CHAPTER 5

MARICOURT

In spite of his comparatively 'cushy' existence, McGowan had been yearning for more specialised work and on several occasions had written to his father with requests for signalling manuals. In September, when orders were published requesting skilled volunteers from the ranks to transfer to the equipment branch of the R.F.C. he seriously considered applying. One stumbling block was that Colonel Groves would have to be treated with the utmost diplomacy to sanction a transfer.

After about seven weeks by the Somme, the battalion went north on Sept. 21st to take over trenches 28 – 35 from the French between Machine Gun Wood and Maricourt Wood in front of Maricourt Village. By chance, McGowan avoided the upheaval of the move as for three days he had suffered from his aching tooth. Having ascertained the whereabouts of the nearest dentist, Dr. Costello sent him off to the clearing hospital at the railhead some twelve miles back. McGowan quite enjoyed the half hour run in the ambulance from the collecting station as a brightly shining full moon illuminated the peaceful countryside.

Eventually he found himself in a large rectangular hospital room, thirty yards by eight, equipped with twenty iron bedsteads, mattresses, snow white sheets and mosquito nets. Most of the patients occupying the half filled ward were already asleep though it was only 9 p.m. After having had some chicken broth and an aspirin, McGowan too dozed off only to be woken with the late arrival of a stretcher case who had received a head wound. In the morning, McGowan the only officer who could get up partook of his solitary breakfast seated at a small table in the centre of the room:

> ...There is apparently a big medical staff here, for as I sit here two fresh
> doctors & nurses are making the morning round of visits, taking
> temperatures, testing pulses, dressing wounds, a serum injection as
> protection against lockjaw after a shrapnel wound. This is of course not
> as comfortable a place as Mont Noir & much more methodical &
> practical for which I suppose the womenfolk are responsible. The nurses
> are not a particularly attractive lot, but I expect very clever & useful. I
> notice one at least is wearing a military medal.

11.30 a.m.

> Well I've seen the dentist and parted with the tooth that was causing the
> trouble & am to see him again at 2.30 p.m. to have my gums treated. He

111

says I'm suffering slightly from pyorhoea (I don't know how to spell it) but it sounded something like that & advises Kolynos Paste as an excellent thing for cleaning my teeth with, so will you please send me a tube of it in your next parcel. He has cleaned the broken tooth but can do nothing further with it here. It will require crowning & I shall have to wait till I come on leave to get that done. I am not to leave here until tomorrow to give the swelling of my face a chance to subside.

2 p.m.

...I'd quite an exciting little encounter with the powers that be last weekend. On Friday I sent in an application for transfer to the equipt. branch of the R.F.C. & this application reached the C.O. about 2 hrs before a notice from the Brigade asking for a name to be submitted for the Bd. Tunnelling Section. My name was sent in without any mention of the matter to me personally & the first official intimation I recd. was a telephone message ordering me to report with batman & baggage to the R.E. Tunnelling Sect. I straitway paid a visit to our Hd Qrs. feigning mystification on the grounds that I'd made no application for the job, was not qualified for, did not want the job & in accordance with my Territ. agreement could not be forced to take the job. This upset the 'heavenly twins' somewhat & the explanations given were truly amusing. The outcome was that I personally took a note to the Brigade explaining that my name had been sent in under a misapprehension & that I was an engineer only in so far as it concerned the telephone. I saw the Staff Captain first & then the General. The latter was exceptionally nice, asked me, first, would I like to try the mining job & gain the experience as I went along. I said I would, only I thought I should be more useful where I could apply my telephone knowledge & told him that I had sent in an application for transfer only two days ago. He wondered that the applicn. hadn't reached him (I didn't) asked me to have a drink & a smoke & questioned me as to my telephone experience. When I'd finished he said "Undoubtedly you would be wasted underground, send in a full statement of your qualifications & I'll see it is forwarded to the proper quarter". So I left the Bde. feeling very pleased at the unintentional opportunity afforded for furthering my wishes for transfer to the Army Signals R.E. or the Equipt. Branch R.F.C. Of course I may lose my sappers, but even that is not certain for Capt. Bourne, to whom the C.O. intended handing over the Sapper Section, is awaiting the result of an application to the Divisional Tunnelling Section. The C.O. has admitted, time & again, that he is very pleased with my work as Sapper Officer, so if Capt. Bourne leaves us he'll probably consider it best to leave things as they are at all events until I hear the news of my application.

Don't be alarmed & think I've been cheeky or wilfully getting across with my superiors. It so happened that I held the trump card & was forced to play the hand in self defence.

(McGowan, Sept. 21st)

On volunteering it was understood that the Territorials had certain rights, e.g. no overseas service and no transfers to another unit without their consent.[1] But in May 1915, the War Office ordained that for the war period the T.F. rules were to be similar to those for the Regular, and that a C.O. had power to transfer a man from one corps to another without his consent merely noting any objections. [2] Perhaps McGowan was not aware of this. When it was generally known the order was widely resented.

When the time came to vacate Vaux, Heald felt quite sorry to leave and though he still felt like having a scrap, life at Maricourt soon became increasingly dismal. For the next three days it poured down incessantly while the alien trenches which were seemingly complicated, quickly became soggy alleyways engulfing the walkers ankle deep in thick slime. Dug by the French, the trenches were made for offence not defence, and were constructed in the shape of a long 'T' having a fire step in the small advanced cross trench with no elaborate sandbag parapets. At the saps some of the forward listening posts were dangerous to man, though they had been covered by wire netting to try and minimise danger from enemy bombs. Heald found he was dug in to a poor kind of 'bivvy' with no chance of getting dry:

Fine at last. The trenches are in an awful mess. Our push seems to be progressing fairly well but the French in Champagne are right through and still advancing. They are fine in attack.

In the evening I had to go out and reconnoitre an old advance trench in front of our lines to see if it is occupied by the Germans. I crawled out with three men and we got quite close to a German working party. We heard a man sneeze three times, I think he must have been one of the men covering their working party. We crept down to this old trench but found nothing there. We made a plan of it, and took bearings.

(Heald, Sept. 26th)

---

[1] T.F. Regulations 1912, para 3.
[2] Army Order 188, May 1915.

After four days in hospital McGowan trudged along the muddy roads with his batman towards Maricourt. From the signs they saw en route, they speculated how soon they would be ordered across the space between their own trenches and the German's, and hastening their steps they took care to arrive before sunset when they feared all would be confusion.

As expected, McGowan no longer had charge of his sappers; he was back again with 'C' Company who were guarding the village almost in the front line. Among the desolation of wrecked houses about four remained habitable, though others, badly damaged, still had hearths to boil a pot. The Germans who had despatched their heavy guns elsewhere now sporadically lobbed over small shells which did little more than break a hole in a roof or outer wall.

On first catching sight of McGowan, the Adjutant said: 'Hullo, you're back again are you? Well, you'll be leaving again shortly, you're to attend a Medical Board on Monday with a view to transfer to the R.F.C.' As the A.S.C. had taken off all the battalion field kit to near the hospital, McGowan was glad at least to know that he could retrieve his warm gear. Hardly anyone had carried with them a change of clothes and few had more than a thin waterproof covering for the night.

In spite of his boredom at Vaux, Heald sickened anew of trench warfare. He had been saddened with the news of a 'Liverpool' patrol ambushed back in the marsh; one officer he knew called Greenhalgh had been killed with a further man wounded and another missing. Because of his poisoned hand he had missed attending a course of bomb instruction and had not been appointed Brigade Bomber. Another minor misfortune occurred when the Sergeant Major burnt the feet of his spare woollen socks when he was drying them, leaving Heald with only one thin wet pair. A cushy wound and Blighty was all he wanted; a chance which straight away appeared to be sent by their General:

The G.O.C. sent a Daily Mail which was shrieking good news up with instructions for it to be put in the German trenches or on their wire. I and my sergeant thought we would have a try to do this. We heard a cough about 30 yards away to our left, and judging this to be a listening post we crawled about another 20 yards to our right. Suddenly I heard another cough about 5 yards away on my left. I nearly jumped out of my skin. We heard them move in their post so we put the paper on a long stick with the headlines showing and stuck it in the ground just by their post. We crawled back safely. In the morning we saw the paper on the stick just outside their wire. They crawled out and got it during the day.

(Heald, October 1st)

Farcical newspaper games had not escaped Hodgkin's notice on June 24th, 1915 when the 2nd A.C. propaganda sheet publicised some messages as examples of bad discipline among the enemy:

'Send us English papers. Our ones are lying in front of your trenches, but don't try and get them for there are some fanatics here who will shoot you. We should like some cigarettes. Look out for papers coming over soon.

We have thrown you over some newspapers. Have you received them? Throw us over some news too. Don't look out, the Lieutenant won't have it but it will be all right at noon today. You needn't be afraid, we shan't shoot.

Your Comrades.'

After Heald's nocturnal foray it grew cold and he felt miserable with dysentry but his good servant managed to get a stove going to warm up the bivvy and sat up with him all night. Most of the men by now had become infested with lice, and the rats growing daily more numerous became unafraid, pestering the dug-outs and rear trenches, letting no one rest with their squealing and careless scampers. Well aware of their discomfort in the trenches, Dr. Costello arranged hot water for the officers, and Heald lapped himself in a bath tub at headquarters where it seemed that abundance overflowed:

The C.O. is living in luxury. Carpets, sofas, fires and beds just the same as at home. He sits down and carves his joint and has his wine at night. No wonder he does not want to move out.

(Heald, October 11th)

McGowan and his engineers had managed to rig up a bath house for the men with two boilers and half a dozen wood tubs so that there was hot water and a change of underclothing. Despite diminishing brick stocks they also beavered away to fortify underground dug outs and stocked them up with provisions and water ready to stand a siege:

You say "What will they do for a Sapper Officer when I'm gone". They'll find another I expect very quickly if Capt. Bourne doesn't turn up again. There never was a man yet in the army who could not be replaced by another, better in some ways, worse in others. I shall be quite sorry to leave my Sappers though. They are a mixed crew. The original 24 were a reckless, undisciplined lot who volunteered for whatever the job might be in the hopes of avoiding the monotony of sentry duty in the trenches. Eight of these have since been replaced by casualties that I sent back as unsuitable. Naturally when a company officer is asked by a specialist officer for men to fill vacancies in the latter's complement, the former, if he can help it, does not let his best men go, but rather his worst (that is to say those *he* has most trouble with). So you will see why they are a mixed crew, but they are all excellent workers & I've very little trouble with them, providing I keep them busy; it is when the battalion is at rest that they need a lot of looking after. Here they are as happy as pigs in clover. They've got one of the best billets they've ever had, a wire bed each & a stove on which they cook unofficial meals when work is over for the day. I really must inspect one of their dishes some evening for I hear a lot about them — apple & jam dumplings made from breadcrumbs & bacon fat seems to be the most popular.

(McGowan, October 9th)

Out again wiring at night in front of an advanced post, Heald had accompanied Lieut. J.D. Salmon who got a bullet through both his hands:

The top slipped off the maule with which he was driving in the posts and he made too much noise. We took him in and carried on and just as I was wiring the last post a bullet passed right under my instep and did not touch me. It would have been a beautiful 'Blighty' and I should have got home for winter.

(Heald, October 10th)

Having a care for his officers, Colonel Groves now forbade Heald to attempt any further nocturnal wiring, though he managed to rig up an observation post in a haystack hoping the enemy had not spotted it.

Life all at once took on a more rosy hue, he learnt that he had been promoted to Lieutenant antedated to March 20th, and that the C.O. had recommended him for some Russian or French decoration. With this news, and when he heard that he was to go on leave on October 26th, Heald's spirits rose with the eager anticipation of the lights and music in London. He was only sorry that others had not also received their well deserved promotions because of wounds.

In honour of the promotions on October 16th, Heald stood the other three officers in his trench a dinner of seven courses with 'fizz', coffee and liqueurs.

Maricourt

The following was the menu:

Hors d'oeuvres
Consommé Argentine.
Lobster Mayonnaise.
Pâté, Canard rotie au 'George'.
Petit pois. Sauce des Pommes.
Pomme de terres brouille.
Fruits, Gateau.
'Un petit piece de moutard'.
Liqueurs. Café. Music.

Not bad for the trenches. We held it in the largest dugout and it was a
huge success. Our batman turned up trumps and everything was very
good and went smoothly.

(Heald, October 16th)

The following day he constructed a bomb trap in an old trench which they
suspected the Germans were using, but the wedge must have slipped as it
went off ten minutes later. Undeterred the next evening he set the trap
afresh.

Working with such unstable weapons was always hazardous and sometimes
tragic. October 23rd was a real bad day. At about 9.15 a.m. somehow or other
some of their own bombs exploded in the dugout of Heald's grenadiers:

Eight of them were badly wounded and worst of all Sergeant Harrison
died of his wounds. Poor chap he had been with me ever since the war
started & had always gone out with me on any patrol or bit of dangerous
work that wanted doing. He was one of the finest men in the battalion &
I was very fond of him. His loss is irreparable & I feel it very keenly.
To think he should be killed by a pure accident when he was just the
sort of chap to win a V.C. This war is cruel. All the best seem to go &
one wonders what sort remains.

(Heald, October 23rd)

Thanking heavens he was starting on leave the next day, Heald had a hot
bath and some good food at 'transport' before leaving at four the following
morning. It was terribly cold and his teeth were nearly shaken out of his head
in an unsprung limber box during the thirteen mile ride into Amiens. At the
station he saw King George V leaving the special train for his car. He had
been inspecting some troops but there was absolutely no ceremony, just a few
sentries around with fixed bayonets.

For a few hours, Heald spent time breakfasting on three omelettes and sprucing himself up with a shave and haircut. He started to cheer up considerably on the train with the lively company of two jolly nurses. Although he was disappointed at not sailing with them on the afternoon boat, they all met in London the following day for tea and a show at the Gaiety: 'Tonight's the Night'. Starring Mr. George Grossmith as the hero and Mr. Leslie Henson with his comic frog like face, it included such names as Miss Moira Mannering and Miss Haidée de Raince who came of an actor family. The show had already been running since April 29th, 1915.

During the three days rush up north, there was hardly time to look round, but on the last evening he managed to fit in another show: 'The Girl in the Taxi'. A very popular spectacle, already it had enjoyed a long run, having opened at the Lyric Theatre on September 7th 1912. One of the main stars was Miss Amy Augarde who was dark and very vivacious, a type which Heald particularly admired.

Leaving for London from Liverpool's Lime St. Station, Heald found himself surrounded by a bevy of girls he called a 'beauty chorus' which livened up the journey. Not giving himself time to think he went off shopping and to a further show at the Coliseum before departing at Victoria for the return to Maricourt.

Although McGowan no longer had charge of the sappers, he worked busily with them supervising the laying of bricks and drains in the floors of the saturated communication trenches. Plentiful materials were to be found from the walls and rafters of the skeleton buildings in the shell wrecked village. Once more a platoon commander of 'C' Company, he nightly patrolled the trenches while the enemy fired shells into the village on the lower ground. He took with him a 'verey' pistol and lights in case a sentry should spot the Germans repairing their barbed wire which had been sporadically smashed by the British artillery.

One evening all the British guns in the neighbourhood fired one round at the German trenches, and immediately afterwards the infantry fixed bayonets, fired a volley and let forth a cheer. This ploy fairly put the wind up the enemy, who thinking they were 'for it' became unusually excitable for some time afterwards. Waiting for the noise to subside, McGowan with 2nd Lieutenant O. Johnson retired to Captain Davies's dug out to keep themselves awake in between patrols with a game of bridge. Playing for love, McGowan proceeded to win heavily, but he knew he was not meant for gambling as however small the money staked he invariably lost. 'Don't be alarmed' he told his parents, 'if not playing for love, we only play for small stakes to make a little battle game of it'. Later on as amusement they spent half an hour trying to kill the rats, but without much success as the animals had become old and wily. It was only after the bleak hour of dawn they retired to the village dropping on the floor in their wet clothes to sleep till lunchtime.

In his free time, McGowan wrote letters at H.Q. amidst a regular and confused din. He sat in the safe corner of the room away from the shutters of the exposed window through which the enemy rifle and machine gun bullets could penetrate. A telescopic attachment for a sniping rifle was a recent novelty sent from Brigade; McGowan tried it out while the Armour Sergeant and Sergeant Major were resting it:

> My word if the Germans have had instruments like this in use for long
> (& I don't doubt they have) it's no wonder we dare not show a hair
> above the parapet. It doesn't take an expert shot to hit the mark at 600
> yds. when the telescope is attached.
>
> (McGowan, October 9th)

Heedless of the ubiquitous bullets, a big 'funk hole' was being constructed and almost complete. This shelter could accommodate over one hundred men in the standing position and nearly fifty lying down, the whole measuring about eight feet high and fully eight feet below ground besides many other little rooms and passages. McGowan thought that under the supervision of the C.O., his experience as Sapper Officer in dugout construction would prove very useful in later years:

> 11.00 a.m.

> This morning I've been a round of visits with Capt. Hartley &
> discovered that Chavasse with his usual energy & resource has
> established a recreation room for the men in a little cottage with a hol-ly
> roof. (sic) Here a gramophone was playing & men inside reading or
> playing games. Outside on a noticeboard were pinned up copies of all
> the latest telegrams from the scene of the push. This is a fine thing, for
> it gives the men a little incentive to stick, whatever unpleasant tasks they
> get, in the interest of a tangible cause. Chavasse in one of his sermons a
> few weeks ago instanced the remarkable fact that along the whole front,
> in the ruined villages & towns one notices innumerable Calvaries
> standing unharmed, although everything around is devastated & in the
> same way, often, in churches, hopelessly shattered, the crucifix above the
> altar remains unharmed. His inference of course was that just as God set
> up those likenesses to remind us of the trials & sacrifices of Christ in his
> combat against sin, so he allows them to remain as a sign of the ultimate
> triumph of right over wrong.

This morning I came across what was once the church of this village,
but now nothing remains of it but four broken walls but on one of them
still hangs unscarred a plaster calvary.

(McGowan, September 25th)

Lance Corporal Bolton related that he bought cocoa for ½d. and 1d per cup
and ate 'fairy' cakes in this much talked of reading room where papers, books,
games of darts, dominoes and draughts were supplied:

I have often read of these places for Tommy's comfort but this is the
first I have seen & I believe this is some of the good work of our
Chaplin who says he loves his bhoys (sic) & as you see his is not all talk
but practices what he preeches. (sic)

(Bolton, September 23rd)

Partly by mud walking and partly in a Field Ambulance, McGowan made
the going to and from the hospital for a Medical Board for the R.F.C. Apart
from a stringent eye test to be taken later he thought that his Board had been
successful and hoped to wait a few weeks only before his transfer matured.
After dinner that night the doctor in a whisper asked McGowan, still
besmirched with mud, to go across to his billet to make a four for bridge. Dr.
Costello's secret haven was known only to a few and to McGowan's delight
he found a beautifully furnished room with a bright fire burning in the grate
and the table set with coffee for four. The next door house was quite roofless,
and Costello's cosy billet, where all the furniture had been abandoned by the
inhabitants had remained unnoticed. This rare interlude poignantly
reminded McGowan of the home he had not seen since June, and he was
engulfed by a wave of homesickness.

Besides setting up recreation facilities for the men, the Chaplain had
transformed a small wooden hut into an attractive miniature church:

I was surprised when I went inside this morning, for Chavasse has
equipped it beautifully — quite a church in minature. Round the walls &
above the little altar are hung a set of plaster models, portraying the
story of the cross. These were rescued from the wrecked church here, as
also were the chairs and hassocks but in addition Chavasse has had made
a lectern, a number of kneeling rails of wood, & a small side table for
the holy vessels. It is wonderful when you consider that it stands so
close to the actual front line that the outside wall has to be barricaded
with sandbags to stop stray bullets from penetrating & we were
cautioned to sing hymns in piano, so as not to attract the attention of the
enemy without. However long this little chapel may fulfil its mission, it

is well used at present for Chavasse has arranged a daily evening service at 6 p.m. & Holy Communion on two days of the week so that troops going to the trenches at the week-end may have opportunities for attending when they are free to do so.

(McGowan, October 3rd)

With the profligate numbers of casualties draining the Army during the first year of the war, further labour was urgently needed for road and rail making, water supply and second line trenches behind the front line. McGowan, who had talked to an officer of one of the eight labour battalions sent from England in the Summer, felt it was very unfair that these men were paid three shillings a day as opposed to the one shilling received by his engineers who, besides doing construction work, had also to fight with the infantry. He thought it a big waste of government money. There was no conscription in 1915 and the increased money presumably was an inducement to entice older men overseas. They wore the badges of the R.E's and were officered by civil engineers, whose colonels and adjutants were Regular or Special Reserve R.E.. Labour battalions also included other nationalities such as Chinese and Indians.

McGowan did not have long to wait. On October 12th he was summoned for a personal interview with the O.C. (Lt Col. J.F.A. Higgins) of the 3rd Wing R.F.C. at the 1st Aircraft Park, St. Omer. Borrowing a bicycle he pedalled off in haste after Sunday lunch to the Corbie railhead for the evening train to Amiens. Unluckily he missed the connection which delayed his arrival at the park until the following midday:

Unfortunately the O.C. himself was away for the day, & although I expressed my willingness to wait until his return, his adjutant, after asking me a few quite unimportant questions, said there was no need whatever for that, so I couldn't press the point further. I learnt from him that if transferred to the equipment branch it would in all probability mean England for a few months at all events. Strange as it may seem to you I didn't fancy the idea of that a bit & said that I'd hoped to have remained out here & taken to flying ultimately. He said that I could, of course, become attached to them as an observer & if successful ultimately become a pilot, but advised me if the O.C. agreed to recommend me for transfer to the equipment branch to take that as they were in need of competent officers for that branch & my prospects of success would be better there. He promised me, however, that if for any reason the O.C. did not recommend me for the equipt. branch he would recommend that my name shld. go forward as an observer, so I'm pretty certain of one or the other now, but had I seen the O.C. himself I shld. have known definately — such is the reward for being zealous not to lose any time. Had I wasted a day in (A) I shld. probably have seen him without difficulty.

(McGowan, October 12th)

Hodgkin who met Lt. Col. Higgins R.F.C. (By then Brigadier Higgins) on October 23rd the following year described him as: 'A sarcastic person, very amusing but bad to serve under I am told'.

Shortly afterwards McGowan got his transfer to the 3rd Wing on the recommendation of the Adjutant, and without many regrets took his leave for good of the 5th Cheshires.

During the first week, unused to the new job he worked hard trying to master the novelties of wireless telegraphy. He half hoped that the 'powers that be' would permit him to become an observer and ultimately a pilot but whatever happened he had no wish to return to his regiment.

Besides acting as a general depot for every kind of store, No. 1 Aircraft Park handled most of the R.F.C. wireless organisation originally set up by Captain B.E. Smythies, a former officer of the Royal Engineers. The park encompassed clear level fields of grass or stubble suitable for landing grounds, and portable aircraft hangars made of light detachable wooden framework covered with canvas easily transported on lorries. There were also some fixed wooden sheds for workshops.

McGowan was billeted with a Madame Joly who plied him at breakfast with omelettes and coffee. Regularly every evening he dined at a café in St. Omer where for four francs, exactly the same fare was on offer. Madame Joly and her eldest daughter looked after a printing works in the town while her husband was away in the trenches. McGowan visited the local catholic church but as a low church protestant, he was struck forcibly by the seeming lack of sincerity in the form of worship. He confided in his parents that he preferred the plain unvarnished religion of the Plymouth Brethren: 'I dislike especially the sight of a lot of mere children toying with strings of beads & bobbing up & down & moving about the altar as though on a stage platform!' (McGowan, October 29th).

While on duty as orderly officer at the aerodrome, McGowan encountered Robert Loraine, the actor airman: 'He had just brought in a machine & looked a fine specimen of manhood, strong healthy face & clothed from head to foot in leather overalls' (McGowan, October 29th). In November 1914 while flying as an observer in a Henri Farman Reconnaissance machine, Loraine had been wounded by a bullet from an anti-aircraft shell which had pierced his lung. Loraine, holding his machine gun, was positioned underneath the pilot who sat as though on a trapeze above him:

> Had I been standing or walking I would have gone out right away, as the excessive bleeding would have suffocated me. Being seated, I found that by leaning forward and not attempting to breathe with the injured lung but being content with small gasps with the uninjured one, I could conquer suffocation for a time.[1]

As the doctor had given up all hope of his life he twice received the Last Rites.

Besides being a handsome and acclaimed actor manager, Robert Loraine, then thirty-nine years old, had already cut a dashing figure in the army and had been awarded the Queen's Medal with three clasps as a machine gunner in the Boer War. In the R.F.C. he appeared to have a charmed existence, gaining the D.S.O. and M.C., besides being mentioned six times in despatches. Flying under the pseudonym of 'Jones', on July 16th 1910 Loraine, against all advice, was the sole contestant in an event at a 'Flying Week' at Bournemouth, where in appalling weather, he managed to pilot a flimsy kite-like Henri Farman bi-plane and land precariously at Needles Down, Isle of Wight. Possessing a charismatic personality, he featured in many star theatrical roles of all kinds on both sides of the Atlantic. He was known as a fearless if somewhat ruthless pilot who did not always endear himself to those under his command. When McGowan saw him, Loraine who had been appointed Flight Commander on September 13th was in 'B' Flight, patrolling with No. 5 Squadron. He was in charge of one of the new Vickers Fighter biplanes, feared by the Germans before October 1915; after which the German Fokker E III monoplane, fitted with a machine gun that could fire through the arc of the propeller arrived in numbers, and achieved temporary air superiority. Lieut. the Hon. Eric Lubbock was Loraine's observer.

At St. Omer there were a number of B E 2c aircraft used for reconnaissance. In 1915, the B E 2c was the basic equipment of two thirds of the R.F.C. squadrons, it often carried a 'C' type camera shaped like a square mahogany box clamped to one side of the fuselage from which the pilot would have to lean out to change the plates. To sight the camera he had to lean over the side and look through a ball and cross wire finder. The reconnaissance pilot had to fly the machine with his left hand, arrive over the spot he wanted to photograph, put his arm out into a seventy mile an hour wind and push the camera handle back and forward to change the plates,

---

[1] W. Loraine, *Robert Loraine* p.77.

pulling the string on the end of a cord between each operation to make an exposure.[1]

Though McGowan did not state the make, he enjoyed his first trip in a plane. The flight only lasted half an hour but he thought it grand: 'The pilot who took me up knew it to be my first flight thought to upset my liver by a few ocean wave effects, spiral descents etc., but not a bit of it, I thoroughly enjoyed the trip, that part of it especially & I'm looking forward to another tomorrow' (McGowan, October 29th). As it was a warm day, McGowan went up bareheaded. Usually it was impossible for pilot and observer to communicate as ears and mouths were covered by leather caps and eyes protected by goggles. In cold weather, the freezing air whistled through the strutts and wires of the flimsy planes, their wings of canvas stretched over maple wood battens.

About two and a half years later Heald was taken up in an R E 8 which largely replaced the B E 2c as the standard equipment of corps squadrons. Like the B E 2c it was rather a slow machine lacking manoeuvrability, designed for observing artillery shoots and reconnaissance. Owing to the design the R E 8 was difficult to land and the pilot's vision was somewhat restricted:

> I did not feel at all ill, and I was not at all cold. In fact I was warmer
> than down below. We had no machine gun so could not venture over the
> Boche lines.
>
> (Heald, February 19th 1918)

At the aerodrome, McGowan marvelled at listening to the news: 'Radiated through space from Nordlich in Germany, Eiffel Tower Paris and Poldhue in Cornwall'. He recounted that he heard beautifully clear signals between Nordlich and Madrid in international morse code though it was as yet a little too fast for him to 'read'.

When McGowan had first arrived, the Lieutenant acting for Major F.L. Festing who was away on leave, had expressed surprise when he learnt that McGowan knew nothing about wireless. However, he decided to send him for a weeks instruction to Captain Smythies who, pleased with McGowan's aptitude recommended he should remain a further week. On Festing's return from leave, the matter was reported to General H.M. Trenchard who had taken command of the R.F.C. in France on August 19th. According to Festing, Trenchard considered that McGowan had been trying to foist himself on them under false pretences and gave orders for his immediate return to his regiment. Abruptly Festing confronted McGowan: 'Why did

---

[1] C. Lewis, *Sagittarius Rising*, p. 60.

you say you had a knowledge of wireless?' McGowan did his best to explain that he had told the Adjutant of his inexperience in the first interview. After referring to McGowan's papers, Festing ascertained that indeed McGowan had made only a general application for either the Equipment Branch of the R.F.C. or Army Signals R.E. Feeling apprehensive that the R.E. might abruptly decline his services without an interview and fearing that he might be returned to the Cheshires, McGowan felt shocked that this misunderstanding might disrupt his hopes through no fault of his own.

CHAPTER 6

THE BOMBING SCHOOL

After his brief vacation Heald's train pulled into Amiens in raw November weather. There was no transport at the station, so he was forced to ride on horseback for thirteen miles back to Maricourt where he found the others in a nearby village. The Germans were tending to be fairly jumpy so it was a relief not to be living in the water logged trenches. With his grenadiers he practised bombing attacks and on the 9th held a test which sixteen of them managed to pass. As usual the rain was lashing down in torrents and those up manning the trenches paddled round in long rubber thigh boots and large macintosh capes.

A few days later, the battalion was relieved and went back to Suzanne by night. As the snow started to fall, Heald learnt that he had been appointed as instructor to the newly formed 5th Divisional Bombing School, and though happy in the thought that he would have a good job in comfortable winter quarters, he was sorry to hear that his smart grenadier section was to be disbanded. The men were very sorry for themselves as they would have to revert to the drudgery of duties in the line, but Heald still felt keenly the loss of Sergeant Harrison and was glad of the change.

On November 21st, he left for the new school at Chipilly on the north bank of the Somme where he found himself among a congenial group who had been out since Mons in 1914. Speedily with his sergeant instructors he laid out a section of trenches dug by fifty men from the Guards Entrenching Battalion and had his work syllabus approved by the General. Having rigged up a comfortable room and kitchen for the mess, Heald cycled off to Corbie for some liquid refreshment to greet the new class. His return journey incurred a precarious ride of well over six miles along the banks of the Somme, the sun had just broken the top of the frost, but despite the slippery surface he managed to keep a hold on a precious bottle of liquor he had purchased from an obliging old woman. He felt a great sense of triumph in his bargain, as the town had been placed in the spirit restriction zone. As Heald would have seen it, Corbie situated at the junction of the Somme and Aisne rivers was a quaint and ancient little place and the fine Benedictine church, the Abbaye de Saint Pierre founded in 657 was still intact. In 1918, the church suffered heavy damage when every other historic building was also seriously wrecked, the medieval timbers spilling out forlornly all over the narrow cobbled streets. Pedalling along, he heard some German aeroplanes dropping bombs on the nearby railhead and he hoped they would not spot their newly dug trenches.

Shortly afterwards, he took to his bicycle once more and rode off in the opposite direction along the winding river bank to Bray-sur-Somme to visit the Cheshires. He thought Bray rather a large place with nothing much to recommend it. There was a long uphill village street at the bottom of which at a cross roads was a fine old church with a pointed gothic tower (later destroyed in 1918). By the river there was a meadow where the French and British troops used to congregate to listen to the regimental bands in the summer.

Everyone in the battalion was plunged into gloom. News had come through that henceforth the 5th Cheshires was to be converted into a Divisional Pioneer Battalion with a vast deterioration in status:

> Everybody was on the verge of mutiny. It was the C.O.'s fault too. I suppose he saw a chance of saving his own skin for the war and he made an application to the General regardless of anybody else's wishes. He is about the most putrid thing in this war. Thank heaven I got out in time. Three officers have already gone. Transferred and most of the others are thinking of volunteering for Servia. Poor old 5th Cheshires. It was hard luck having to have such a washout as Groves in command. The General sent all sorts of complimentary messages to us on leaving the Brigade on the good work we had done. Of course he said it was because there were no other territorial battalions good enough for the job but we did not join to dig for others. Perhaps after the war this C.O. will know what he has done.
>
> (Heald, December 1st 1915)

Officially the battalion was selected for pioneer duties on account of the reputation it had gained in trench construction and pick and spade work. In spite of the fact that Territorial Battalions were not supposed to be appointed as pioneers to regular divisions, the 1/5th Cheshires were told to carry on with their pioneer duties until January 25th, 1916 when they were appointed Pioneer Battalion to the newly formed 56th (London) Territorial Division. The concept of Pioneer Battalions was completely new to the British. They were to have a dual role having to fight in the line and to carry out engineering works, chiefly trench constructions and roadworks in the battle zones. Their duties involved them in long and arduous marches at night to the front line under shell fire in pitch darkness. It was wretched work in the eternal mud.

Four days later at Chipilly, courses started at the bombing school. Just as Heald was giving his first lecture the following morning, an old woman started to kill a pig at the door of the barn which served as a classroom.

The Bombing School

Quickly ending his lesson and overcome by the noise, Heald provided a counter attraction in the form of grenade throwing.

As usual, many of the weapons were unstable, while testing some new rifle grenades Heald somehow escaped with his life as the first one exploded at the mouth of the rifle. Inevitably next day there was a useless casualty though every precaution had been taken, the rifle being rigged up with string around a corner, the grenade burst in the air:

> A sergeant of the Devons was firing at the time and he got very seriously wounded. It's not right to send us these things for test when they are as dangerous as those grenades without warning us.
>
> (Heald, December 9th)

A further accident occurred on December 24th when another instructor was badly hit by a bomb fragment, but although a court of enquiry was held no effective conclusion could be reached. It was a gloomy and frustrating period not helped by the weather as during the fortnight up to Christmas the rain poured steadily down flooding the trenches and interrupting the training. One of the officers who ventured into the German line found enemy trenches as dismal as theirs and totally deserted:

> A terrible calamity has happened. Grower our mess president had just cashed all the mess bills and had five 100 franc notes in his hand. Just then the post came in and he took off the wrapper of a newspaper, crumpled it up and threw it into the fire with the notes.
>
> (Heald, December 17th)

As this was worth about £125 and a Second Lieutenant's pay in 1916 was 7/6d per day, it was indeed a misfortune.

For Heald, Christmas 1915 was a lazy one. He slept by the fire and wrote letters. The class having departed the previous day the school invited some Divisional Cyclists to dinner when they had quite a good spread with a ration each of plum pudding. A new class arrived on December 26th, they seemed a nice lot, among them being Hodgkin's friend Woolley V.C. who had survived the fighting on Hill 60. After the rain, Heald managed to set a hundred men to clean up the trenches while he amused himself on a borrowed horse which gave him a sense of freedom. He felt well pleased that their manual of training had been accepted by the Divisional Staff as 'excellent' and was going into print. But as soon as the school was running smoothly they heard they were on the move once more: 'It is annoying just as we have got so nicely settled and comfortable. It is always the way though. The same old game of "silly fool". It's just as if the authorities came up to you and said "Oh you

129

thought you were comfortably settled here for the winter did you? Well you're not, Out you go". (Heald Dec. 28th)

Martigny their next location was a pretty enough Somme village a few miles from Bray. In the second week of January, the removal of the few school's possessions was effected by two motor lorries and two general service wagons. Another huge château had been requisitioned for their billets, evidently it was the property of a rich but absentee landowner and was surrounded by a large but rather neglected park. The walls of the outsize rooms with their high ceilings consisted of almost nothing else but large doorways and long windows which had the effect of making the whole place exceedingly draughty. But Heald felt content in his airy bedroom, his bed was comfortable and he slept well.

It seemed just about the limit when they heard a rumour of another imminent move. Heald had only just completed the designing and siting of the new instruction trenches. Was the C.O. off his head? More likely he too, was the victim of the huge impersonal machine that ground up the lives of those at the front. As it happened the school eventually was designated to be enlarged for general instruction with seven additional staff:

> Military etiquette will have to be strictly observed as in peace time and I shall have to take squad drill in addition. The objective of the school seems to be to teach these new officers how to behave to their seniors and to their men. I loathe etiquette. I am getting rather fed up with this life and should not mind rejoining my regiment. When one is in the trenches you do feel that you are in the right place, somehow. There's one thing I shall never be and that is a peace soldier. When the war is over I shall become a civilian again with feelings of relief. I don't mind fighting but etiquette and red tape worry me.
>
> (Heald, January 15th)

Heald found all these vacillations unsettling and increasingly tedious. Whenever he could, he borrowed a horse and worked off his frustrations with a good gallop; without proper exercise he was always miserable. With the arrival of a new class of forty-four there was not much time for anything and he was usually up by 6.30 a.m:

> I have been made Mess President, a job I loathe. The other two Grenade Instructors have got to take squad drill in addition to grenade instructions. I suppose because they are Regulars. I am senior to one but he is put down on the list first. I shan't say anything because I get out of the squad drill. Military red tape is in full swing. I really think that life in the regiment is preferable. They are in the trenches now having

been taken off pioneer work. The only thing is the conversation of the Staff Major who is running the show is so intensely interesting. He knows a lot of the things hidden to ordinary mortals. Besides I want to learn the course. It will be useful for teaching the others when I get back.

(Heald, January 22nd)

In 1916 Haig and many army generals nurtured in the tactics of earlier wars still put their faith in the use of cavalry on the western front. Like any other star performers, it is imperative that units of cavalry must have continuous practise in their art if they are to be one hundred per cent efficient. Thus on January 27th these dashing soldiers, so little employed, were glad to have the opportunity to show off their prowess in an exercise against the school's defended positions. Closing in at full gallop they made a fine sight as they charged the practise trenches with ferocious precision. Had they not realised that already they had become an anachronism in such warfare?

At the end of January, in a sudden flurry of attack amidst heavy gunfire the Germans captured Frise on the south end of the Somme from the French. As the counter attacks did not make much headway, Heald felt that the old trenches occupied by the Cheshires across the river at Vaux and in Maricourt would be barely tenable. In any case it was always a bad salient.

In Amiens, the French had recently set up a camouflage workshop in which they devised a wide variety of dummies to deceive the Boche. Heald was most impressed by the ingenuity of the objects and afterwards was happy to sit down with the rest of the school in one of the big restaurants to a good dinner. On a bright moonlight night some two weeks later, German aeroplanes dropped about twenty five bombs on the city and damaged the magnificient cathedral:

It is a shame. They evidently meant to hit it because they got their bombs on it. It was a bright moonlight night too, so they must have seen it. They are swines, what good can it possibly do them to spoil the beautiful place.

(Heald, February 21st)

With only twenty four hours notice, the school yet again was uprooted, though Heald, who had suddenly received orders to rejoin his regiment was not sorry to leave the red tape and vacillations he had encountered. During the move to Picquigny, his congenial fellow instructors stood him the best lunch in Amiens he had ever had, as a farewell.

131

Heald found his battalion at Hallencourt where it had joined the 56th Division composed of first line Territorial units recruited from the City and County of London and County of Middlesex. While the C.O. was away on leave Heald was appointed Assistant Adjutant. The men were supposed to be training but morale was low and there was little enthusiasm; after teaching his classes, Heald thought them pretty slack. By way of improvement he prepared a schedule of training and explained it to the junior officers with the help of demonstrations by the Sergeant Major.

The weather was as cold as in the previous February at Neuve Eglise and for two days it snowed hard grinding everything to a halt. In spite of this they were ordered on once more and starting at 9 a.m. for Domart they took seven hours on the march. As slippery as glass, the roads were fearful so the usual transport was out of the question.

Just as dark was falling they had a hard job to find billets but Heald located a welcoming house where the owners made him at home in the warm kitchen:

> This must be a charming town in the summer. It is in a valley with the Church on a hill. The whole lot surrounded by high hills. The houses are rather quaint and dilapidated. Chiefly made of wood and plaster. Very many are empty and our men are billeted in them. If a bit of plaster is knocked out we get a huge bill for damages. Some of these people must live on the proceeds. I am sure the 'Maire' of the town gets part of the booty for 'certifying'.
>
> (Heald, March 2nd)

Once more, he had been appointed grenade officer, though he was heartily sick of grenades:

> ... but I suppose its my duty and must be done. I am also appointed Signalling Officer. Incidentally I know nothing about signalling. I may go to a course. I am also Mess President of the H.Q. Mess and am learning Adjutants work as I am a kind of Jack of all trades.
>
> (Heald, March 9th)

Like a wandering caravan in the desert the battalion left Domart, moving to Authuille on the eastern bank of the Ancre on March 12th and three days later near by to Grand Rullecourt. In addition to everything else, Heald was appointed Billeting Officer, he had a terrible time as accommodation in all the villages was at a premium, and biking on ahead uphill all the way to Grand Rullecourt, he thought he would die of the effort. Fortunately several units had just moved out so he managed to get hold of the pick of the billets.

Recently awarded the C.M.G. the C.O. returned fresh from leave in high spirits wearing his new acquisition. 'Two new Captains have been sent out from England. It's a bit thick. We have absolutely no hope of promotion now. The sooner we get into action the better it will scare some of them home again' (Heald, March 9th).

In its new rôle as pioneers the battalion was detailed to give Grand Rullecourt a thorough spring clean. Stables were built, incinerators erected and sanitation improved. Already very dirty, the small village streets had been churned up by heavy lorries, a number of six inch naval guns and some huge twelve inch howitzers drawn by traction engines with caterpillar wheels. Lt. Col. Groves was appointed the commandant of the area:

Our men have done wonders in clearing up this village. Really our C.O. is very good when he is on work of this sort. I think the Pioneer work will suit him. Spent this day finding trenches for grenade work. Went to the cinema show tonight. Quite good.

(Heald, March 17th)

Delighted to escape it all, Heald departed on leave:

Instead of going the stereotyped way we (I and Johnson) got a motor lorry to Doullens. There we saw a hospital train going to Rouen so we bribed the sergeant in charge to put us on. He put us in a sick ward and presently a nurse came along and enquired whether we had had dinner, she seemed surprised when we answered no. I think she smelt a rat because in a few minutes an orderly came and wanted to see our cards. We had to confess. The M.O. then came and chucked us out. We had lunch at Doullens and A.S.C. car took us to Amiens where we stayed the night.

(Heald, March 22nd)

We caught the leave train at 11 and got to Havre about 9. No boat; submarines in the Channel. Went to a hotel and stayed the night.

(Heald, March 23rd)

CHAPTER 7

BRIGADE SIGNAL'S OFFICER

Before McGowan finally left the aircraft park at St. Omer the previous November, he had tried out a few runs on a new 1915 'Triumph' motor bike which was on charge to the Flight Sergeant. Having stalled the engine McGowan had found difficulty in re-starting the heavy machine on an up gradient, but when questioned on his abilities for a post of Brigade Signalling Officer he felt confident enough to answer that he could drive a motor cycle and ride a horse. Contrary to his more pessimistic forebodings, he had a satisfactory interview with General Fowler, the G.O.C. Signals and after a spell of leave reported back for further orders:

> The Colonel did not interview me until after dinner in the evening, probably the delay was intentional just to impress on me the degree of importance he attached to my coming. However, he was quite nice & decided to send me for attachment to the 48th Divisional Signals.
>
> (McGowan, Nov. 14th)

Duly arriving at Souastre he reported to a Major Brown, a friendly enough man, for a month's probation as B.S.O. Souastre was about four miles or so behind the line, and had not received a shell; it was another typical small place consisting of scattered uncared for cottages and a few farms with outhouses adjoining the road. From the hill outside you could see Gommecourt towards the east while the village was linked by road to Fonquevillers lying to the north west of Gommecourt. Although there was the usual grand château, McGowan did not find it as large and ornate as the others he had seen. A few days later, Brown sent McGowan forward to the trenches in front of Gommecourt Park wood which stuck out as a salient from the enemy line, Hébuterne village to the south west had been badly damaged.

McGowan was detailed as assistant to Captain Foreshaw, B.S.O. of the 145th Brigade. Foreshaw was a gentleman farmer from Berkshire who had knocked about abroad a good deal. McGowan thought him 'exceedingly nice but as hard as nails'. They lived in comfortable dug outs specially built for the Brigade H.Q. staff with whom he messed and McGowan felt he would have to be on his best behaviour. When the 145th was relieved by the 144th, McGowan who was handed over as 'part of the trench stores' stayed in the Gommecourt sector with a new set of officers, who were rather more businesslike and not as homely:

I'm fairly moving about in high circles at present am I not? & a very fine education it is too to be dining each day with a General to say nothing of Bde Majors & Staff Capts; of course I say little except when spoken to but there's always plenty of interest to listen to. General McClintock is a dear old man who has seen service in quite a lot of places. He's short, stout and enjoys his food, but is none the less very energetic & very considerate to those under his command.

(McGowan, Nov. 20th)

In spite of the age of the 'high ups' the mess did include younger men of McGowan's age and he felt confident that the length of time he had been in the country gave him quite a lot of standing:

Talk about war time economy! You should just see some of the meals turned out by the cook of the 144: soup, fish, meat & 2 vegs. boiled pudding & milk pudding, entrée cheese, desert, coffee & everything excellent. Of course we have to pay for it something short of 6 frcs. a day but I suppose we can well afford it.

(McGowan, Nov. 20th)

The stationary warfare of 1915 had produced a period of evolution in army signal practise in the field. With his pre-war training, McGowan naturally found his new work very interesting and he spent his time at Gommecourt examining the wiring at Brigade H.Q. and the various Battalion H.Q's. Telephones had been generally introduced and experimental work was underway devising cable routes underground.:

One of the battn. signalling sergts. is a very smart chap at his job & has devised quite a cute little telephone exchange to enable him to work his battn. lines more efficiently than is possible with the apparatus supplied officially. He was quite pleased that I showed interest in, & was able to appreciate, his idea & especially when I suggested a slight improvement to it, which he quickly put into operation & found satisfactory.

The outside wiring I'm not so much interested in. It's just a question of maintaining satisfactorily a network of insulated wires joining up the various Bn. offices with the bde office, some are run overhead some are buried & some are run in trenches & in this type of trench warfare it's a case of devising the best system to preserve the lines from breakage due to enemy shells & bullets, & still be able to get at your lines for testing purposes. Tracing lost wires is a job that, at this time of the year often takes you knee deep in mud.

(McGowan, Nov. 20th)

Immense expenditure of time and labour had been spent in constructing cable trenches and test boxes; the experimental buried system was found to work fairly well until the dislocation of divisional boundaries and disruption in the Somme battles. Sometimes the telephone stations were encased in wood and set into the sides of the trenches, the tops covered with layers of sandbags. A pigeon service had been organised in April 1915.

It soon appeared to the keen volunteers of the early Territorials that they were fast becoming a poor third to the Regulars and the currently more glamourous Kitchener's Army. Since arriving in France, Territorial casualties had seeped away their strength and their often scanty replacements had received little training.

There had been a great deal of criticsm in the Cabinet about Kitchener's waste and duplication of recruiting methods. His disapproval of the Territorials was well known, he regarded them as playboys and amateurs joining the army in a holiday spirit. Instead of making use of the County Associations already set up for recruiting the Territorial Army, he appealed for the first 'Hundred Thousand' volunteers on August 7th 1914 to form a 'New Army'. This appeal was followed for a further two hundred thousand. The two organisations continued side by side but the 'New Army' enjoyed the monopoly of favours. During the first eighteen months of the war out of almost two and a half million volunteers, roughly seven hundred and twenty six thousand were Territorials whose numbers considerably dwindled as time went on.

McGowan was concerned that he had never had promotion: 'These K.A. officers are alright in their way, but not so fine as the old regular or territorial officers. They are all full lieuts. but really junior to me in date of gazette'. (McGowan Nov 30th). He put his case to Col. Groves:

> I was glad to get your letter and to hear how you were going on. We have been taken out of the Inf. Brigade & turned into a Pioneer Battalion, so had you remained with us plenty of scope would have been found for your energies & pre-war training.
>
> With regard to promotions, I will see that your name goes in with the next batch. So far as I can make out you have not been passed over.
>
> (Lt. Col. J.E.G. Groves, Dec. 21st)

McGowan who had surmised the Cheshire's fate from Major W.A.V. Churton wrote:

> They will cease to exist as a fighting unit & become the scavengers of the brigade. If this is so it's a shame, for no battn. has done better in the line than the 5th Cheshires. But I understand that it is what is happening to most of these Territ. Battns. that came out early in the war & have gradually become reduced in strength without an adequate supply of reinforcements.
>
> (McGowan, Nov. 30th)

At the beginning of December, McGowan at last obtained a permanent position when he was appointed B.S.O to the 90th Infantry Brigade of the 30th Division then at Corbie. He felt delighted with his good fortune as the Brigade comprised the 16th, 17th and 18th Battalions of the Manchester Regiment (K.A.) in which many of his school friends had enlisted. These particular Kitchener's Battalions were known as the 1st, 2nd and 3rd 'Manchester Pals' while the 30th Division, formed by Lord Derby was called 'Lord Derby's Own'. It contained two Manchester Brigades and one from Liverpool, part of the famous 'City Battalions'. The 3rd Manchester Pals had been recruited from the 'Clerks and Warehousemen of Manchester' and like many of the other 'Pals' from the industrial north were a close knit community from the same district or occupation. Brigadier General C.J. Steavenson commanded the 90th Brigade, McGowan affectionately called him 'the old soldier':

> I am now feeling quite at home here. Gen. Stevenson, (sic) unlike most Generals appears to like youngsters in his mess. At our permanent H.Q. when I joined the mess comprised 10 but now it is reduced to 8 which will be permanent I expect.

> At present we have quite a small room with two tables. The smaller one is known as the children's table and accommodates Capt. Blacker (Bde Mach. Gun Officer), 2/Lt. Harris (the General's aide-de-camp) and Mons. Bullie (the French Interpreter). They are known to the General as 'the babes' & he is already planning as to what form their Xmas stocking shall take.

> Capt. Blacker should of course be in my place at the other table with the staff and an R.C. Padre, but he rather enjoys his posn. as 'chief babe' & won't change.

138

The Staff Captain known to the General as 'Sir Arthur' addresses
everyone in the mess (except of course the Gen.) as 'old boy'. He is
certainly a good example of the English aristocrat. In fact in every way
it's quite a high- tone but very sociable mess...

(McGowan, Dec. 11th)

The Staff Capt. Arthur Taylor lived at Dunham and McGowan said he was
quite a man of importance in the Manchester district. The General and the
Brigade Major (both regular officers) were always teasing him about his
belonging to the fortunate class of the idle rich.

McGowan was in charge of all the communications between the brigade
and its battalions. Besides the telephone there was a motor cyclist service
which was used to link up any two units on their front. Known as the
Despatch Rider Letter Service, it was often termed the 'Dam Rotten late
Brigade' and though General Steavenson was prepared to overlook the
inefficiency, Staff Captain Taylor was apt to become annoyed at the least
hitch:

The front line is well nigh impossible & the communication trenches are
from knee to waist deep in many parts. They seem to have put a lot of
work into their efforts to drain them, but I shld. imagine they let the
water get a footing before they started to drain seriously.

It's an actual fact I believe that one man was actually drowned in a
trench not far from here & there have been several of men leaving boots
& trousers in the mud when pulled out of a partic. bad place by their
pals.

It's impossible to keep men in the trenches more than 48 hrs. for even
the dug-outs are becoming waterlogged & still it's wonderful what good
spirits the men keep who mudlark all day long. There is a battn. in the
bde to wh' we are appd. that is comprised almost entirely of London
stockbrokers & solicitors & these are the men who in this 20th century
of civilisation are spending day after day like rats in sewers thanks to
this war of nations. It's wonderful there is not more sickness than there
is.

(McGowan, Dec. 11th)

As B.S.O. McGowan was entitled to a groom, a batman and two horses. In
the appalling mud he found horse riding much quicker than a push bike and
could cover thirty miles cross country in one day. The German trenches were
as bad as the British:

139

'A German who surrendered to us not far from here a few days ago gave as his reason for crossing over that he was 'D-fed up', & when asked why he didn't surrender before said he did cross over to our trenches one night, but found no one about & everything looking so miserable that he went back again.

(McGowan, Dec. 11th)

In spite of McGowan's inexperience as B.S.O he found himself taking over probably the largest brigade section in the British Army with a staff of unfamiliar operators and linesmen only just out from England. He worked strenuously for five days at fifteen hour stretches to restructure the brigade control exchanges:

You may wonder at their being so much work attached to the taking over of a front line brigade signal office, but the reason of it is that after so long a period of stationary warfare, the telephone communication to battns, & artillery & all the other specialist units which go to make up a modern infantry brigade, has increased tremendously that each signal office becomes equal to a *busy* local telephone exchange without the help of all the modern apparatus. The number of messages dealt with per day average 10,000 to 12,000.

Before I forget, I must tell you that the last long list of soldiers mentioned in despatches includes Col. J.E.G. Groves & Captain Bengough (Adjutant), no other officers. I think this must be taken as a compliment to the battalion as a whole rather than a personal reward.

(McGowan, Jan. 10th)

In the same vein, on Jan. 2nd 1917 Hodgkin wrote: 'The honours list is out today; the higher officials of the Army have done well; not so the more humble ones. The list always gives rise to more ferocity among the expectant but disappointed than any Boche atrocity'.

CHAPTER 8

A DIVERSIONARY ATTACK

Heald always enjoyed a light hearted show on leave. It helped him take his mind off the trenches which seemed like a nightmare. In a way it was the same feeling of dread he experienced before leaving home for Shrewsbury School where he had never been happy except for the games, and where the food was invariably so bad that the boys went hungry unless they could afford to buy it out of their own pockets. Some of the performances he saw in London were what he termed 'leg shows' with a befrilled black stockinged row of chorus girls, others were lavishly dressed revues with romantic music and sparkling lyrics. On the way back to France he bought a ticket for 'Bric-a-Brac', which he found a diversion before the long journey ahead. 'Bric-a-Brac' had opened on Sept. 29th of the previous year. One of the leading ladies was Miss Gertie Millar and another a lively French actress called Miss Gina Palerme. A popular member of the cast was Miss Teddy Gerrard whose telephone exchange in the Soho area was called Gerrard, and was the theme of one of her songs:

"Now then Teddy Bear said my friend,
On the telephone,
I've a million or two to spend,
Must I do it alone?
No or Yes?
Well, I guess,
We are in this world to help each other.
Everybody calls me Teddy,
T.E. double D Y,
Yankee, Swanky, full of hanky panky, With the R.S.V.P. eye.
All day long my telephone keeps repeating hard,
Are you there little Teddy Bear?
Naughty, naughty one Gerrard!"

After twelve hours in the train without food, he felt the whole business of these short leaves hardly worth the effort. His parents lived in a conventional Victorian house with heavy furnishings where the quietness seemed uncanny. His mother, a strong-minded handsome woman adored him, but even with her it was impossible to discuss his emotions and unless he was perpetually occupied his thoughts scarcely left the prospective battle. Alighting at Frévent on the way to Doullens he had to bed down on the floor of a wooden hut, the only protection against the cold being a filthy blanket covered with lice.

He found the battalion scattered over the countryside doing fatigue work. Like all the others, Heald was sick and tired of mending roads, after all he had volunteered in the Territorials to fight the enemy in an infantry battalion and he too was aggrieved that the Government had put aside the Territorial agreement.

By the beginning of May, the various units included in the 56th Division had arrived in the area so that by May 5th it was up to strength. The division was a fine one composed of nearly all professional and commercial men. As Divisional Pioneers the Cheshires were now doing the 'navvy' work besides carting the supplies up to the site of work and back, almost always at night and under shell fire. They still kept the same specialist fighters, the Signallers, the Bombers and the Lewis Gunners as they had to stand and fight with the infantry battalions when required. With the landscape disfigured by shelling, it was often impossible to find the way in pitch darkness to an obscure map reference. But then they had experienced all that before:

We move tomorrow. This division has only two battalions in the line. I suppose we are going to push soon...

Battalion marched to a place called Souastre about four miles from the line. This place is packed with troops, but does not seem to have been shelled. The billets are very scarce here, I share a room with another officer but we have no beds. However I managed to pinch two wire netting beds. This is quite a small place, in a hollow like all French villages. If you stand clear of a village and look round the country you cannot see a village at all, although in the clumps of trees or woods about two or three miles apart from each other there is invariably a village of which only the church spire is showing.

The people in my billet are very decent and their little girl Georgette has quite adopted me. She is six. She puts flowers into my room every day.

(Heald, May 5th, 6th & 7th)

It went very cold which was unfortunate as all the blankets were withdrawn. Heald, detailed to be temporary Adjutant found it exceedingly dull especially as kept down in the office he had little exercise. On riding the four miles over to Hébuterne he learnt that the big guns were arriving with all hell to come. 'B' Company was working on the trenches outside the village and it felt like old times to hear the shells whistling overhead and the bullets zipping over the trenches. The company was digging some forward lines about 500 yards towards the enemy, they all knew this was usually a sign for an offensive as it was done at Loos.

There was no time to undertake the laborious effort of mining operations as used at Ypres. In front of the 56th Division, no man's land measured roughly eight hundred yards, a gap too wide for the infantry to proceed safely during the initial attack. Therefore in spite of the enormous serious risks involved, Major General C.P.A. Hull, the Divisional Commander took a chance in ordering an entirely new trench to be dug in front of the British line:

> I am going with 'B' Coy. to help dig a new trench, in front of our present line some 400 yards nearer the German trench. I think there will be something like 5,000 men out. If the Germans spot us there will be hell to pay. However the trench has got to be dug whether they spot us or not, so a lot must be left to chance. I went up today and inspected the trenches and had a look at the ground. Last night we carried out a rehearsal on ground in the rear. We have got lots of heavy guns to back us up. We shall need all our strength though. 5,000 men will have to be very quiet within 200 yards of the Germans not to be spotted.
>
> (Heald, May 25th)

Two weeks previously, the 167th Brigade under Brigadier General Nugent had been sent on ahead to reconnoitre, his group consisted of one company of Cheshires plus five battalions of infantry. On the night of the 25th May, Heald and the covering parties went forward followed by half a company of 2/2nd London Field Company R.E.'s, the latter staked out the line with 9 inch long stakes (the bark still attached) plus jute twine prepared with loops to mark angles of bays and traverses:

> We do it tonight. I hope it rains hard. The sky looks cloudy. It is our best chance. I think this is about the most colossal bit of cheek the Army has attempted yet. Let's hope it comes off. By Jove the Germans will be surprised when they wake up and find our trenches up against theirs. There will be some shelling.
>
> (Heald, May 26th)

The night went off very successfully. We assembled in an orchard in Hébuterne. We got started about 11 o'clock. Luckily there was a bit of ground mist so Fritz did not spot us. Just as we were going out a deuce of an artillery scrap started on our right. I thought we had been spotted, but no. This proved a blessing in disguise to us because the noise covered our movements. We had no casualties. One man was hit full on the helmet by a bullet but the steel turned it and saved his life.

(Heald, May 27th)

The covering parties consisted of sixty officers and men in six groups who carried full fighting kit and one day's rations. The taping, digging and wiring men (one hundred per battalion) carried only their loaded rifles plus ten rounds and one bandolier. For each battalion 10% carried picks and specially sharpened shovels. Each man had three sandbags wound round his shovel and pick to muffle the noise. Ten exits were made from the trench where steps and trench ladders were provided and marked with white boards; by 2.30 a.m. it was complete, fully stocked with water, rations and shovels, plus the installation of telephone lines.

The trench was photographed by the R.F.C. on completion:

Last night we had a much worse time. We had support lines to dig and the top of our communication trench to finish. Fritz was uncannily quiet at first. He let us get well out and then he hailed shrapnel shells and machine gun bullets on us for about ten minutes. The air was one mass of bursting shells. Luckily we had a little cover. I was just spacing our men out to dig when it started. The trench was about two feet deep. We had no one hit which seemed to me absolutely marvellous. Our helmets are splendid. Our men dug like they have never done before. When it stopped the other regiments took rather a lot of casualties especially when they were working on new trenches. They gave us four or five more of these bursts of fire. I was very lucky the last time. I had picked up a shovel, when they started. The trench was enfiladed. I got down as low as possible and put the shovel in front of me. A shell burst in the air about three yards off and pieces came all round but I was not touched. With luck I might have been back in England now with a 'blighty'. Everybody got mixed up in the trench and we had a job to sort them out. We got home quite safely after about as exciting a night as I have ever had.

(Heald, May 28th)

Thus the 56th Division started its battle career by constructing and wiring two thousand nine hundred yards of fire trench plus one thousand five hundred yards of communication trench in no man's land within less than four hundred yards of the enemy. If things happened to turn out badly the Corps Artillery had been ordered to stand by to put up a barrage; while helping to cover up any noise, carts full of biscuit tins were driven up and down the shell stricken village of Hébuterne. The gap they had to cross was

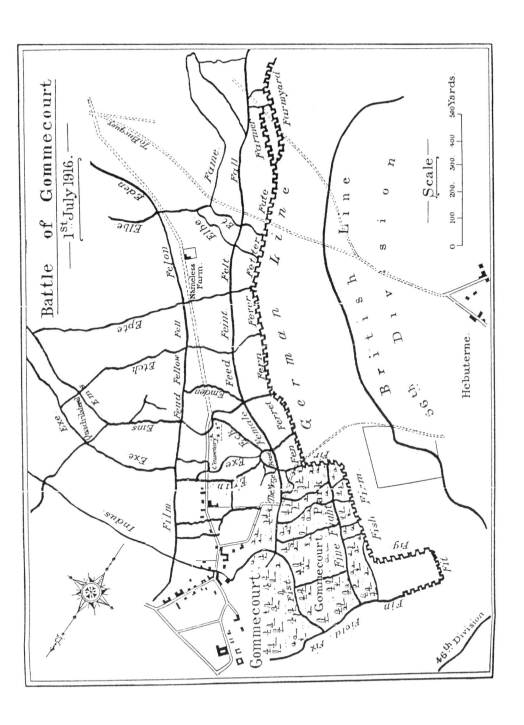

Battle of Gommecourt

— 1st July 1916. —

Scale

0   100   200.   300.   400.   500 Yards.

Hébuterne.

56.th Division

British Line

German Line

Nameless Farm.

Gommecourt Park

Gommecourt

46.th Division

still too wide, but with the onset of bad weather there was no possibility of a second effort. As Heald noted on May 31st, in addition to their exertion on the forward trench, all the emergency roads had to be made good, as well as the existing fire and communication trenches. However willingly and hard they worked, they could not achieve the impossible.

Little did the unsuspecting soldiers of the 56th Division realise that the attack soon to be launched on Gommecourt was merely a diversion. A diversion to attract the enemy's attention away from the main attack of the Fourth Army to the south. Only a short time before, on March 23rd there had been a Franco/British raid to test the salient so it seems hardly possible that G.H.Q. were unaware of the strength of the German defences.

In Gommecourt Park, an intricate warren of dug outs was strongly fortified and often forty-feet deep hidden by a dense mass of trees. The Germans having been in occupation so long had constructed comfortable electrically lit quarters with kitchens and other amenities. Connected by passages which lead out into the rear trenches through the Kearn Redoubt, further entrances ran into the front line encircling the edge of the Park. To the rear, Gommecourt village, acting as the core to the salient, had been turned into a miniature fort, its defences proof against the worst of the shell fire. Well over two hundred yards to the east of the village lay the Quadrilateral, another formidable strong point connected by communication trenches 'Exe', 'Ems' and 'Etch' to the three parallel German front line entrenchments. The whole area was criss-crossed with well dug fortifications.

Learning of Haig's plan for the attack on Gommecourt by the 46th and 56th Territorial Divisions, the 3rd Army Commander, General Sir Edmund Allenby felt uneasy. In particular he disliked the mile gap to the south which left his flank exposed and the fact that he was given no reserves to back up his men. But whatever his feelings in the matter, his objections appeared to have been over-ridden.[1] With the paucity of his resources and the short time for preparations, the Corps Commander, Lieut General Snow (who had elected to go on leave for ten days while the preparations were being discussed) ordered that there should be an assault on the salient from each side, the 46th to attack the north and the 56th the south. It was deemed that these troops were adequate to join up behind the park, clear the wood and then take the village.

On June 4th, having found the C.O. in a moment of good temper, Heald was granted leave. He spent a tolerable night on the crowded boat as he had managed to get hold of a cushion. Next morning however, an air of gloom pervaded the ship; Kitchener, the nation's hero who had just sailed for Russia on the *Hampshire* had been drowned off the Orkneys when the boat

---

[1] B. Gardner, *Allenby*, p.91.

had been struck by an enemy torpedo. Aching for the bright lights and feverish distractions, Heald managed to squeeze in two shows before going north.

For the next few days he went out on the golf course in the June weather but he played badly. Ever a perfectionist, at twenty-six years of age with handicap of scratch, he would have been one of the foremost competitive players in England except for the war.

Once more the dreary train across France returned him to the battalion at Gommecourt. Two fifteen inch howitzers had arrvied at Souastre and had taken up their positions outside the village. The news had swiftly got around that the division was going to 'push' and that they were 'for it'. On return he found himself attached to 'B' Company at Hébuterne and he didn't like it. He noted that there were now a devil of a lot of guns and that it was going to be hell. 'Oh for a blighty one'. It was as if a legendary giant was about to unbar his cave of thunder and winds. They were hard at work deepening the old communication trenches and completing new ones, if the Germans had known, they would have put a barrage up to stop them. He couldn't understand it:

Was working all night, and Fritz was very active with whizz-bangs and minnies. Minnies are huge trench mortar bombs that make a terrific noise and tear up a hole about 12 ft. by 8ft. deep. Luckily you can see them coming, and often can avoid them. They are very nerve racking.

(Heald, June 21st)

Tomorrow is the beginning of the show, viz. 'V' day. The attack proper starts on 'Z' day. We are to have a six day bombardment. This billet is just in front of our guns. The noise will be awful.

(Heald, June 22nd)

It has started and shells go screaming over our billet all day. You can hardly hear yourself speak. We have to work as usual in the trenches expecting the Germans to bombard at any moment. He has been very quiet so far. We had a terrific thunderstorm this evening which has flooded our trenches to a depth of two or three feet. It also carried our observation balloon over to the German lines.

(Heald, June 23rd)

We managed to get to sleep in spite of the noise. Our bombardment has not been so intense as I expected. I don't like visiting the trenches as I have to. It's beastly expecting a shell at any moment. I have been given my job in the attack. I have to fix up notice boards in the German lines denoting the names of the trenches as shown on our maps. At Bayencourt between Souastre and Hébuterne a battery of 9.2. howitzers bombarded Gommecourt Wood every five minutes. The London Scottish were also involved with the digging operations which would bring the front line now three hundred yards nearer to the German lines.

(Heald, June 24th)

A beastly day. The noise is awful. I was visiting one of the working parties and I had got to an exposed part of a trench. A shell came and the concussion knocked me down. I was not hurt. I hear we do a sham attack tomorrow with smoke and bombardment. We shall get into our funk holes and pray that they don't hit us.

(Heald, June 25th)

The sham attack went off very well and put the wind up Fritz properly. Our artillery shelled hard for thirty minutes then the smoke wallers let off smoke and Fritz bombarded us. Our trenches had been cleared of troops so we had not many casualties but the smoke wallers had a bad time. I only got one shell close to me. After things quietened down we had to go and dig out the trenches again. Directly Fritz saw earth being thrown up he shelled so we had a rotten time. However that is our work to keep the communication trenches clear. The wet has made it much worse.

(Heald, June 26th)

Our artillery keeps on giving intense bombardment and we discharge smoke to puzzle Fritz. I think he is too clever to be caught napping though. I think we make a mistake showing him exactly what we are going to do. The trenches are in an awful state. Men keep on getting buried by shell fire and we have to keep on digging them out. It's awful — poor beggars, most of them are dead when we get them out. The noise of our guns is very trying.

(Heald, June 27th)

The show starts tomorrow. Davies and I spent the morning in an artillery observation post finding out the various German trenches and where we are to put up the sign boards. I wonder how the show is going to go off. We are still working on trenches. I am not feeling well tonight, I have got a chill with the wet.

(Heald, June 28th)

A Diversionary Attack

The show has been postponed two days owing to a German spy getting information. I hear ours is only a first push though, the main push is further south. We shall get hell from Fritz when we do go over. I have got a high temperature 103. The doctor is going to send me down. I am disappointed as I should have liked to have been in the push. Arrived at Field Ambulance feeling very bad.

(Heald, June 29th)

Transferred to Casualty Clearing Station Doullens on stretcher by motor ambulance. Glad to be between sheets.

(Heald, June 30th)

CHAPTER 9

GOMMECOURT

On the morning of July 1st, at 7.30 a.m. units of the 56th Division clambered over the parapets of the trenches which had been dug in such haste over four weeks before. Each man carried two hundred rounds small arms ammunition, a waterproof sheet, haversack ration and the current day's ration, two or three sandbags, two tube helmets and a proportion of wire cutters, bill hooks and other tools. The attack was fully expected by the Germans, who had put down a heavy barrage at about 4 a.m. on the assembly trenches causing numerous casualties among the patiently waiting troops.

Detailed to position sign boards in the enemy trenches, two platoons of 'B' Company, of the Cheshires (attached to the 167th Brigade), were ordered up to stand fast to fight as the situation was deteriorating. Met by a hail of fire, Second Lieutenant F.A. Davies, who had replaced Heald was instantly killed in no man's land while leading his platoon. His grave lies close to the spot where he fell in the Gommecourt No. 2 cemetery, off the Hébuterne Bucquoy Road. Heald's high fever had saved his life.

All the other Cheshire platoons ordered over the top suffered high casualties and only one met with success. Owing to the density of the entrenched enemy defences (many of which survived the gun barrage) amongst the splintered desolate trees of the wood, and the intense machine gun fire which poured from both flanks, the attackers found it almost impossible to bring up ammunition and supplies across 'no man's land'. Alerted by the usual barrage, the Germans had strongly reinforced their troops to contend with Haig's plan of diversion which successfully drew the enemy fire on to the two hapless divisions.

Led by McGowan's friend P.B. Bass, no. 4 Platoon of 'A' Company (attached to 'C' Company of the Queen's Victoria Rifles) was ordered to proceed through the German communication trench and consolidate the enemy strong points at the village cemetery. Private H. Lancaster who was under Bass's command described the scene:

> I went over with the platoon and lost them in the smoke. I got into the first wave with the Q.V.R. and Q.W.R. and opened fire on bombing parties of Germans in the first German trench. I was in a shell hole with a Q.V.R. We got the order to advance and got bombed again so we got down and opened fire near the German front line trench. I looked to my right and saw Lieut. Bass with Private Clifford going over some high ground near the German 2nd line. I made my way to join him and found Clifford waiting. He said that Lieut. Bass was reporting to Capt. Cox of the Q.V.R. Lieut Bass came back and gave orders to three of us, who were there to make a fire step in a trench running through the Cemetery. As we were digging, some bombers passed along and one accidentally dropped a bomb which exploded. Lieut. Bass was hit in the eye and Clifford was wounded. We bandaged them up but could not stop Lieut. Bass bleeding and I went to find some one to report. An officer of the Q.V.R. said 'come along with me'. We found Capt. Cox and reported what had happened.
>
> (Private Lancaster, July 1st)

In order to make for the strong points, Bass and the others would probably have made their way down 'Ems' communication trench which ran through the centre of the cemetery. One of Lancaster's comrades, Private E.J. Brown, said that after following 'C' Company over the parapet, they reached the enemy front line, but could'nt see anything of the Q.V.R. in the turmoil so started letting into the Germans:

> Then we got to the 2nd line and started letting into the Germans again, but Mr. Bass stopped us and told us to get into the trench and wait orders. We got into the 2nd line trench and sat down. Mr. Bass took the first man and told him to come with him. Whilst Mr. Bass was away we set at work to reverse the parapet. Sergt. Lancely went up to the 3rd line to 2nd Lieut. Arthur, and then we went up to the 3rd line and attached ourselves to 2nd Lieut. Arthur. We started cutting a piece out of the travers or block for the Q.V.R. and we placed a man on guard in the communication trench. Whilst he was on guard some Germans came up. We cut the piece out and went down the trench and helped to pass the bombs up. We then had

orders to retire. I never saw Mr. Bass after he had taken the man away. He
went up to report to Captain Cox, of the Q.V.R.

(Private E.J. Brown, July 1st)[1]

Whether Bass died of his head wounds in the communication trench or was
afterwards blown up is not clear. His name is carved on the Thiepval
Memorial to those seventy three thousand and seventy seven missing in the
battles of the Somme.

Second Lieutenant G.S. Arthur from Halifax of 'A' Company, though
wounded in the arm found himself leading a part of Queen's Westminster
Rifles. They had been ordered to send a section of bombers up the German
trench behind Gommecourt village to attempt a link up with the luckless
46th Division who had launched an abortive onslaught on the other side of
the park. But short of the appointed rendezvous with the 46th Division, in
the menacing confusion Arthur encountered a strong party of the enemy.
Abandoning his pioneer tools he stood alone and fought to cover his party's
retreat. Like Bass, Arthur was never seen again only the sound of his last
stand rang in his men's ears. His valour remained unrecognised.[2]

Corporal H. Wolfenden of No. 2 platoon 'A' Company had been ordered to
consolidate the junction of 'Indus, Fillet' trenches in the third line, but
having gone over about 8 a.m. they lost five men before attaining the first
line. The others, reaching the second line found the trench full of Queen's
Victoria Rifles, with no room for the Cheshires to shelter. As a result twelve
further men were killed. Trying to find their way, in the mêlée one of the
sergeants shouted 'Come on boys I've got it' and they reached a trench
junction branching to the left called 'Fillet' and the communication trench
'Ems'. The platoon due to proceed up 'Fillet' could not reach the point
where they had to work owing to the Q.W.R. bombers blocking the way in
front of them. Joining up with No. 1 platoon instead they worked on the
maze of trenches in the 'Quadrilateral'. In the mounting chaos, Wolfenden
only saw one officer, Second Lieut Arthur. Eventually running out of
ammunition, his party was forced to retire, with the Germans in hot pursuit
firing down Ems. Soon after this the order was passed down: 'Every man for
himself', and Wolfenden made for a gap in the German wire.[3]

Corporal Ratcliffe observed for a Lewis gunner of the Queen's
Westminsters in the second line, and together they fired on the Germans for
twenty minutes until his companion was sniped. Obeying a call for
reinforcements in the third line, he survived there for one and a half hours

[1] Lancaster's and Brown's accounts, Public Records office W095/2443.
[2] Middlebrook, *The First Day on the Somme*, pp.171–3.
[3] Public Record Office, WO 95/2943.

using up six magazines in enfilading the Germans who were to the right of them. Many of his comrades were wounded. After using up the last of the magazines and bombs, eventually they were ordered back down the communication trench, to the first line which they proceeded to man and reverse the parapet. Here, while losing many of their comrades they lay with their feet towards the wire, but shortly after they decided that the wounded should crawl through the wire as they soon found themselves almost stranded. About five in the afternoon, they heard the Germans bombing the dugouts and later saw them take in some of the British wounded.[1]

Such was the complete confusion on that day that Sergeant J. Robinson the no. 1 platoon sergeant of 'A' Company couldn't tell if they ever reached the Quadrilateral though he certainly spotted Ratcliffe making good use of his Lewis Gun. His platoon commander, Second Lieutenant E.I. Andrews had lead them over the parapet shortly after 7.30 a.m. Amidst the smoke they managed to get over into the German lines and man the fire step but Robinson was delayed owing to Andrews being wounded in no man's land. Eventually forced to retire, Robinson had no further clear idea of events. His men became scattered and soon after 'every man for himself', the survivors reached their own trenches alone.

Second Lieutenant H.W. Glendinning of 'D' Company who had joined the battalion at Ypres on April 30th 1915, had been ordered to take a party of fifty-five men to remove some barricades across the Hébuterne/Bucquoy road. Having started off at 7.45 a.m. They succeeded in dismantling one only as they too were heavily attacked. He returned the remnants of his party to the rear but was immediately ordered to advance again when possible. Later he reconnoitred the barracades himself but shells still rained down unceasingly. During these proceedings he had lost over half his party.

Another Cheshire's officer, Second Lieut, H.R. Leigh was badly wounded in the arm. With part of his platoon (No. 3, 'C' Company) he had been ordered to reinforce the London Scottish to the right but due to appalling shelling he had been turned back with his party on reaching the German wire. His party suffered twenty two casualties. Only one Cheshire platoon, commanded by Second Lieut. S.D. Salmon managed to complete its allotted task. Brilliantly destroying the barricades with gun cotton on the Gommecourt road they threw their bridges across the enemy trenches enabling the troops to cross them.

Apart from the platoon under Leigh, the rest of 'C' Company remained wholly in reserve. With the others they had moved into an assembly trench at Hébuterne on June 30th. where they had been shelled all day. Lieutenant J.H. Joliffe, second in command of the company, stayed in the trench helping

[1] ibid.

No 2 Cemetery, Gommecourt in 1986, those who fell on July 1st, 1916.

with the four wounded, discussing the rumours, reading *Pickwick Papers* and watching the activities of a fat grey rat.[1] When darkness fell they got back through the blazing ruins of Hébuterne to Battalion H.Q. at Souastre. Of the Cheshire Pioneer Platoons detailed to fight that day at Gommecourt, six officers and one hundred and ninety seven men were casualties of this diversionary attack. The 56th Division, one of the finest Territorial Divisions in the Army suffered a total of over four thousand six hundred. Those who doggedly attained the third line were left unsupported as nothing could be done to help them. The 46th North Midland Division on the other side of the salient suffered just over two thousand casualties, having been mown down on reaching the massive wire in front of the enemy trenches. In a communiqué to the 56th Division, Snow the Corps Commander though deeply deploring their losses assured them their attack was 'of material assistance to the success of the plan of operation'.[2] Allenby had been given

---

[1] Letter, J.H. Joliffe to Martin Middlebrook dated February 2nd 1970.
[2] War Record the 1/5th Battalion the Cheshire Regiment, p.53.

Gommecourt Wood in May 1986.

little say in the plans for the Gommecourt offensive, and the division had been told to make their preparations as obvious to the enemy as possible to draw their fire. What in retrospect was there to say to these Territorial Divisions about this massacre?

Recovering from his fever, Heald had been sent to a large general hospital by the sea at Havre. He had been carried on to the hospital train as a stretcher case with the first batch of wounded bound for home from the battle. Somehow he felt a fraud only having 'flu' among the wounded even though his nerves were badly frayed. He wished he was back with his friends, as a letter from the Adjutant had arrived full of bad news. Somehow the division had got to know that their rôle was only one of a decoy to enable the main attack to succeed. He was told of Davies being killed and that 'A' Company was nearly all wiped out, and he wanted to be with the survivors. Shakily he got up and went for a peaceful walk on the beach in lovely weather. In the

156

little town flags were waving in the breeze; it was France's day, July 14th and everyone was on holiday.

Leaving the hospital that evening he reached Rouen early next morning to report to the Base Depot. About two miles out of town the camp accommodated drafts of men waiting to replenish their depleted regiments and as far as the eye could see huts and tents stretched into the distance. The parade ground about a mile square accommodated thousands of troops which Heald noted were just reinforcements for a few divisions. Before they left the camp for the front, the newly joined recruits, were strictly disciplined and given courses of drill and instruction on the huge parade ground, commonly called the 'Bull Ring'; Heald felt that though such training was necessary, the poor devils didn't know what they were in for. Seventy new officers had just arrived in the mess from England but after seventeen months of trench life, to Heald they looked very young and he wondered if they could be much good. Cynically he supposed all the public school type was exhausted.

With the numbers increasing to over ninety, trying to get food in the mess resembled fighting in a rugger scrum and Heald grew weary of the place. He went off to look around Rouen and found some tranquillity in the wonderful cathedral with its delicate stone tracery: the light shone through the richly rose coloured window above the organ, flooding the cool peaceful solemnity of the interior. Rouen was a magnet for shopping and having seen that his name was on the notice board to stand by for the front, he took care to stock up with supplies. The contrast between abundance at the base and scarcity in the line was an old story and the place abounded with old 'dug-outs' living it up.

Collecting up the new drafts for his regiment, Heald marched the three hot miles or so to the station and shepherded them into the train. On finding Battalion H.Q. still at Souastre he learnt that he was to command 'B' Company now in the line at Fonquevilliers another desolation of ruins. It was fairly quiet now after the Gommecourt battle, and only the odd shell lobbed its way over, keeping them on the alert while they worked away on a communication trench and a palatial new dug out. From where they were, they could see the whole battle raging away to the south, it was one line of bursting shrapnel with the accompanying thunder of the guns. To Heald, the battalion so much part of his life had changed drastically as so many faces had disappeared forever.

Back in reserve, the 'Bow Bells' the 56th Divisional concert party a lively lot did their utmost to take their minds off the future. As rather a connoisseur, Heald even thought their performances much better than a lot of the London shows he had seen. In particular the costumes were marvels of creation considering they had to conjure them up on the spot. The group played in a makeshift theatre, the talented 'females' being impersonated by the men. One chap even played the piano standing on his head. Two years

Active Service Concert Party

D
I
V
I
S
I
O
N.

B.E.F.

D
I
V
I
S
I
O
N.

B.E.F.

EVERY COSTUME WORN IN THIS PRODUCTION IS DESIGNED AND MADE BY Ptd. Cpl. DREW.

SCENERY & PROPERTIES MADE AND PAINTED, STYLE & ARRANGEMENT BY Ptd. H.C. SCREWS.

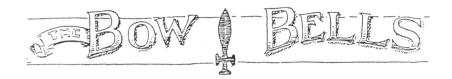

THE BOW BELLS

Opening Chorus

A band of merry folk we come
With dance and frolic gay
We pass the time along with song
And drive dull care away,
Though tomorrow may bring toil
We'll raise a laugh today
Bringing mirth and harmony
Into our joyous lay.
Let's have merry fun and laughter
Fill the hall from floor to rafter
Turn all strafing into laughing
In the merry BowBell way.

WE ARE ALL —

— BRITISH TOMMIES TOO.

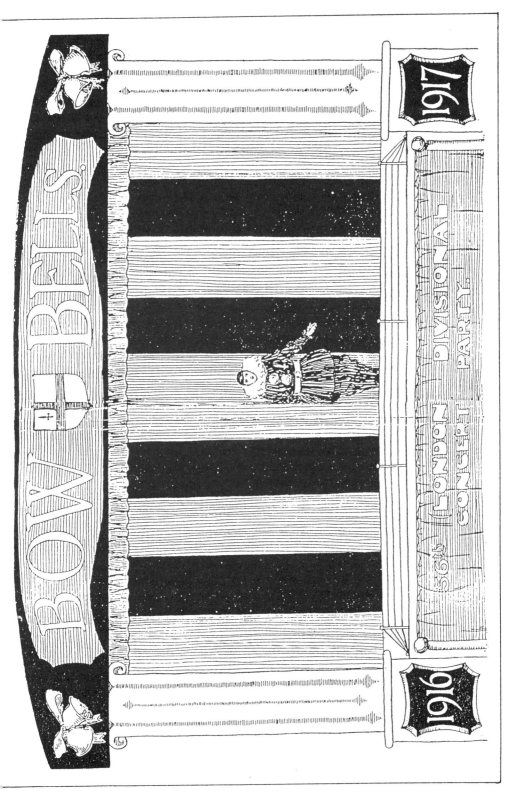

later on June 4th 1918, Heald saw the concert party once more. 'They put on a very good show. A little too vulgar perhaps — there were some 'sisters' there which was rather a pity'. (i.e. hospital sisters)

Many divisions ran their own concert parties; after Hodgkin returned to France he went to see a Canadian company calling themselves 'The Volatiles' in a revue called 'Take a Chance' at Camblain — L'Abbaye:

> Anything better one could not possibly wish to see. The "leading lady" was simply delightful, & as Davies, who is a bit of a Lothario, remarked would stand out favourably in any London beauty show: "she" was exceedingly pretty, answered to the name of Kitty O'Hara, & had a delightful Canuck accent. What the "ladies" look like in uniform I can't imagine. I fell very much in love with "her" & am going to take the Company to look at "her" tomorrow. I gathered that the "chief exports of France since 1914" were "officers going on leave & Blighties" & that the "chief sports of France since 1914" were "grousing, swinging the lead, hunting by candlelight, & Crown & Anchor". There was also a pirate who sang "The good ship Yacci Hicci Dula" in most engaging & blood thirsty fashion. The house was most enthusiastic over the whole performance.
>
> (Hodgkin December 3rd, 1917)

Two nights later he visited the Volatiles again and was as much entranced as ever: 'But with "her" wig etc off not much to look at, as I saw for myself in the green room afterwards.'

At the end of July in high Summer heat, Heald had to oversee about two thousand yards of trench excavations. Unused to such labours some of the newly joined men found it hard gruelling work. Increasing the tempo of shelling, 'Fritz' was becoming unbearable, badly wounding one of the diggers with a 5.9 and blowing in about a hundred yards of parapet. After a desultory rumour that they were 'for it' and that Gommecourt was to be attacked again using gas, they were put to work on emplacements in the gun steps for gas cylinders. For his part, Heald thought it fairly useless as gas was as dangerous to the users as to the attacked. Gloomily he wondered about the great push to the south, no news was usually bad news.

Hignett who had been in hospital, took over 'B' Company: 'It always seems my fate to be under him, he is only senior to me because his name happened to come before mine in the Gazette'. (Heald, August 2nd). But Hignett who had joined up with Heald still did not seem too fit and disappeared once more for a month's course at the Army School.

For the next two weeks the wind remained unfavourable for gas but two men in the trenches were lost, knocked out by enemy shells. Rumours of a move south materialised and on August 18th they were on the march once more, relieved by the Staffords Pioneers who had come from Deville Wood.

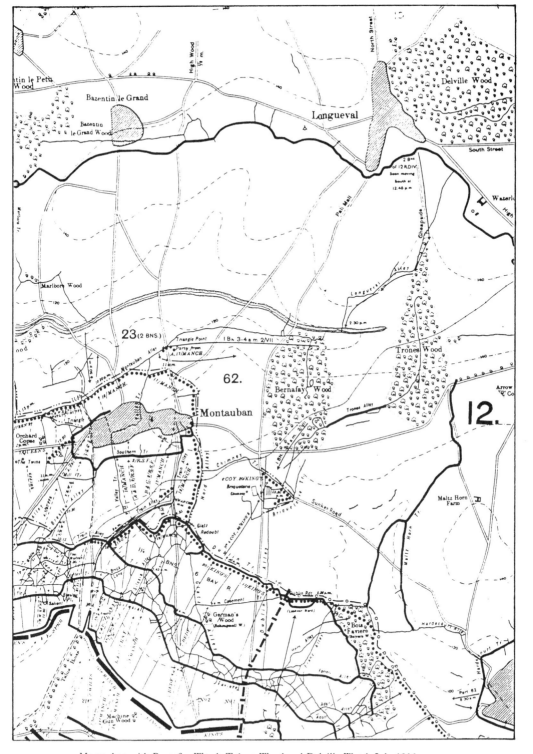

Montauban with Bernafay Wood, Trônes Wood and Delville Wood, July 1916.

CHAPTER 10

MONTAUBAN

On July 1st 1916 naturally McGowan with the 30th Division knew nothing of the fate of his old battalion. The 90th Brigade had been ordered to the south of the battlefield, but soon afterwards the name of Gommecourt became associated with sinister and ugly implications. Bad news travels fast.

Situated next to the French 20th Corps the 30th Division on the extreme right of the British line had its own problems. The 90th Brigade had been ordered to capture and hold the village of Montauban, (between Guillemont and Mametz) passing through the 89th and 21st Brigades whose task was to pave their way.

For several weeks the roads leading to the front line were packed for twenty four hours at a time with cursing transport drivers churning up the ground for miles back. Like Heald who longed for a scrap spurning the interminable dreariness of manning trenches, McGowan, seeing such preparations on a vast scale became infected with the fervour of war. As tensions grew he told his parents that they were on the eve of a great battle probably the greatest of all the many encounters of the greatest war the world has ever seen.

Step by step in accordance with the timetable fixed for the actual day, the brigade practised its part in the big offensive, studying the maps of no man's land, enemy trenches and the village of Montauban which had been drawn up from aerial photographs. McGowan had no doubt of overall success, and he had a sure faith in God's will which he cherished more than a steel breastplate or deep dug-out. But he could not allay his apprehensions about fearsome casualties even though he felt the sacrifices would be worth while if the whole ruinous struggle could be shortened by even a few weeks.

Divisional signals three miles to the rear were in the shelter of a quarry where a palatial dug-out was well stocked with furniture and footstuffs.

McGowan found the communications between Corps and Division many and safe, and fairly reasonable between Division and Brigade. Those lines forward from Advanced Brigade H.Q. however, the most exposed to danger, had been left to the last, and the cable had been so lavishly used to the rear, that those in the front who would need all the cable they could get for extending the lines forward had been left ridiculously short. As usual the guns preceding the attack made their deafening display. As Brigade Signals Officer, McGowan did not go over in the initial attack, but followed on his horse at about 4 p.m. having sent up the bulk of his section to their Battle H.Q. at 'B' Copse a little earlier. Previously he had been impressed by the variety of novel alternative apparatus for communication: aeroplanes, kite balloons, lamps, shutters and even wireless which he thought made the war very scientific.

Before setting off, McGowan had taken a quick glimpse of Montauban over the top of the parapet, but owing to the bombardment all the familiar prominent features had disappeared and he hardly recognised it. With the guns hammering away for all they were worth, he told his parents that he rode his trusty horse forward as far as he dared as he was heavily laden with kit: 'I really felt as though I was going into battle proper for the first time when my groom went back with the two horses, wished me luck.' (McGowan, July 6th, 1916)

Had it pleased the Germans to devote a little attention to 'B' Copse there would have been enormous casualties. Although a hive of dug-outs housed the H.Q.'s of the 90th and 21st Brigades, there was not enough shelter for McGowan and his forty-five men, but somehow he managed to fix up his section before the General and Brigade Major arrived at 10 p.m. He then felt at liberty to leave and place several of his men in different observation posts to watch out for the visual signals when battle commenced. Taking precautions in case of a heavy barrage, he sent some of his specialists to a forward dug-out which they anticipated occupying after the advance. As the time of the attack grew close, the battalions filed into their assembly trenches specially prepared for them in a stretch of hollow by Cambridge Copse between Brigade H.Q. and the front line:

> There was one little dug-out for each Battn. Commander & a telephone line linking him up with both Bde Hd Qrs. & the Advanced dug-out. I visited them all just before dawn & they seemed quite cheery waiting for zero. The hour of zero had just been made public i.e. 7.30 a.m. Every one was very pleased & amazed to know that there had not been a single casualty in the Bde in reaching these assembly trenches nor was there one at all before the actual assault, which proves the Boche was hard put to, for he knew of those trenches. Altho' newly dug they were shown on certain maps taken from Boche prisoners — the aeroplane again, and must have guessed their purpose for he's no fool. Still from information received from prisoners taken we probably have the 48 hr. postponement to thank for that. Boche spies had obtained the date of the original Z day but not the news of the postponement & consequently we took him more or less by surprise.

> (McGowan, July 6th)

Just after dawn, McGowan ate the few remaining sandwiches he had with him and lay down on the floor of the dug-out, but sleep was impossible as the guns were working up to their grande finale. At 5 a.m. a misty haze heralding a glorious morning lay lightly on those waiting in the assembly trenches. Aeroplanes hovered about waiting to report progress and McGowan's visual signallers exchanged 'calls' with their particular machine by lamp signalling devices with ground sheets and large ground signalling shutters.

> At 7.20 a.m. all watches were synchronised by telephone & at 7.30 to the dot the guns lifted off the Boche first line & the first waves of the 21st and 89th Bdes advanced to the assault across the 'racecourse' (the new name assigned to no-man's land). Minute by minute the news came through from the O.P.'s (all of which were connected to Hd Qrs. by telephone) reporting progress — German first line entered — second line reached — little opposition — Glatz redoubt reached — some opposition — Gunners apply further persuasion — opposition overcome — objective reached — consolidation begun. Intermixed with these messages which immediately concerned us were items of information from other divisions on our right & left. Mainly satisfactory, but the Bde on our immediate left were badly held by hostile machine guns. It was now nearly 8.30 (zero 1 hr) the time at which the 90th Bde was to advance through the 21st & 89th Bdes to the 30th Division's ultimate objective Montauban. Would the opposition at Glatz Redoubt be overcome in time, for if not our troops must be held back. Yes at 8.30 Glatz Redoubt is reported in our hands, so there is no need to hold our men back, but the Adjt of one of our battns. in the assembly trenches reports that one of our forward batteries firing very low will have to be stopped before his men can leave the shelter of their trenches. This little matter is soon attended too — thanks to telephone facilities.
>
> (McGowan, July 6th)

(The Germans fortified strong points around Montauban included 'Glatz Redoubt' south west of the Briqueterie by 'Dublin Trench', 'Pommers Redoubt' and the 'Castle.') The three waiting battalions of the 90th Brigade were due to forge through the first attackers being the 16th and 17th Manchesters and the 2nd Battalion the Royal Scots Fusiliers. These battalions assembling in the positions known as 'the Grid' had first had their rum issue. They were in high spirits as they had been told there had been little opposition to the other Brigades:

> ...so the trench ladders being in position, a few lively spirits in the first wave get up on top & start a game of football in the hollow with a paper ball until the whistle warning them of the time brings them back to their position. The C.O. of the 10th Battn. Col. Petrie, D.S.O. lights a cigarette, drinks a last toast with Capt. Worthington who commands the

first wave of the RT. Battn. waits with watch in hand until it shows 8.30 & then with a wave of the hand starts the first line off, accompanied by a hearty cheer from those in rear who are to follow a few moments afterwards & so line after line advances to the assault with the same precision as if on the training ground & little occurs to stop them until they reach the racecourse. Here machine guns & shrapnel take their toll, but as one falls another takes his place & so they proceed yard by yard as nobly as did regular troops of the finest if not the largest army in the world. The German support line is reached & now real trouble appears. The front line troops of the 21st Bde are in occupation & have laid trench ladders across for our men to pass over, but their left flank is exposed, the 55th Bde on our left has not made good their ground & there are Boche Machine Gunners with their infernal machines sending a stream of bullets across our front. There is a temporary check but Colonel Petrie, D.S.O. decides at once that (although this proposition never cropped up during training) there is only one thing to do that is to press forward & he himself comes up to give his men the example. Now, the casualties are many & Capt. Worthington falls with a bullet through his chest. He is placed in a shell hole there to lie for nearly 36 hrs until the stretcher bearers are able to carry him in. However, the 'green line' is reached in time & here both battns. 16th on the left & 17th on the right reform & wait in trenches, or what is left of them until the barrage from our guns lifts from the village & the instant it does on they go in style the like of which has never been seen before (so say those who witnessed it & have witnessed other assaults also) & the village is entered, — each officer, or if the officer is not, the senior N.C.O. marshalls his men together & leads them to the particular strong point or advanced post that he is detailed to consolidate. The houses, the roads & the trenches of the village have been battered out of all recognition by the intense fire of our guns & nothing remains but bricks & dust, but the direction instilled into all ranks during training still holds good & there is little confusion. Meanwhile immediately behind the two assaulting battalions, the supporting battalion of Jocks (2nd Royal Scots Fusiliers) has advanced & one company detailed as nettoyeurs proceed to clear the village of what remains of the Boche, but their task is not as great a one as was expected for the guns have done their work well & either killed or frightened off defenders. Nevertheless many prisoners are taken and marched back to our lines by escorts, the majority looking very pleased with themselves & gaily distributing souveniers to their captors. Included among our prisoners was an artillery brigadier & his staff, a nice old man who gave one of my runners, who was on the spot at the time, a photograph of himself & his family. The remainder of this battn. proceeded to dig themselves in just outside the village. Accompanying each of the two attacking battalions were platoons of the 18th Battn. carrying stores to help in the consolidation & sections of R.E.'s to give expert assistance while another company of the 18th followed the supporting battalion with more stores & ammunition to be dumped at the village & then return for more. The remainder of this battalion were in reserve & proceeded to dig themselves in behind the Boche support line, but coming under heavy shell fire they were obliged to retire a little but to the shelter of some existing Boche dug-outs a little further back. The task of consolidation was a most difficult one, for the Germans knowing the village was in our hands straitway turned their guns on to it and kept them so. It had to stop when we did for those of our troops who advanced to the most forward posts, say the Boches were fleeing backwards in hopeless confusion, & our men thoroughly enjoyed themselves trying to stop their flight, still Montauban was our objective & it would have been no good going further forward without help & co-operation on the flanks.

(McGowan, July 6th)

In addition to Capt. Worthington, all the leading company commanders in the attack had been killed or badly wounded. Lt. Col. H.A. Johnson of the 17th Manchesters was wounded in Talus Boisé plantation. Once Montauban was captured, no immediate attempt was made to exploit this hard won gain. This decision was disastrous for the Manchester men.

At the signals office in 'B' Copse, McGowan at first was not able to witness the initial advance of the attackers: but his observers in the O.P.'s had a good view as they were situated overlooking the ground between their original front line and Montauban about one thousand five hundred yards away. Every attacking infantryman carried a sheet of yellow cloth and a bright tin disc on his back which made it comparatively easy for the observers to watch and report their progress up the level slope. About 10 a.m. around the time the first wave had reached their objectives, McGowan visited one of the visual signalling posts. He was surprised to see all those not on duty out on top watching the show and saw groups of artillery observers with their telescopes fixed in the open instead of from the small peep-hole in the dugouts:

A certain F.O.O. kept his lamp going all night & it was from him we got most of the news "Enemy assembling between X & Y — attack imminent — barrage falling short — lengthen range etc.' & to confirm these messages one of our battns brought its red lamp into play & with the prearranged signal called for barrage. The consequence was the artillery kept at it continuously & were forever asking when they might slacken off as they feared for their supply of ammunition. A great feeling of relief was experienced when just before dawn two of my best linesmen succeeded in getting a good new line through to Montauban to which all battns. joined up & the staff were once again able to speak with Battn. commanders & learn the true state of affairs. The effect was instantaneous, the guns slackened off, & comparative peace reigned. It appears the Boche had attempted a counter attack but was easily driven back by bombers, but the O.C. Montauban didn't feel disposed to stop the guns as a slow barrage was required to keep down the fire of enemy batteries & so enable them to get on with the consolidation.

(McGowan, July 7th)

With two stalwart linesmen at Montauban, two in the Boche dug-out and two at H.Q. McGowan saw to it that they were never cut off again until relieved.

Lt. Colonel Petrie C.O. of the 16th Manchesters, by now relieved from Montauban came to give them the graphic details of the defence of the village sustained under heavy shellfire. It seemed that the single German machine gun (noted by McGowan) blasting away between the German lines and Montauban had mown down many of the attackers until silenced by a Manchester Lewis Gunner. McGowan said that the casualties to both battalions were sustained in the ruined village itself, though it was difficult at that point to particularise, he had gone up soon after to inspect the telephone wires with his relief and witnessed a little of what they had had to endure for upwards of twenty-four hours:

The first battn. H.Q. I dropped across was the 2 R.S.F They were all squatted in a low trench just outside the village with no roof cover at all and crumps following quite close, in fact one (a dud) actually fell into the trench not 10 yds from them. The ditch which had accommodated the 16th Battn. for 24 hrs. was now blown in, so the Wilts who relieved them had housed themselves in what remained of a cellar. The 17th Battn., spent the bulk of their time in a large deep shell hole, & it was from such positions that the command exercised control of affairs all day & night & day again. I was jolly glad to be able to tell them that there was every prospect of relief that night.

(McGowan, July 7th)

Some had already pressed forward beyond Montauban having occupied a long communication trench behind known as 'Montauban Alley' at about 12 p.m. Looking over beyond the Montauban ridge there was seemingly peacefully wooded countryside stretching forward with a sight of the enemy retreating into the distance. But the Germans soon made a further attempt to retake the village and the hoped for relief was slow in coming. Due to enemy gun fire, one battalion of the relieving force lost thirty men in the packed valley leading up to Montauban in spite of a retaliating barrage put up by the British Artillery. But compared to the fate of McGowan's old battalion with the 56th Division at Gommecourt, the 30th had at least won success in gaining their objective.

Almost dead with fatigue, McGowan felt drained of all reason as he handed over to the signallers of the new brigade. Slowly at sunrise the worn out troops dragged their way from the front line to the rear. They were able to file their way freely across the top without being led by officers or N.C.O's many of whom had become casualties. The Germans temporarily had disappeared over the sky line and the British guns had taken up forward positions.

McGowan's stores wagon was waiting at 'B' Copse and with it his horse. Wishing to check the bivouacs, he left his men in charge of the Sergeant and galloped to the rest camp in 'Happy Valley', close to Mametz Wood. It was a bleak unwelcoming spot about two miles from the original line, the only protection for the men being slits in the ground. There was a strong stench of half buried dead animals:

When I reached the camp I found just a few tents erected for the Officers, one available as a signal office, but none other for the men. Fortunately it was fine & everyone too tired to bother about anything but sleep & my men were soon stretched out on the ground & fast asleep. The first thing I did was to have a good wash & shave. The first of either for 72 hrs. & then I lost no time in getting into my fleabag but for some unearthly reason I wakened again at noon. I think we expected to move further back to billets, but if so t'was a false alarm & after lunch I lay down again intending to write to you in time for post at 3 p.m. but I dropped off again & the next thing I knew was the announcement that dinner was ready. This meal we had out of doors, but it was becoming overcast & cold, so I advised the men to rig themselves up some temporary shelters, & it's as well they did for it rained during the night with heavy thunderstorms next day & Happy Valley became a morass of mud.

(McGowan, July 7th)

On making enquiries about certain of his friends in 'The Pals' he was very grieved that so many were dead or wounded. Waiting around in the muddy camp they anticipated a move forward once again at short notice.

> I can't say there is great enthusiasm in this brigade to be at it again, but if it's the best thing to do I know we'll all be ready when called upon & with God's help we'll keep up the good name we've earned.
>
> (McGowan, July 7th)

McGowan ended his twenty-eight page narrative:

> From now onwards I expect to be busy again so I'll put this away for a while trusting as before I'll be able to continue the narrative after battle No. 2.

> With fondest love & God bless you both, always your Affectionate Son,
>
> George.

To the east of Montauban, Bernafay Wood had been captured by two battalions on July 3rd with only a few casualties though fierce shelling continued. At that point, had advantage been seized in the sweep forward, the infamous Trônes Wood (connected by a trench known as Trônes Alley to Bernafay Wood) could probably have been put in the bag without much harm. But those commanding the army strategy allowed some five days to elapse before going further, thus losing the momentum and allowing the Germans, who had been largely shelled out of the wood to reoccupy it.

CHAPTER 11

TRÔNES WOOD

After a wet night, July 8th the day of the second attack dawned fine and warm, though underfoot the trenches squelched with mud and their surrounding tracks oozed like quagmires, disabling the transport. By now the German guns positioned in Longueval by Deville Wood to the north, and in Guillemont to the east overlooked the area at close range. Pear shaped Trônes Wood, torn up and pitted with shell holes was criss crossed by splintered fallen tree trunks strewn over a web of ruined trenches, unseen pitfalls for the unwary. Whole regiments lost their bearings in the darkened maze whose dense undergrowth had not been cut for two years. The area was divided laterally by the old line of the Montauban Guillemont railway.

After only four days in 'Happy Valley', the 90th Brigade was ordered forward again into its second battle, and its grim task, to take the wood:

My Dear Mother & Dad,

It is now practically a week since we were withdrawn from the line after
our second fierce battle in connection with the present offensive but
until today I have not had the least inclination to put on paper the
impressions & experiences of those terrible 2 days, in fact, I in common
with everyone else concerned, have striven to forget the whole business
& enjoy to the full the quiet restfulness of the back area where we now
find ourselves.

(McGowan, July 17th)

Ordered to join the H.Q. of the 21st Brigade in 'Train Alley', McGowan with seven of his men, followed in the wake of Major General J.S.M. Shea, the Commander of the 30th Division, and the Brigade Major who were crossing the original 'race course':

This was the neighbourhood of the Glatz Redoubt which had received so
much attention from our heavy guns just a week previous. It was
amazing to see the size of crater produced in the soft ground presumably
by our 8″ shells. You could have put a horse & cart in some of them &
so close were they together that it is nothing short of a miracle that
anyone in the neighbourhood lived. As we got nearer to TRAIN
ALLEY, so the congestion increased, until when we turned the corner
close to the dug-out in use as a Bde HQrs one could hardly move, & just

171

at this instant one shell came over, only one, a small schrapnel, but it took as big a toll as probably ever a shell of the same explosive power took before. It exploded just head-high in the trench outside the Hd. Qrs. dug-out & accounted for two Colonels, a Captain & about a dozen N.C.O's & men, while a second one which followed it close wounded an officer & several men of the Bde Section we had come to relieve who had rushed out to assist in clearing the trench of the dead & wounded. It was a most gruesome beginning to our second battle for both the Hd Qrs. dug-out & the signal office were temporarily full of badly wounded cases groaning in a most unnerving manner. The Boche might have known, though it's difficult to know how, that there was a relief out and that the trenches were crowded for he continued to shell this particular spot & altho' no further casualties resulted it was thought advisable to move the Hd Qrs. to another dug-out not receiving so much attention.

(McGowan, July 17th)

McGowan, who had moved his office up to a dug out behind the old enemy support trench struggled to mend the shattered telephone lines; those few remaining unharmed were always blocked. As no contrary message had been received, on July 8th they relayed an order for the artillery to start up their half hour's intense barrage on the Wood and the Maltz Horn Farm (by now a heap of rubble) and Trench to the south of it:

The 17th M/crs were to go for TRNES WOOD & the 2 R.S.F. for MALTZ FARM & TRENCH, and they got both objectives in pretty short time, the latter position offered little resistance & yielded some 100 prisoners but not so the Wood. This was a position much prized by the Boche & he wasn't going to let it pass from him without a fierce struggle. In fact we know from prisoners taken that their orders were to hold the Wood at all cost & 'to the death' was their oath. It is no use my trying to write a history of what actually did happen for in the first place I don't know the sequence of events, no-one does. It's all the Bde Major can do at present to submit facts culled from messages sent & received & from the information of officers who were on the spot & have lived to tell the tale. Secondly this is not intended to be a history of events, but merely a private diary of the show as it concerned me, sufficient it is for me to say that that bit of a wood accounted for the best part of perhaps 12 battns. before it was finally cleared of the Boche & as you may be sure, the enemy suffered every bit as heavily as we did you can quite see why it became known as the cemetery and why newspaper correspts. described it's interior as the 'craters of Hell'.

(McGowan, July 17th)

Trônes Wood

To advance in strength proved impossible. In order to dodge the bombardments the German machine gunners in the wood retreated into their dugouts, coming to life when it grew quiet, to mow down the attackers, who,losing their way in the gloom, made for any glimmers of light to find their bearings:

> The 1st battn. to attempt this was the 2nd Wilts of the 21st Bde, the early morning of the day we moved up. They were so badly hit that our 18th Bn. was sent up the same afternoon to reinforce them in holding positions on the rear outskirts of the wood. It was while receiving order from the G.O.C. 21st Bde, that Col. Smith of the 18th Bn. was mortally wounded & Capt Godlee was called upon to take command. Next morning shortly after dawn, our 17th Battn. pushed through the wood, but were unable to keep together & hold the ground gained, were heavily shelled & forced to retire from the wood with heavy casualties. It was now up to our artillery to shell the place again before the 18th Bn. advanced, but they too suffered badly & were not able to stay there. In some mysterious way, the Boches who were quite familiar with this wood again succeeded in surprising them on all sides. Many & fierce must have been the hand to hand fighting in that battered bit of wood.
>
> But altho' little ground was gained some valuable information as to the haunts & habits of the Boche came to hand and a battn. of the South African Bde holding Bernafay Wood on our right were called upon to make good the gap between what remained of the 17th & 18th Battns. & the Scots Fusiliers on their right. I'm afraid quite a large number of the 17th & 18th battns acting on a false order to retire straggled some distance back towards Bde Hd Qrs & some considerable difficulty was experienced in getting them together & forward again. I came across the signalling officer of the 17th Bn in a half dazed state with 3 signallers & no equipment who tried to tell me that the whole battn was wiped out. It appears he was suffering from shellshock so I gave his Corporal a telephone & some wire & sent the three men back to their hdqrs, leaving Kerr to sleep in a dug-out until he's recovered.
>
> (McGowan, July 17th)

Such was the wholesale confusion, that McGowan sent up four pigeon flyers and runners to the Briqueterie south of Bernafay Wood before dawn on July 9th, hoping to set up a visual station:

> My word it was a nasty spot was that brickyard. Formerly a German strong point, where on July 1st a Boche General & his staff surrendered

to our 89th Bde. We went there across the open, for you soon decide that it's preferable to make a dash across the open in double quick time, than to crawl along a trench of doubtful protection. The Boche evidently guessed we were making use of the protection accorded by the BRIQUETERIE TRENCHES & dug outs for day & night he kept a slow barrage on the place. It's a marvel there were not more casualties, for as is usual where trenches exist, there was not room to move for scores of troops waiting in reserve were lying or sitting in niches dug into the sides of the trenches, or standing ready to crouch low whenever the whistle of a shell was heard. The dug-out used now as a Bde report centre & a Battn. Hd Qrs. was a wonderful sight. Three flights of about a dozen steps led down out of a deep trench into a covered passage-way off which were 2 small dug-outs & two little stalls that served for the signal offices. Every staircase was blocked with waiting troops seeking cover from the shells & in consequence the atmosphere down below was anything but fresh. I had just left with two men & signalling lamp to establish a visual station when one shell landed plumb in the trench just outside the dugout, again a lucky shot for the Boche, for it took its toll of our men & filled the underground office with smoke & fumes. I didn't waste much time searching for a visual station & after fixing on a reasonable post sent the two men back to shelter with orders to man the post only if absolutely necessary, for it would have been manslaughter to have kept them there on the off-chance of other communications failing, as it was, one of them was wounded (fortunately not severely) before they got back to shelter, this I learnt when I got back to Bde Hd Qrs. after an exciting dash across the open with shells falling in front & behind but fortunately not near enough to puncture my orderly or myself.

(McGowan, July 17th)

All that day the merciless battle ebbed and flowed. Inadvertently the 17th Manchesters in retiring from Trônes Wood left stranded a band of forty men to their fate as the messenger sent back to recall them had been killed. Meanwhile further reinforcements waiting in Bernafay Wood were shelled with gas and forced to withdraw. Back at Brigade H.Q., McGowan, now in sole charge of the signals office, recognized the disastrous plight of the battalions. And he knew more than anyone, that because of the random slaughter of the forward patrols the true state of affairs had not been properly ascertained. In spite of this, an ill judged order was given for guides to lead forward the luckless 16th Manchesters who had formed up in the sunken trenches close to the brickworks:

While they were getting into posn. patrols were sent out to try and ascertain the true state of affairs in the wood before the artillery preparations for a further assault began. Some of these patrols came back with useful information, others didn't & finally 9 p.m. was fixed as the time for the assault. Just about this time the Division decided that Bde Hd Qrs. should move up nearer to the scene of operations, & the only place to move to was the notorious brickyard. Now from the point of view of communications alone, a move at this time would have been most disastrous for even while the 16th Battn. were waiting to attack, the Boche launched the first of several desperate counter attacks from the wood, but failed to dislodge our troops from their line of defence along the South and Eastern outskirts & suffered accordingly. Therefore after explaining the situation as far as possible it was decided that we should remain where we were until the 16th Bn had made their effort. After good work by the artillery three companies each with its definite objective attacked the wood & got through, but almost immediately the Boche turned his batteries on, exactly as our guns had been firing half and hour before & as it was impossible to dig cover two of the three companies were forced to retire to the Southern edge & there commence to dig themselves in some 50 yds in front of our former line. The third company did not return. What exactly happened no- one knows probably a strong party of Boche came out from underground & attacked them in the rear.

(McGowan, July 17th)

Late in the evening General Steavenson, as vigilant of the battle as he was considerate of his brigade, strode out in the open to make his second visit to the brickyard. Shortly afterwards after midnight, McGowan followed him with dogged perserverance in a further attempt to establish his report centre. The last time he had tried this route was by day, but in the dark with only a mystified guide, his party hopelessly lost its way in the maze of bombed out trenches. Eventually emerging above ground, dodging in and out of craters he located the brickyard by noting a distant point appearing to be a target for enemy shells:

My word it was a gruesome spot of H.Q. Outside in the trench one had to step over the forms of wounded & dying & inside was more packed than ever with men alive but exhausted. It was absolutely necessary for us to clear our passage way to let in a bit of air & to allow officers & orderlies a clear entrance & exit. It is no use trying to describe in detail the next 24 hours. It was just one continuous strain for all. The Boche counter attacked 6 times in all, but never succeeded in occupying the

Southern corner of the wood, but the front line troops were put to a severe test & several times reports came through that parties were returning, but each time they were collected & sent forward again. That night I lost my best linesman Spr. Angus. A man absolutely without fear & one who only needed to be told what to do & I felt sure it would be done whatever the difficulty. He had been with me only a couple of months, passed to me from Divn. under a sentence of 6 mths imprisonment for drunkeness. As is usual the man who can get really drunk when the opportunity offers proved himself the best possible soldier under fire & I was sorry indeed to lose him. I have sent in a special recommendation that his sentence be repealed and he be reinstated to his former rank of L/Cpl. The fact to be permantly recorded in his papers for the sake of the wife & 3 children he left behind. He was killed close to our new Hd Qrs by a shell while on his way to repair a line.

(McGowan, July 17th)

The H.Q. was a hive to which a constant stream of officers and runners homed in to report. Those who had been in the thick of the fight were pale, bathed in perspiration and had fixed stares. McGowan who conjectured that their mien was not from bodily exertion but mental strain was thankful that his place was mainly in the dug out:

I remember well a Major commanding a Coy. of the 18th L'pools who was detailed to make a further attempt to drive the Boche from one of his strongholds within the wood. I saw them leave after receiving his orders with a smile on his face, half-an-hour later we heard that the attack had been beaten back and Major Higgins was severely wounded & the horrible part of it all was that each side in turn bombarded that slip of a wood they well knew that many of their own wounded were still there.

(McGowan, July 17th)

On July 10th the 89th Brigade sent by degrees to relieve them in their turn exhausted themselves in the wood. Until General Steavenson left the dugout at 1.30 a.m., the place teemed with his jostling staff whose preparations for departure obstructed the entrance of the newcomers. Emerging from the mêlée an hour later, McGowan passed by the body of Angus lying where he fell and as yet unburied; though he realised an isolated funeral service was out of the question the sight distressed him a great deal.

Trônes Wood

In the dawn, the trip back to Château Keep at Maricourt was refreshingly pleasant, they left with the sound of the guns ever pounding away on the north of Trônes Wood and shell still falling on the pulverised brickyard. The dugout at Château Keep resembled a palace, though previously they would have turned up their noses at its discomfort. The battalions' billets consisted of their old original dilapidated front line trenches. One thing was certain however, they would not be over crowded for it was pitiful to see two battalions go by, each no stronger than a former company. Such was the result of two short battles.

By the time the 90th Brigade had been relieved on July 11th after those terrible days of fighting, it had lost nearly eight hundred officers and men and the 30th Division over two thousand of all ranks. In spite of this slaughter, Trônes Wood was still uncaptured except for a small portion to the south of it. Only after further suicidal attacks and hundreds dead did the area fall to the British forces.

In finally vacating the wood, the Germans retreated northwards, then streamed out to the east across open ground to Guillemont. A terrible sight met the gaze of the incoming forces into the 'craters of hell'. German and British dead and wounded, their bodies pinned by fallen trees, lay tangled in the equality of common suffering. Many of them had been shelled by their own sides, each of which in pounding remorselessly their respective enemies unwittingly killed also their own comrades.

Even as far back as Maricourt, had it not been for a stout brick wall, McGowan would have lost his beloved section as a volley of four shells pitched less than ten yards away from them. He was thankful to mount his horse and canter back to Bois des Celestines, a haven of rest with a chance to wash, have dinner and listen to the gramophone. There was even a bed to sleep on "though most of us had nightmares I believe and small wonder if we did".

> Knowing that in comparison with our first battle we had gained but little ground from the Boche & that at a much greater cost, we were a little doubtful as to how the higher command would view our efforts, hence it was with great pleasure that we received a copy of a telegram from the C. in C. in which he congratulated the 13th Corps on their excellent progress in that they had attained every objective asked of them & what is more held them in face of desperate counter attacks & particularly the 30th Divn for their defence of TRÔNES WOOD by the 90th Bde. This is the first time a Bde has been specially mentioned in a congratulatory telegram from G.H.Q., so we had every reason to feel justly proud of ourselves.
>
> (McGowan, July 17th)

Only one night was spent in the Bois. They left the following day for Daours, a small village south of Guerrieu, where the remnants of the brigade were addressed by Major General Shea. All could hear him clearly as he had been trained in elocution:

> He thanked us for the way in which we had proved our worth as soldiers & conveyed the news to us that whereas other divisions with losses less heavy than ours had been indefinitely withdrawn from the fight, the Corps Commander had said that he could not & would not do without the 30th Div. & so, as a reward for our value as soldiers, we were to be reinforced as speedily as possible so as to be ready again for the fray at an early date. I know a large section of the men didn't altogether appreciate this reward for they'd had quite enough for a time, but as I explained to my men afterwards, all fights would not be so trying as the last one, & there was a good deal to be said for the job as a fighting unit as against that of a unit that was only good enough to hold trenches probably in flat Flanders.
>
> (McGowan, July 17th)

For McGowan that Sunday at Daours was for once a real sabbath day. In a field in front of the small château which served as Brigade H.Q. a band played martial music. 'I expect most of us thought with regret of the large number who were with us at the last parade service and have since made the supreme sacrifice in the country's cause'. (McGowan, July 17th)

The next day, training began once more in earnest. The 90th Brigade receiving a massive intake, was nearly up to strength but sadly the Manchester battalions had few Lancashire replacements. The majority of the new men were old soldiers from the base who had left their own regiments some time ago wounded or sick. They resented being transferred and felt a loyalty to their previous units. This deliberate policy by the War Office to create an 'Army Spirit' rather than a regimental 'Esprit de corps' resulted in a deep deterioration in relations and loss of enterprise. Nearly every street in the cities and towns of the "Pals" battalions had suffered appalling losses. By mixing up the replacements, the casualty lists from a specific area would not appear so blatant, but the main damage had been done. Unexpected new orders reached McGowan at 9.30 a.m. on Wednesday July 19th to the effect that once again they were to move back into the battle area via the hutments at Bois des Celestines. Nothing was right. The brigade was far from ready for action, as only four days was allowed for re-organisation. The original troops were not fit physically or mentally. They were completely worn out. The officers had not had time to ascertain the capabilities of the reinforcements and the C.O's knew little of their new officers:

> Yet if they need us (& they don't really for England has troops in abundance both at home & abroad) we'll try our best again to keep the good name we've earned & may God give us all strength, wisdom & courage to carry out what is requd. of us in the sure hope that we are fighting against evil for his sake for it's difficult to endure the sight of such terrible slaughter of human life without some such faith.

> This brings my third chapter to a close. & again I express the sincere hope that God in his mercy will grant me his help & protection that I may be able at some future date to try & record our further experiences.

> With fondest love & best wishes & may God continue to bless you both now & forever.

> Always your affectionate son
George
>
> (McGowan, July 19th)

Given these dire conditions, the prospect was bleak for those north country battalions. It was some time before McGowan could bring himself to describe the further onslaught:

> My Dear Mother & Dad,

> Now that a week has elapsed since the end of our third battle I am feeling more disposed to put down on paper my experiences of quite the fiercest & most bloody fighting I have yet experienced...
>
> (McGowan, August 7th)

The reconstituted brigade so hastily cobbled together, had marched back to Happy Valley to stay only for forty-eight hours. It was one huge camp packed with thousands of men. Soon McGowan was back in the area of the Briqueterie — a place he had hoped never to see again after the unforgettable experiences of July 9th and 10th. But somehow the gruesome sights of their last visit were not immediately apparent as the stretcher bearers had carried away the dead and wounded. Based in the old German line the Brigade H.Q. was in the deep dugout of a former dressing station which contained a kitchen, office and served by two entrances. On the way there McGowan had noticed the light railway in evidence working up to Montauban and the desolate ruins of Mametz and Carnoy villages. As none of the communication lines were functioning up to the battalions, and the operational orders most indefinite, he felt unhappy to be working so much in the dark. But deciding to see for himself, he set off down the 'Sunken Road' with some linesmen from the R.S.F. who knew the ground towards the south edge of Trônes Wood. It was the first time he had set eyes on 'The Cemetery' at close quarters:

> As we left the cover of the Sunken Rd & climbed to bleak open country 400 yds. due N. could just be seen the S. edge of TRNES WOOD & it was across this bit of shell ploughed ground now showing not a sign of life that our brave fellows attacked & reached the wood, only to be overwhelmed & forced to return very much depleted in strength & finally to dig themselves in as close to its edge as possible. Just how many hundreds fell here I can't say, but there was now as little superficial sign of death as of life, for the battlefield has been cleared, so it was only when you walked among a trench constructed by joining together a series of shell holes that you found signs both of life & death.
>
> A small working party completely hidden from view busy sapping forward preparing trenches in which troops would shortly assemble prior to another attack would unearth the body of some unknown hero, who wounded in the attack, had dragged himself into a shell hole for cover and then while unconscious (let us hope) another shell falling near had buried him only partially but sufficient to prevent his being uncovered by the clearers of the battlefield. So, many days, perhaps weeks after they have fallen are missing soldiers identified & a record of their last resting place filed for the information of relatives & friends after the war. Some will have had funeral rites, some will not, but all will be equally welcome to their place in the Kingdom above, with this one big sacrifice looming large to their credit.
>
> (McGowan, August 7th)

Not a living soul was in sight as they walked down the eerie valley road which ran to the north east, parallel to Maltz Horn Trench. About two hundred yards in front of them they spotted a waving blue and white signal flag held by an entrenched operator sending morse code to the south. Making for the flapping flag they heard a voice calling 'keep low if you don't want to be sniped'. Looking up, they realised they had almost stumbled into the enemy lines. The signaller's trench, originally dug by the Boche was now occupied by a battalion of stout hearted 'Bantams'[1] who had held it for over a week attracting heavy shell fire on themselves while other troops attacked through them.

During his gruesome walk McGowan continously checked his cables and searched for suitable places for his visual operators. Passing the notorious Briqueterie and Train Alley, the shells fell thick and fast.

When he returned about 4 p.m., he learnt that the 30th Division was to attack Guillemont south west of Montauban that night. As usual a heavy barrage heralding the offensive broadcast the news to the enemy, but once again fresh orders postponed the assault. McGowan felt this only wise as his signals plans had no possible chance of success in these hasty decisions. During the waiting period in their dugout, in spite of the acetylene lamp being extinguished with each reverberation from a 6inch gun, they managed to feed, snatch some sleep and remain in good temper:

> During the day the troops could do little except crouch down in the trenches & endeavour to keep clear of the shells. There were quite a score of casualties on the R.S.F. alone who were quartered in Train Alley & adjoining trenches. As soon as dusk fell working parties set off to dig assembly trenches & cable trenches. Officer's patrols went out to reconnoitre no man's land & the assembly positions. They always came into the H.Q. dug-out before starting off to receive instructions from Ramsden & incidentally a drop of his famous patrol medicine as supplied by FORTNUM & MASON.

> We were all getting to feel the worse for our confinement & on the morning of the 26th there being no news of active operations the Division agreed to the General's suggestions the 2 battns. should march back to Mansel Copse for exercise & training. Accordingly the 2nd R.S.F. & the 16th Mchrs left their trenches about 9 a.m. I too thought a little exercise would be an advantage especially taken rearwards & as I had several things to see Molesworth about I ordered my horses, met them at Talus Boisé & rode to BRONFAY FARM. For once the Divisional H.Q. had not such comfortable quarters, They were mostly in tents & subject to the shrapnel of shells not aimed at them but near enough to be unpleasant & dangerous.
>
> (McGowan, August 7th)

McGowan suffered considerably from the gruelling events which followed. Situated in a forward trench as Brigade Signals Officer he was forced to relay

---

[1] Men not less than 5 ft. or more than 5 ft 3 inches in height, sanctioned to enlist in March 1915.

many of the ill judged orders despatching his comrades into disaster. He did not conclude his narrative until two months later.

Before the divisional attack on Guillemont, wishing to bury as deeply as possible such scanty cables as he had been allotted, McGowan assembled a party of two hundred infantry to accomplish the task. Shrouded at one point by a thick early morning mist, they achieved some lines forward to a new Brigade H.Q. at the Briqueterie and to an advanced report centre at Maltz Horn Trench:

> About midnight we down in the dugouts began to smell gas, not the lachrymose variety, but a new type of gas shell with a more or less pleasant odour. We immediately donned our helmets. I personally used one of the signallers box respirators, that being far more comfortable & less suffocating. We were just waiting for a meal, but had to forego that pleasure & sit waiting for the fumes to evaporate. I went up to the top several times to see if all was clear & heard these little gas shells popping off all around. It had the effect desired by the Germans, who evidently knew we were anticipating an assault & the troops moving up to the assembly positions with helmets on, were considerably delayed & exhausted.
>
> (McGowan, October 9th)

Around 3.50 a.m. there was a bomb store explosion close to the Briqueterie and the resulting sparks set alight some sandbags close to about a hundred yards of unburied cables which were consumed in the blaze. During that early morning McGowan's section at Maltz Horn Trench were badly shelled, some were half buried and several were wounded, despite this he managed to keep one forward line open and by 7.50 a.m. all the lines of the 89th & 90th Brigades were working.

McGowan learnt that the leading companies of the R.S.F. attacking at 4.45 a.m. having reached Guillemont suffered severe casualties, though taking fifty prisoners:

> They waited on the line of the church for the barrage to lift & then pushed on to E. face of village & started consolidating. The two rear companies reached & held the Western edge of the village. During this time 2 coys of 16th had advanced S. from their assembly posns. E. of Trônes Wood in 4 waves & on reaching the Rly had left formed & attacked S. of station. They reached the wire at this point but were very heavily enfiladed by M.G. from the Station which 2nd Divn had failed to take & were forced to retire.
>
> (McGowan, October 9th)

The tattered remnants of these companies were placed in a trench east of Trônes Wood for better safety; meanwhile two forward companies of the 18th Manchesters reached a trench on the west face of the village taking several hundred prisoners. They too were cruelly enfiladed, this time from machine guns in 'the Quarry' and in their turn forced to retire. Two companies of the 17th Manchesters who had been sent to contact the R.S.F. and somehow to reinforce the 18th, were the target for hails of bullets from the machine guns both from the Station and 'the Quarry'. In spite of a heavy advance bombardment much of the wire had remained uncut and many were mown down in front of it.

Few of the 2 R.S.F. came back, they were cut off in Guillemont. Of the 18th Manchesters only a pitiful handful returned. The enemy by now counter attacking through the village put down a heavy barrage between it and Trônes Wood. Scarcely any patrols returned from the inferno, and by 10 a.m. no information was to hand:

> The situation remained unchanged throughout the day with very heavy shelling along the line held by the remnant of 90th Bde E. of Trônes Wood along the Maltz Horn Valley rendering the taking up of Ammunition a difficult task most ably carried out by a Coy of 23rd Mchrs. under Lt. Somerville. It was impossible to maintain telephone communication forward of HAIRPIN BEND despite constant effort by the best of linesmen & the expenditure of 6 mls of cable. At 5.30 p.m. news of probable relief by the 164th Bde was received with relief. Certainly the few hundred of our troops still left could not of withstood a strong counter attack...

> I went out on some business or other & was amazed to find the Sunken Rd deserted — not a soldier in sight between the BRIQUETERIE & MALTZ HORN TRENCH. Knowing how weak our bde was I wondered what would happen if the Boche really broke through. We few at the BRIQUETERIE would have had an exciting time.
>
> (McGowan, October 9th)

Relief by extra troops having arrived around 3.30. a.m. the following morning the sad survivors of the botched up 90th Brigade wandered back about two hours later. McGowan was met near Train Alley by his groom with his horse Lottie who carried him back to the remnants of the brigade at Mansel Copse:

> The operations against Guillemont were not successful in spite of most gallant behaviour by our troops. It is not difficult now to locate reasons

for the comparative failure. (1) Between the 12th & 19th July the Division had been refilled with drafts of many different regts. The battns. that went into action before Guillemont bore little resemblance to those fine battns. that began the push on July 1st. The South country reinforcements did not mix well with the men from the North & many officers & men were complete strangers to one another. (2) The Divn was fighting with mixed Artillery, it's own Divl. Artillery was resting after heavy strain from before the 1st July. (3) The various changes in the attack orders, though unavoidable naturally lead to some confusion & had a wearing effect on the Bde as a whole. The time given for Battns to make their dispositions was somewhat short. Naturally conditions did not & are not likely again to allow of the thorough preparations made before the MONTAUBAN push, but if there had been more artillery preparation, a better system of assembly trenches nearer the village & a more intimate knowledge throughout of what was happening at Montauban. Though not officially verified it is pretty evident that at the time of our assault the Germans had massed large numbers of troops & considerable artillery behind Guillemont in anticipation of a counter attack, which had it taken place at dusk on the 29th would undoubtedly have proved successful for TRNES WOOD & MALTZ HORN TRENCH were then held by two tired battns of Bantam who had staunchly held on there for nearly a week. As it was our attack surprised & nipped in the bud this counter attack probably to be delivered at the same time as our attack, with resulting heavy losses to both sides.

Apart from Transport Officers, Quartermaster & Second-in-Command, who do not normally go into action, the number of officers left in the Bde of those originally with us on July 1st can almost be counted on the fingers & the loss in men is proportional so can you wonder that I didn't attempt to write about it until a week afterwards & am only just completing it now 2 months later while waiting orders to move forward to battle again.

At noon on the 31st July I was awakened from a heavy sleep by Major Davies of my regt. 1/5th Cheshires who it seems is now with a kite balloon section operating close to Mansel Copse. I accepted his invitation to dinner next evening & thereby learnt quite a lot of news about the old crowd. Poor old Bass is missing & believed killed. I remember how right from the commencement he anticipated being killed & was I'm sure quite prepared for whatever befell him.

184

Trônes Wood

You can hardly imagine what a delightful sensation the after-battle feeling is, with a promise of a long rest & probably leave. No end of amusement can be obtained out of things that would only provoke a grouse under ordinary circumstances. On the afternoon of 1st Aug we received orders to the effect that the Brigade would entrain at Méricourt railhead at noon next day...

What a delight it was to leave Mansel Copse & the battlefield behind us at dawn next morning. The journey to Longpré by train was a very slow & uncomfortable one in cattle trucks, but I don't think anyone minded. I don't know who was responsible, but there wasn't even a coach for the Brigadier. I shall always remember 'Sir Arthur's' outspoken indignation to the R.T.O at Méricourt. However, the staff were spared the indignity & drove to Longpré by car. We reached our chateau at Verlaines about 5 p.m. Quite the finest Bde H.Q. we have ever had & we only hoped to stay there for a month or so. The weather was glorious & Walker & I pitched tents on what was once the tennis lawn close to a tip-top bathing spot for our morning bath. The battalions were all just as comfortably situated, so of course we were not surprised to receive orders next day for entrainment N'wards (Bethune district). Knowing what I did of Flanders I anticipated a dreary winter in muddy trenches which compared rather unfavourably with the 6 wks resting & reorganising which we had expected somewhere on the Somme. The 3rd of August was a delightful summer day. I had a little correspondence to deal with which included sending in 3 names for awards (Pte Irvine, Spr Gannon & Cpl Davies) & for the rest I did nothing but loaf & bathe in the sunshine. It's a remarkable fact but it was 12 mths to the day since I first arrived in the Somme district from Flanders. Next day the Divn left by train for Flanders. Our train left Longpré 3.41 p.m. & arrived Berquette 10 p.m. A slow but quite comfortable journey as there were two first class carriages for Bde H.Qrs. The General, Bde Major Harris, travelled in one, Walker, Pemberton & myself in the other, but we joined together for tea & dinner served enroute, but as it wasn't a corridor coach the goods were passed from the kitchen to mess by the skill of the waiters on the footboards.

(McGowan, October 9th)

In spite of his apprehensions about Flanders, McGowan found the countryside of northern France clean and pleasant. After a convivial week with a family in a small village farmhouse, he moved to the fair sized town of Béthune, marching in early on August 11th to escape the heat of the day.

185

Surrounded by poplar forests and fields drained by dykes, to McGowan's mind, Béthune a bustling centre of communications near La Bassée canal was a jolly place. Encompassed by squat old houses, its square medieval belfry jutted out from narrow streets. There were plenty of well dressed civilians about to please the eye and several really good shops including an excellent patisserie. The Prince of Wales, who, in 1915 was sometimes billetted in the Hotel de la France, used to frequent the Globe café in the market square where he was heard to be indignant that General French would not allow him to go up the line. The day McGowan arrived, both the King and the Prince paid an unofficial visit to the town probably to inspect the shell damage done during the previous Sunday. Another favourite rendez-vous was the public swimming baths containing horizontal excercising bars. The municipal theatre had been commandeered by a tip top troupe known as 'The Pedlars'.

McGowan stayed with a Madame Pacquet of 44 Rue de Sade Carnot. It was one of the finest billets he had encountered since leaving home and he mentioned a Mlle. Emilie Droy who was especially kind to him.

It was ill luck one day when an enemy shell landed on the house adjoining the Brigade mess in the Rue de Victor Hugo. By now thoroughly set on edge by the random shelling, the staff hastily repaired to a mean little farmhouse, the only available billet outside the town. As for McGowan, he was always riding out on horseback or bicycle ostensibly on business, occasionally ranging eastwards towards the trenches, but more frequently straying back to the pleasures of Béthune. Presently they moved once more to a large and comfortable château not far away:

> During this time the General & Beaumont were both in hospital &
> afterwards on leave & on the 23rd Aug. Capt. Taylor left us in an
> ambulance with internal trouble. He ought never to have retd. after his
> illness in April, for he's never been well since, but his interest in the
> 90th Bde attracted him. Few realize how much he has done for this
> brigade. He practically raised it in Aug. 1914 & has ever since given it
> his unselfish attention. We were all very sorry to lose him, for he's
> finished with the Army for good now & likely to be confined to his bed
> in England for many months yet.
>
> (McGowan, October 9th)

Having relieved the 93rd Brigade, after a fortnight they became optimistic on spending a really comfortable winter. But all at once their hopes were destroyed when an order came for them to turn back once more to the south:

> Such is the reward of the good soldier hard work, constant moving, &
> plenty of fighting, leaving the soft jobs for the untried & found wanting.

Trônes Wood

We left the Bethune district by train from Chocques at 2 p.m. on the 18th Sept. arriving Candas 6.30 p.m. I don't think there was one among us that wasn't sorry to leave that neighbourhood for as far as we could see it would have given us most comfortable winter quarters, the billets were so good, & the people so very obliging.

Freddy & I did the detraining again at Candas & rode together with column to Beauval, arriving 10 p.m. This was the village I visited 12 mths ago regarding my transfer to the R.F.C. which didn't come off & I'm not sorry for I've had a far wider experience as Bde Signalling Officer, than I should have done as Asst. Equipt. Officer with the R.F.C.

We remained here 3 days only but were thoroughly at home at our billet. Capt. Fearenside who was temporarily replacing Capt. Taylor celebrated his D.S.O. with champaign for the mess which lasted 2 nights & each evening we had our private orchestra playing for us in the drawing room of Madame. Both Madame & her 13 year old daughter Madelaine enjoyed the programme of music as well as we did.

(McGowan, October 9th)

On Thursday September 21st the Brigade moved to Flesselles, receiving and training further hapless newcomers. Many of the supposed billets allotted to them had been used as stables by a squadron of cavalry but McGowan was fortunately situated in the comfortable local château. Here General Steavenson was taken seriously ill with kidney disease, the aftermath of a bout of trench fever:

He left us the same day & I'm afraid he'll never return for we heard from his wife that he is still too ill to be moved to England & she has been allowed over to France to see him. I remember the time when I didn' care for the old man much, but that was because he was rather up against me due to his natural antipathy to Sappers, but ever since the first attack at Montauban, he's been exceptionally nice to me & I, like everyone else in the Brigade, came almost to love him. In the mess no General could have been nicer, he loved company & in consequence we were probably one of the happiest and most united Bde staffs in the army. His successor, Lt. Col. Lloyd of the 1st K.O. Lanc. Regt. arrived very quickly only 3 days after Gen. Steavenson left us. Naturally we were all critical but I don't think we shall have much cause for complaint. He's jolly enough at mess but it's not so spontaneous a jollity. In one respect he's the exact opposite of C.J.S. He's very reticent about forthcoming moves & loves to attend to details himself whereas C.J.S. had such confidence in his subordinates that he rarely bothered about anything personally except to bark when things went wrong, hence his general light heartiness as compared with the absorbed expression of General Lloyd. We're curious to know what the new Brigadier will be like as a commander in action. Personally I think he'll be rather callous as to the loss of his officers & men. He has not yet made a point of knowing all his battn. officers as C.J.S. & naturally not knowing them all personally as did C.J.S. he'll not feel their loss so keenly & is not likely to write letters of sympathy if one of his best officers is lost.

(McGowan, October 9th)

Anticipating his fourth attack, McGowan became more forlorn with the passing of each day. After twenty months of war he was dejected in mind and fatigued in body and he left restless and irresolute. In spite of this, sustained by his fundamental Christian faith and the high moral qualities of his east Lancashire upbringing, his outlook was still forbearing:

I certainly have had my share of front line work & should welcome a permanent job in the back areas, but would it be good for me morally? from what I've seen of these back area jobs, there's plenty of opportunity for kicking the loose-leg, & not a particularly good class of officer as companion. On the other hand I think I personally could find plenty of useful recreation to occupy any spare time I had, such as rubbing up the technical knowledge I once had, but have now forgotten. I should however be very sorry to leave this Brigade & my own section, though not quite so sorry as I would have been to leave 4 months ago, when it was practically all intact as I had known it when I first joined it & then going into real action for the first time. It's a good brigade still, but much changed & gradually becoming more "ordinary" & the thought of attacks is not so inspiring a thought as it was before the 1st July.

While at Flessells I had a short 2-day course with the No. 3 Squadron R.F.C. at La Houssoye during which time I learnt a little about the liason work between infantry & aircraft illustrated by one short flight & a great deal about the inner life of the R.F.C. Their's is a nerve wracking job if taken in large quantities, but they watch that that doesn't happen too often. About 2 to 3 hours in the air per day as a maximum & the rest of the day is spent playing cards, reading or talking. They always have comfortable billets & plenty of leave, but all the same I wasn't envious, but I do know this if I was an ordinary platoon commander I wouldn't rest until I got a transfer to the R.F.C.

188

Trônes Wood

We left Flesselles on Oct. 4th by French motor lorries. The whole Division less transport was moved by road to the Buire district by these lorries. Here we stayed for 2 days, but on the morning of the 6th Oct. I left about 5.45 a.m. on horseback for Longueval & spent morning & afternoon reconnoitering the new front line at the point we expect to attack from.

I retd. about 4.30 p.m. to Fricourt Camp which an Anzac Bde. had just left. Apparently they have no difficulty in getting stores for the whole camp was left strewn with stores of all kinds including detonated bombs, one of which exploded as the 18th Mchrs marched into camp after dark & resulted in 10 casualties. Major Goodlee wounded, Lieut. Crichton killed, 1 O.R. killed, 7 O.R. wounded. Nevertheless they were very hospitable to the General & myself who arrived hungry, & gave us a welcome meal under difficult circumstances.

This camp is situated just where our front line used to be between Mametz & Fricourt, which two villages & the ground between is typical of all the land wrested from the Boche during the last 3 mths. Just one vast shell-packed wilderness, studded with many black spots which represent the site of a one time village or wood.

Well orders have just arrived to say that we do definitely move tomorrow early, so I must cut this short & hope to be able to enlarge upon these notes at a later date. I trust I shall have strength & courage given me to carry through whatever tasks are allotted me to the satisfaction of my superiors & myself, & may it please God to protect me from the many dangers to which I shall undoubtedly be exposed. No one knows better than I do myself how particularly fortunate I have been this far, but I quite recognise that at any time it may be my turn to become a casualty & am quite prepared for whatever be my fate, but life is sweet & I sincerely trust I shall be spared to enjoy many more years of active useful life & may God grant that my dear Mother & Father remain to direct me in the right path.

(McGowan, October 9th)

CHAPTER 12

BOULEAUX WOOD

When Hodgkin returned to the front after five months he was detailed to join a unit specialising in water purification duties where much of his time was spent in a barge near St. Omer. This new job was not at all to his taste, he missed his friends and increasingly he disliked being behind the lines; but however bored he was, his sense of humour never deserted him:

> I have never wasted — absolutely — and — without — any — extenuating — circumstances — wasted 5 months & I am sick and tired of it.'
>
> (Hodgkin, May 1st)

He did not like the filter unit officers either whom he thought seemed to run a kind of republican and democratic show with their men.

At the end of May by chance he met Hatt-Cook of the 1/5th Cheshires now a Town Major in St Omer. Hatt-Cook regaled Hodgkin with all the gossip up to the time he left the battalion on April 29th:

> 'If only Col. Groves would go sick, I would go back to the Regiment at once as I feel a beastly slacker here. Hatt-Cook says he gets more and more disagreeable as time goes on'.
>
> (Hodgkin, May 26th).

Working with the purification unit, Hodgkin took no part in the battles of the Somme, but on August 9th he visited Suzanne which the Cheshires had occupied the previous year. He saw the French building a causeway in three days across the river and noted that the imposing château where McGowan had lodged was almost in ruins. Fourteen months later on a further visit he glimpsed the owner's car standing outside it. No doubt the Marquis was visiting his ancestral abode. The château despite being pitted with shell holes still served as an H.Q. and was overseen by a dear old French commandant with whom Hodgkin struck up an acquaintance.

As the summer of 1916 wore on, Hodgkin felt so keenly that he was not with his old comrades during the big push, that he even took the step of writing personally to Col. Groves to ask for a transfer. In his reply, it did not appear that Colonel Groves at Divisional H.Q. was aware of his battalion's dislike of its pioneer status:

Barge near St. Omer

In the Field
22.8.16

My dear Hodgkin,

I have your letter and am glad to hear news of you. I quite appreciate
the situation and can assure you that you need not worry. We all know
you too well to think for one moment that you would not be glad to be
back with us sharing our toils and honours, for I can assure you that Bn.
has done well and more particularly so since it has been turned into a
Pioneer Unit. We are of course Divisional troops and I personally do not
come very much in contact with the Brigadiers. We like our General and
his staff and in fact are very happy. All ranks now fully appreciate the
change to Pioneers as it gives all our skilled men a chance of showing
what they can do. You will, of course return to us after the war but
before it is over I hope. All old friends join in kind remembrances,

Yours sincerely,
John E.G. Groves, Lt. Col.

Bouleaux Wood

Eventually after eight months of boredom, on August 29th Hodgkin shook off the dust of St. Omer and after suffering two punctures arrived at St.Pol where his undoubted abilities and qualifications entitled him to wear the blue tabs of Assistant Chemical Adviser at Third Army H.Q. Henceforward for the rest of the war, he was destined to work on the use of chemicals and gas in warfare.

Despite his new staff job and the change of scene, he still felt he was getting nowhere; there seemed no chance of promotion and he found the work dull. 'I have never been satisfied since I left the Regiment; and my chances of getting back there seem remoter than ever' (Hodgkin, November 3rd).

While on leave on November 18th he learnt that Brunners (Brunner Mond & Co.) where he had been working before the war wanted him to return, or said they did, which he deemed rather different. He couldn't afford to tell Brunners that the last thing he wanted was to go home, and he hoped that the General when requested for his release would refuse to let him go.

In fact he had worried unnecessarily. On November 28th he left St. Pol with all its comforts and motored via Doullens to Toutencourt, a little village

193

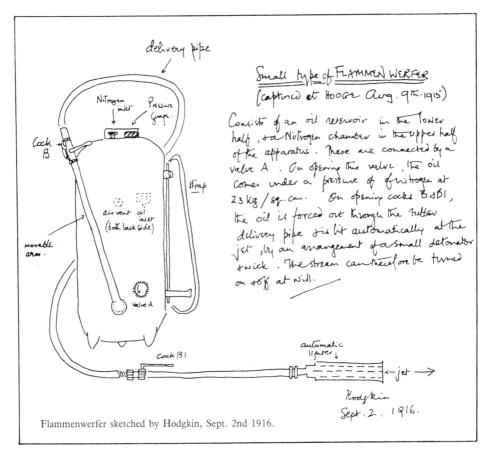

delivery pipe

Nitrogen inlet. Pressure Gauge.

Cock B

air vent oil inlet (both back side)

moveable arm.

Strap

valve A

Cock B1

automatic lighter

←—jet —→

Small type of FLAMMEN WERFER
(captured at Hooge Aug. 9th 1915)

Consists of an oil reservoir in the lower
half, +a Nitrogen chamber in the upper half
of the apparatus. These are connected by a
valve A. On opening this valve, the oil
comes under a pressure of nitrogen at
23 kg/sq.cm. On opening cocks B & B1,
the oil is forced out through the rubber
delivery pipe & is lit automatically at the
jet, by an arrangement of a small detonator
& wick. The stream can therefore be turned
on & off at will.

Hodgkin
Sept. 2. 1916.

Flammenwerfer sketched by Hodgkin, Sept. 2nd 1916.

which he said looked absolutely filthy. Here he was detailed to be the Chemical Adviser to the 5th Army commanded by General Sir Hubert Gough, who at that time was based in a farmhouse on the outskirts of the village.

After they were relieved on August 18th, Heald had marched south west with the Cheshires via Doullens to St. Riquier, a nice quiet place well behind the lines for a week's pioneer training. The men were very tired and suffered from sore feet. He felt sure now that they were being fattened for a further push, and, the C.O. having got them together en masse had the time of his life strafing, Heald thought his voice couldn't last much longer. As a change from the endless drills the German 'Flammenwerfer' was demonstrated, it would have been rather terrifying if they hadn't seen it all before, but the flame only lasted about half a minute and in the event the show was spoilt by a heavy August thunderstorm. On the first Saturday in September Hodgkin also saw a demonstration. He thought it would be a frightful thing in action; as bad, if not worse than the minenwerfer, whose fifteen inch long bomb performed such grotesque somersaults before landing softly to discharge its thirty pounds of dynamite, after a pause of ten seconds:

> It produces a huge sheet of intensely hot flame & immense clouds of black smoke: it is worked by 2 men, one carrying the container on his back, & the other, dressed in an asbestos suit, holding the nozzle. The very largest size carries about 80 yds. I believe. As long as one keeps well down at the bottom of the trench against the parapet, & is not hit by the jet, one can keep fairly all right, but the heat is terrific, & one is apt to lose one's presence of mind.
>
> (Hodgkin, September 2nd)

While stationed at St. Riquier the Cheshires were ordered to prepare a set of trenches, wire entanglements and other obstacles for the British new secret weapon called the 'Land Cruiser' to demonstrate its capabilities:

> It has caterpillar wheel movement and can cross any rough country, trenches & steep banks. It is armed with maxims and six pound guns and in future attacks, it or they will precede the infantry and smash and ride over Fritz's trenches. He won't like it at all. We are coming on.
>
> (Heald, September 1st)

All the infantry brigades from miles around had been notified that the 'Land Cruisers' were to perform daily from nine to ten and two to three.[1] Although they were a focus of intense interest to everyone, the crews felt that the demonstrations hindered their preparatory work and were instrumental in prematurely wearing out the delicate machinery.

On the third day of the exhibition which took place at Yvrench, Heald saw General Joffre and crowds of red hats, but the small boyish figure of the Prince of Wales who had come to watch the show two days before had escaped his notice. Haig who had witnessed a demonstration on August 26th, thought it quite encouraging but noted: 'But we require to clear our ideas as to the tactical handling of these machines'.[2]

The manufacture of the 'Land Cruiser' had been a well kept secret. For several years a band of pioneers foremost of whom were Lieut. Colonel E.D. Swinton R.E. and Captain Tulloch had been working out a design for an engine of war capable of forging across the countryside, with the express purpose of flattening the enemy wire and acting as a mobile machine gun destroyer. The scheme was particularly promoted by Winston Churchill with

[1] Clough Williams-Ellis, *The Tank Corps*, p.26.
[2] Ed. R. Blake, *The Private papers of Douglas Haig*, p.162.

Specimens of Headstones on
graves in NO-MAN'S LAND
sketched by Hodgkin, May 1st, 1916

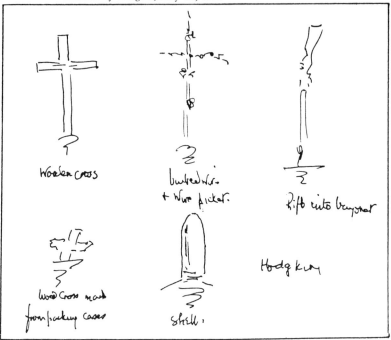

the Admiralty and Joint Land Ship Committee. But many and various were
the obstacles to turning dream into reality, some generals at first being openly
sceptical, Lord Kitchener dubbed the tank: 'A pretty mechanical toy'.[1]
However, in March 1916, Swinton was appointed to raise the 'Heavy Branch
Machine Gun Corps' (re-named 'Tank Corps' in 1917) and the production of
tanks was accelerated.

On February 16th Swinton then the Assistant Secretary of the War
Committee had written a fairly comprehensive paper on how he felt the
'Tanks' should be employed. He insisted that these machines should not be
used in driblets, and the fact of their existence should be kept secret until
they were all ready to be launched together with the infantry assault in one
great combined operation. So secret were they that evidence points to the
general surprise expressed when first in action: 'The other name for the tank
is "hush hush" because nobody is supposed to know about them'. (Hodgkin,
September 15th). Swinton's paper listed the tank's limitations saying that
they performed better over dry ground and could not perform in woods and

---

[1] E.D. Swinton, *Eye Witness*, p. 196.

closely planted orchards.[1] He pointed out that while they could withstand bullets, they would be completely knocked out by shell fire. Above all he wished the generals to wait until the crews be properly trained in England and the new machines to be mechanically sound. It seemed however that Swinton's advice was not heeded as it was decided to bring more than fifty Mark I types over for the late Somme offensive of September 1916.

At the beginning of September Heald knew for sure that everything pointed to a move and right into the thick of it. Before leaving St. Riquier, the usual church parade took place but he could not hear much of the sermon; perhaps the terrible bombardments had affected his hearing, but even if he could have heard, there was too much intonation and 'High Church' and he did not like it. After packing up for their departure on September 4th, they were shunted southwards towards the Somme, back on to the old familiar ground of the Corbie rail head where as usual they arrived in the dark in soaking rain. The billets that night were tolerably good, but it seemed strange to be back once more in Corbie:

> We marched early and after a 13 mile march arrived at a huge camp just
> behind our old front lines. The district here is one huge camp and it
> really is almost like the pictures one sees of war. At night bivouac fires
> and lights twinkle everywhere. Apparently Fritz has too much on his
> hands to shell here. Terrible gunfire is going on.
>
> (Heald, September 6th)

The camp was known as the 'Citadel' near the Fricourt Bray road, an area which also contained the Citadel Military Cemetery where many burials had taken place earler in the year. In May Hodgkin had noted how varied were the headstones in no man's land. Heald saw that the roads to the 'Citadel' were deep in mud, and the camp itself stretched far over the surrounding hillside. Early the following morning, Heald marched with his unit of pioneers to bivouacs in a field near Carnoy north west of Maricourt, now a village devastated by the July fighting. They threaded their way in single file through a mass of dirty carts, sweating men and horses trying to avoid shell holes three foot deep in water. Enormous masses of guns were lined up along the hillside and on a further slope rows of cavalry waited their chance, their horses knee deep in liquid mud:

> We went up this morning to Combles nearby, which place the French
> took yesterday, Fritz is thowing a lot of heavy stuff about. Our Colonel
> took the Company Commanders out and we reconnoitred the ground

---

[1] Swinton, ibid., pp. 198-213.

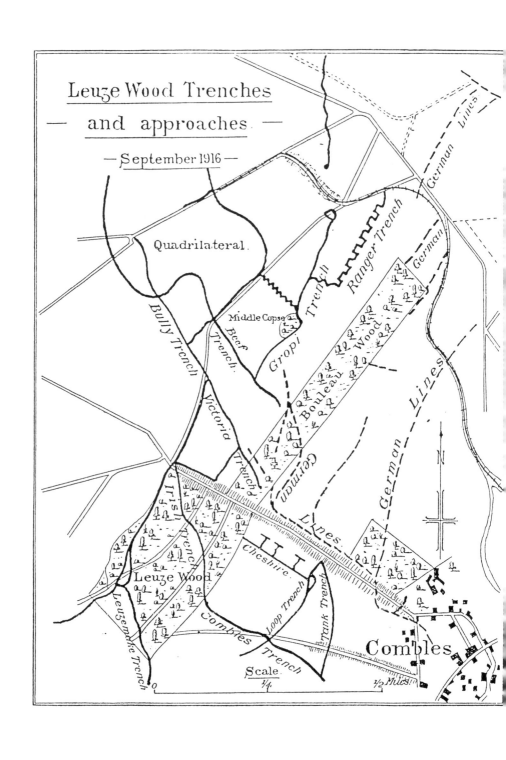

Leuze Wood Trenches
and approaches
— September 1916 —

Quadrilateral.

Bully Trench

Beef Trench

Middle Copse

Gropi Trench

Ranger Trench

Boileau Wood

German Lines

Victoria Trench

Irish Trench

Leuze Wood

Leuzemate Trench

Cheshire Trench

Loop Trench

Combles Trench

Frank Trench

German Lines

N

Combles

Scale
0   1/4   1/2 Miles

over which we have to work. Tonight we went out and dug a
communication trench from Leuze Wood back to a valley. Three
companies did the work and we got shelled very badly. Had about
twenty five casualties. The country we have taken has literally been paid
for by about one man per yard. The ground is torn up by shells and
there are no level spaces so walking over it is very difficult. Was very
glad to get back. We passed over one trench absolutely full of German
dead. This ground had only been captured two or three days ago.

(Heald, September 7th)

[In fact Combles was captured on September 26th]
Leuze Wood presented a grisly scene consisting of splintered shattered tree
stumps, the undergrowth around them tangled up with barbed wire.
Alongside ran the sunken road to Combles which divided it from Bouleaux
Wood strongly defended by the Germans. Excavating the trench up the steep
slope in the chalky earth was really a matter of joining up the enormous shell
holes as the entire area was a moonscape of pock marks. The communication
trench was sited across the notorious 'Valley of Death', an area being a
favourite target for German gunners. An ancient iron cross, rusty and bent
stood ominously on the hillside:

Went out again tonight and constructed a trench to a place called Angle
Wood. We got shelled of course, as the Germans scatter shells all over
the place, but we were not too near the front and so escaped lightly. Am
very tired as it is at least five miles from our bivouac to the lines.

(Heald, September 8th)

Angle Wood was situated in a small valley to the south west of Combles
near Falfemont Farm and the Valley of Death. Some of the 56th Division
were already positioned in reserve, some in shelters dug from the hillside
others in trenches down in the valley:

Had a rotten job tonight. There was an attack going on, and we were
detailed to go and dig a new trench in front of our present line. Of
course no-one knew exactly where the place was and no-one knows
exactly the position anywhere. We had to go out with 300 men and find
out. Luckily the fire had died down when we were getting there and we
had no barrage to pass through only isolated big shells dropping. We
had to stop at every trench we came to and ask our way or get a guide.
It is most awfully difficult to find one's way around over that shell torn
area. There are no landmarks and no-one knows the ground well,
because no-one stays more than 48 hours. They are done by then. We

199

got out eventually and dug it. We did not get badly shelled because the Germans did not know we were there, and so their shells went over us. We had a few casualties. We have lost an awful lot of men there. The ground is strewn with them. Am awfully tired tonight. I hope we have a rest tomorrow night. We are more than twelve hours away on this work each night and its very trying too.

(Heald, September 9th)

Started out early this morning and found our work being shelled badly. We had to make a waggon track. Luckily they stopped shelling soon after we got there. We had a few casualties, four killed, which was unlucky. However day work is much preferable to night work. We get the night in again tonight. Fritz is very active.

(Heald, September 11th)

It was rolling featureless devastated country. Perhaps the chief cause of loss of direction was the shape of the jumping off line which became zig-zag in form and where troops frequently faced east and west and were told to attack north. The attack on September 9th, a wild rush in fading light was in a north easterly direction and the situation remained obscure for several days. At this point the Germans were desperately defending the fortified village of Combles in the valley beyond Leuze Wood. The French Army was on the opposing heights.

September 12th opened with the usual intensive bombardment of smoking shell bursts heralding the news of the main attack three days later:

Had to go with a staff officer to reconnoitre a way for the armoured cars to get up. Managed this quite successfully. Later I took the cars officers up and we got shelled very heavily. Could not get right up — too hot. The French have made a big advance. We do our show in two days. We are quite expecting to go through this time. The cavalry are up and it is going to be a huge push. There will be about 50 armoured cars taking part also.

(Heald, September 12th)[1]

Was out tonight laying a white tape along the line the cars have to go to reach their starting point. Put out about two miles of tape. Fairly quiet time.

(Heald, September 13th)

---

[1] In 1916, the 'tanks' were called by a variety of names. Heald refers to them as 'armoured cars'.

Bouleaux Wood

Although the tank crews had been training in tremendous secret at Elvedon near Thetford, Norfolk, and were well versed in firing the Vickers and Hotchkiss machine guns, some of the officers and many of the men had never been to the battlefields. Their inexperience could be likened to practising first aid bandaging on an unwounded patient and the Mark I machine with its two ungainly tail wheels had never been subjected to the mire of the Somme.

Heald did not say if the tape he had used to mark out the route had been dipped in luminous paint, but this method had been employed in the trials at Elvedon. The eight members of the tank crew needed all the help they could get, as the orders, timetables and maps with which they were issued were insufficient and hurriedly drawn up. The driver's vision was extremely limited, his view being confined to tiny glass slits in the armour or to the periscope. Choked with engine fumes the interior of the vehicle was loaded with thousands of rounds of ammunition, drums of oil, lamp signalling sets and spares for the guns. In addition, there were the tins of food, bread, iron rations, water bottles, field dressings and even carrier pigeons which could be let fly through a slit in the side. The crews wore a variety of service dress and usually sported deep thick leather 'anti-bruise' helmets plus goggles. As some protection against grenades, the top of the tank was partially covered by wire netting spread over a low gabled framework.

By now the Cheshires had moved up to the Bois de Favière, a little over a mile from Maricourt and had bivouacked in some open trenches. On the slope in front of them was an energetic party of French gunners firing off their smooth shooting '75's with obvious enjoyment. For good measure they also operated an old howitzer whose leaping antics provided some light relief. Waiting in the wings the cavalry looked for their chance for action while the Cheshires made a road to facilitate their advance:

> Today is the day. The show started at 6.20 a.m. A terrific noise. We can't get any news. The armoured cars have not been the success anticipated. We saw one come back. It was pierced by bullets. I'm afraid the great offensive has failed. We have taken one or two trenches but have not broken through. The cavalry have gone back. We were out consolidating tonight, i.e. connecting up the captured trenches with our old lines. Of course no-one knew anything or where anyone was. We had a fairly hot time.
>
> (Heald, September 15th)

Three tanks had been allotted to the 56th Division, the objective of the 56th being to clear the strongly held Bouleaux Wood and form a protective flank to cover the lines of advance from Combles. Many of the tank crews who had not heard the noise of deafening guns before had passed a sleepless night in tightening up the loose tracks of the 'caterpillars'. In order to reach their starting points they had had to traverse the ground described by Heald, the type of ground which Swinton said was unsuitable.

One tank attached to the 169th Brigade was in position to attack at 6 a.m. on September 15th from the corner of Leuze Wood. This machine having lent great assistance to the 1/2 Londons, was set on fire by a direct hit from a shell near 'Loop Trench' to the south east of the Wood after having kept its guns firing at the Germans for five hours. Of the two further tanks sent to assist the 167th and 168th Brigades, one split a track while advancing to the assembly position while the other reached the western corner of Bouleaux Wood. Moving slowly towards Middle Copse, it drew considerable enemy fire but proceeded to the edge of the wood where it cruised around eventually becoming ditched close to the enemy front trench. At 11 a.m. a pigeon message arrived at the 56th Division H.Q.; the tank had been destroyed by German bombers and eventually abandoned after all the crew had been hit. The 167th Brigade was ordered to assist them.

In spite of Swinton's insistence, the tanks had been sent out into the muddy shell mangled ground churned up by the endless bombardment and their delicate machinery was soon out of gear. Instead of the anticipated fifty in two companies, considerably less were able to function due to faulty mechanisms. However Haig appeared satisfied with the results as he noted on September 15th:

> A "Tank" has been seen marching through the High Street of Flers followed by a large number of infantry cheering! Certainly some of the Tanks have done marvels and have enabled our attack to progress at a surprisingly fast pace.[1]

J.W. Haddon, the only surviving officer of a Kitchener's Battalion of the East Surreys witnessed the arrival of a tank amongst the rubble of Flers on September 15th. He doubted the vehicle had a particularly devastating impact, the situation was far too tense and the cheering army behind the tank was by a small column of fours which he was mobilising for the gathering prisoners in the street. It was probable that the tank (numbered D 17 'Dinnaken') was commanded by Lieutenant Stuart Hastie and it was in a sorry state. The rear steering wheels were out of action having been hit, and the bearings 'run' in the big ends. Hadden had discussed the next objective with the tank commander but owing to the machine's mechanical plight it was decided 'the old daimler' could only retreat up to the Flers/Delville

---

[1] Ed. Blake, Private papers of Sir Douglas Haig, pp. 166, 167.

Wood road where two hundred yards off the highway the engine finally packed up for good.[1]

Lance Corporal G.L.M. Vine of 3 section, 'C'. Company, Heavy Section Machine Gun Corps taking part in the action wrote to his wife: 'Several of our heavies have been blown to atoms — they received Jack Johnsons on us all the way there and back but we were lucky, tho' our car is marked all over with bullets & shrapnel'. Not knowing what happened in the general confusion, he said: 'Let me have the Daily Mail if there is an account in it will you please? (Vine, September 18th).[2] In spite of the whole dubious venture, the slow and lumbering tank at least convinced the High Command of the potential of the vehicle, even though the surprise element of a mass tank attack had been lost.

---

[1] Quoted by J. Terraine, *The Smoke and the Fire*, pp. 158, 159
[2] Ms. Letter in Imperial War Museum.

Old shells still remain by Bouleaux Wood in May 1986.

At the end of September 1916, Hodgkin had a ride in a tank:

> They are the most uncanny looking things I have ever seen, & reminded
> me mostly of enormous toads with their noses in the air. They told me
> that the only Germans that stood up to them at all were the Prussian
> Guard; & when they found that bombing was useless they turned & ran.
> And I really can't blame them. I understood that Col. Swinton, & not
> Winston Churchill is the chief inventor. Daily Mail says the opposite.
>
> (Hodgkin, September 30th)

After the initial attack, September 16th dawned bright and beautiful, but
later that evening 'C' Company of the Pioneers lead by a bad guide walked
mistakenly into the German lines and Captain Dixon the Company
Commander was wounded. It turned out an awful mess up:

> I have been given command of 'C' Company. We went out to retrieve
> the work of last night. This we did, and dug a trench 400 yards long for

a battalion — the Queens Westminsters to attack from. Very lively time at first but quiet later. We finished our job. Very wet.

(Heald, September 16th)

Christened 'Cheshire' the trench ran perilously parallel to the sunken road at right angles to Bouleaux Wood on the other side. It joined up with 'Loop Trench' recently occupied by the enemy. The scene around Bouleaux and Leuze Woods was a nightmare. There had been no time to bury the dead and corpses lay in heaps half buried in the mud. Each ambulance required six horses to drag it through ground described as worse than a quagmire, while the stretcher bearers stumbled along eight men to one stretcher.

Ever pushing forward, the Cheshires, out two nights later in pouring rain dug a new fire trench roughly parallel to Bouleaux Wood in front of the front infantry:

> Whole battalion dug a new advanced line near Combles. The Company Commanders went on in advance to tape it out and got well shelled. We dug the new line which is intended to enable us to encircle Combles.
> We have not got Bouleaux Wood yet even though the papers say so. The mud tracks are appalling. It nearly kills one getting up to our work and coming back is a nightmare. When one gets in one just drops down and sleeps. It is nearly four miles over slush.

(Heald, September 19th)

Heald and the other Company Commanders had started to tape out the ground as soon as it was dusk. When the darkness could hide them, Major W.A.V. Churton leading the battalion followed with the men trudging forward carrying their tools. It was not an easy matter to lead so many men through the devious miry route and what was worse on arrival at Leuze Wood they found there were no guides.

Heald's small folded map of the area was only a flimsy one and roughly marked (though it can still be deciphered today.) He kept it tucked inside the cover of his war diary. It indicated the trench they had to dig in blue chalk and he had written 'Royal Fusiliers' in brown just behind it. 'Cheshire Trench' by the sunken road had not been drawn, only 'Loop Trench' was roughly shown. No scale was indicated — no wonder it was practically impossible to find the way.

It was fortunate that the watchful Company Commanders could contact their lost comrades and were able to shepherd them up to their nocturnal task. Squatting down in line along the white tape the men proceeded to dig their marked out trench. Hour by hour, in spite of muffled clinks of pick and shovel and occasional whispered comments, the enemy in the nearby wood

205

appeared to ignore them. Perhaps they had their own work to do, but miraculously there was only a single casualty. The thousand yard long trench complete with traverses and approaches was finished. Known as 'Gropi' the subject of their labours combined the words 'Groves' and 'Pioneer'; it was commended by XIV Corps Commander as a perfect example of a battle trench dug in close proximity to the enemy.

The following night, 'B' Company went to dig north west of Middle Copse:

Still raining. This weather has stopped fighting. It is an awful job getting material up and waggons get stuck fast. We had to go up again and dig an advanced post ahead in front of Combles. It took four hours to reach our work. Was dog tired on getting back about 6 a.m.

(Heald, September 20th)

Weather still bad but it is drying a bit. B. & C. Companies dug another advanced line in front of Bouleaux Wood. Company Commanders again had to go and tape it out. This is very dangerous work as there is no-one in front and wandering about in 'no mans land' is no joke in the dark. 'B' Company had a bad time and had four officers hit including Hignett. I'm getting sick of this place. There are strong rumours of a relief.

(Heald, September 21st)

As indicated on Heald's map, strong points that night were pushed ever closer towards the Germans in Bouleaux Wood like a deathly game of 'grandmother's footsteps'. A new trench christened 'Ranger' was dug up to the tram line partly parallel to 'Gropi', the overall idea being to pressurise the enemy by pushing trenches ever nearer the wood.

One of the wounded officers from 'B' Company died shortly afterwards, and 'D' Company, one of whose platoons was forming up wearily to return to base suffered nine dead and four wounded due to an explosion of a large shell in their midst.

Notwithstanding the men were now completely done up, and fatigue had deprived them of force vitality and sensibility, once more on September 23rd they were detailed to excavate another tricky portion of trench ever closer to the enemy. Shells plummeted down on their way up though Heald reckoned this time they had got off lightly. They returned at 6 a.m.

Finally on September 26th, the two 56th Divisions, the French and English, jointly captured the rubble of Combles. Warily they picked their way through the ruined houses, where the rafters lay at weird angles across leaning slabs of brick wall and the occasional pointed iron gate. Previously with his men, Heald had crept round the rear of the village constructing strong points to consolidate their painful gains. But of the enemy there was no sign. Emerging from their deep underground cellars leaving large stores and ammunition behind them they had silently stolen away:

Hear that we have got Combles. Very few casualties considering. I feel very done and need a rest.

(Heald, September 26th)

We moved out this afternoon a few miles back for a day or two's rest. We did not get our field kits until 1 a.m. and no dinner except bully beef and biscuits.

(Heald, September 27th)

As a souvenir the following Christmas the 56th Divisional card depicted a cartoon in Punch commemorating the entry of the village by the two Divisions. Haig was well satisfied, he noted in his diary of Wednesday, September 27th: 'The total casualties for the last two days' heavy fighting are just 8,000. This is very remarkable and seems to bear out the idea that the enemy is not fighting so well, and has suffered in morale'.[1] The correct number of casualties at this point could only be conjectured but the effect of them at home became increasingly horrifying.

Today a narrow tarmac road, gently descending towards Combles divides the dense and leafy trees of Leuze and Bouleaux Woods. Off the road, the adjacent upland field, silent now and smooth, is bounded by a parallel cart track above Bouleaux Wood. Nestling in its grassy verges lie small heaps of rusting shells like clutches of eggs laid by some evil bird.

As the September battles drew to their close, the inevitable rain mist and mud clogged the machinery and fettered the men as the generals martialled their forces relentlessly for the next push forward. Haig considered the task in normal autumn weather well within the capacity of his armies.[2]

Leaving the Combles ravine on September 27th, the Cheshires moved back to Sandpits camp at the cemetery near Méaulte off the Bray-Albert road. The countryside was strewn with army refuse while the village of Méaulte situated in a valley by a tributary of the Aisne presented a gloomy appearance of unwelcoming squalor. The last day of September saw them trudging up to McGowan's stamping ground of Montauban, and forward up to the advanced line by Lesboeufs, in the trenches called 'Foggy' and 'Windy'. New assembly trenches were required at once in preparation for the divisional attack on The Transloy Ridge roughly three miles northwards of Combles:

---

[1] Ed. Blake, op. cit., p. 167.
[2] Edmonds, *Military Operations — France and Belgium 1916, II,* p. 428.

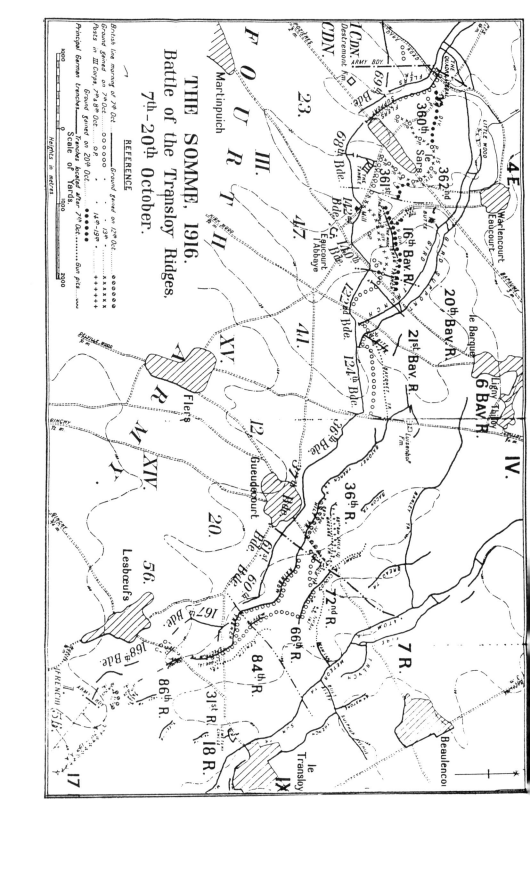

THE SOMME, 1916.
Battle of the Transloy Ridges,
7th.-20th October.

REFERENCE

British line morning of 7th Oct. ⟶
Ground gained on 7th Oct. ○○○○○○
Posts in III Corps 7th & 8th Oct. OP
Ground gained on 7th & 8th Oct. ━━━━━
Ground gained on 14th-18th Oct. ━━━━━
Ground gained on 20th Oct. ●●●●●●
Trenches located after 7th Oct.
Principal German trenches.
Gun pits. ⌣⌣⌣

Scale of Yards
1000   0   1000   2000

Heights in metres

Digging operations again. New advanced trenches. Started at five and did not reach our work until 2.30 a.m. Nobody knew the way. The Germans spotted us digging. We got too near them and we had a hell of a time. They put up a barrage of 5.9 heavy shells — just on us. 'B' Company had to go. We stayed and finished our job. Was nearly daylight when we left. He spotted us again and shelled. An awful night. I did not expect to get out alive. My Company had thirteen hit including an officer. We got back at 7 a.m. absolutely done.

(Heald, October 1st)

More digging. Road awful. It is over five miles to our work through thick mud. Did our work. Journey back a nightmare. The road was lined with men who had dropped in the mud exhausted, and miles of transport carts stuck fast. Got back at 6.30 a.m. Everybody exhausted. These jobs keep us out fourteen hours.

(Heald, October 3rd)

Weather improving. Had an awful time tonight. As we were going up a communication trench to the front trenches Fritz put a barrage up. For a half an hour it was hell. You could not see for smoke and you kept on getting half buried. We had a lot of casualties. When it stopped we went on and did our work, but I had only three platoons left. Got back very tired.

(Heald, October 5th)

Heavy rain had fallen continuously for two days from October 2nd and the Germans appeared to have more guns in action than ever before. Vision was hampered by low cloud so that the position of the British front was known only approximately at Corps and Army H.Q's.[1] The country had become a wide expanse of shell holes in a dark brown almost black morass where no one knew anyone's position. Nevertheless, the assault of the 56th Division on the right flank of the Army took place from the newly dug assembly trenches at 1.45 p.m. on October 7th in full daylight.

Their machine guns inexorably firing from strong points and shell holes the enemy checked the attempted advance to gain 'Hazy', 'Dewdrop', 'Spectrum' and 'Ranger' trenches. Before midnight a general withdrawal to the starting line was carried out. All Heald could do in the terrific din was to help his exhausted men connect up some forward trenches while what was left of 'C' Company tried to consolidate some of the ground. The following

---

[1] Edmonds, op. cit., p. 434.

day at 3.30p.m. the attack was renewed, the experience of the previous day was repeated and the casualties were enormously increased. Lieut Col. A.D. Bayliffe who commanded the 168th Brigade throughout the battle wrote on the spot his recommendations for future lessons for warfare of this nature. The commentary shows how remote was the High Command from the front line and ignorant of the conditions of the fighting men.[1] Two days later the depleted division was relieved and Heald retreated to the transport lines. He needed sleep badly.

On October 10th he marched his exhausted party to the nearby railhead. En route for a week in a rest camp they caught the first supply train available that night, the men riding in open trucks and Heald sleeping in the guard's van, but no one cared. They were leaving the carnage:

> Had a six mile march to the camp at Ault. Men very done. Lovely day.
> This place is on the sea. Evidently a French watering place out of
> season. High cliffs and blue sky. Feeding quite good. We are in tents. It
> is very bracing here. Quaint old houses and up and down winding
> streets. Casino closed. Feel very tired and glad to have some peace.
>
> (Heald, October 10th)

South of Havre, Le Treport, a fashionable nearby French watering place lay near the seaside town of Ault a little way along the cliffs. Although by the middle of October it was quite deserted, there were still some good meals to be had and one night after an amusing cinema show, they came back seven in a cab while feeling rather sorry for the horse.

Heald did not note down the title of the cinema show they saw. Perhaps it was one of the early Charles Chaplin films such as 'The Tramp' made in 1915 or 'The Rink' of 1916. From the Leon Gaumont studios in France Louis Feuillarde's films such as 'Les Vampires' featured the dark haired heroine Irma Vep. This character was in contrast to the demure beauty of Lilian Gish or to the blonde ringlets of the little ingénue Mary Pickford who earned $4,000 a week in 1916. Although the popular and ingenious 'A trip to the Moon' made by Georges Méliès in 1902 with Pathé Frères, Méliés' production of films had waned by 1914 although his displays of camera trickery were still popular.

After six days in Ault, Heald's equilibrium had somewhat recovered, especially as he had stayed a night in an hotel where the sheets felt grand, and there were lovely cakes for tea: 'The food in camp is shocking. They charge us three francs a day and give us bare rations. I don't think I have had more than half a dozen meals in'. (Heald, October 14th)

---

[1] Dudley Ward, op cit pp. 89–92.

By this time the Cheshires had moved to Condé Folie near Hallencourt. On rejoining them once more, Heald learnt that he had been promoted to Captain. A few days later it seemed that his period in charge of a company of pioneers in the trenches had finally ended:

> I have been attached to the Divisional Staff for instruction in General
> Staff work. It sounds good. Perhaps it means I shall get a staff job later
> with red tabs. I was sent to La Gogue to take over some model trenches
> from the Division we are relieving. It was very cold in the car. This new
> district is quite thickly populated and as far as I can see is a beautifully
> quiet sector. I hope we are here for the winter. This must be an
> industrial district as there are numerous factories about. The country is
> very flat and waterlogged so that one has to build up trenches instead of
> digging down. Our sector includes Neuve Chapelle where the battle was
> about eighteen months ago.
>
> (Heald, October 22nd)

Just a little over ten months later on September 3rd 1917 Heald passed through the country over which they fought so bitterly. He found it a poignant train journey. Peering out of the window at the devastation he saw that the grass had grown wonderfully and covered all the shell holes. Still at the front on June 30th, 1918, he wrote: 'I attended a memorial service for the battle of Gommecourt (two years ago) when this Division lost over 4,000 men in one day'. Hodgkin visited the northern part of the Somme battle field on April 1st, 1917:

> After about an hour of walking & threading our way through the
> incredible amount of barbed wire which the enemy thinks necessary to
> put out, we arrived at the scene of the disaster of July 1st 1916, to wit,
> the piece of land between FONQUEVILLERS and GOMMECOURT.
> It had been recently cleared by our men & the only sign of 4,000
> casualties were a heap of web-equipment, a bleached skull, & one
> shapeless mass which it was not well to investigate too closely. Every
> inch of ground to FONQUEVILLERS was pitted with shrapnel bullets.
>
> Our trenches in front of FONQUEVILLERS were smashed absolutely
> shapeless. Unfortunately we had not time to go round to
> GOMMECOURT where the thickest of the fight was, as it was getting
> rather late. So back through FONQUEVILLERS, a heap of stones, but
> with civilians already straying back into it to try & find what used to be
> their houses; & home to FOSSEUX. A most interesting, but possibly
> rather melancholy day; the latter feeling brought about, I think, by the

absolute desolation of miles of country, & the utter futility & waste of it all.

(Hodgkin, April Fool's Day 1917)

To the north of the Gommecourt salient, on the same journey, Hodgkin inspected a little cemetery where the Germans had buried some of the British officers and men on raids: 'Each has a beautifully made wooden cross with the name & regiment & date painted on; they evidently took some trouble about it, which stands to their credit'.

Adrian Eliot Hodgkin (1890 – 1972) when a Captain in the 1st/5th Battalion of the Cheshire Regiment in 1915.

CHAPTER 13

OCTOBER 1916

After Heald and his party departed for Ault, the 56th Division was withdrawn directly from the field of battle; and as part of the 'general post' after their 'holiday' up north the 30th Division was ordered up front to relieve the 41st Division between Eaucourt L'Abbaye and Guedecourt. This was despite the fact that at this stage few battalions could muster more than four hundred men and many of these were only half trained.[1] The war correspondent Neville Lytton described the avenues of graves he saw everywhere after July 1st and the soldiers fresh from the fight who without exception had expressions of tragedy on their faces.[2]

The Official History of October 1916 makes terrible reading. The expected fine October weather never materialised, instead wet spells of drenching rain alternated with dull mist, so that the sodden ground in the battle zone worsened day by day. Unlike Flanders, the roads were not pavé and had become water courses so that supplies forward had to be brought up over the old no man's land where the churned up soil rapidly turned into a morass. Therefore when the moment of assault arrived, the British front positions were a maze of waterlogged shell holes and flooded trenches with enemy wire remaining uncut in many places. Many of the guns had been firing for over two months and were too worn for accurate fire. In spite of all these adverse factors, the High Command appeared to be confident in sending their countrymen into this environment for renewed and relentless frontal attacks, nothwithstanding the tragic failures of October 7th and 8th.

McGowan cycled along the bumpy road to the desolate village of Fricourt, a scene of strife on July 1st when it was part of a notorious German salient. His destination was the ruined château where the 41st Divisional H.Q. resided in the depth of its vaulted cellars.

On August 10th, King George V had stood on top of the hill south of the village overlooking Mametz. From it could be seen Montauban and the grisly jagged stumps of Trônes wood, flashes of gunfire blazed in the distance. Dugouts had been excavated inside the hill:

> These dug-outs on *King George's Hill* are the most wonderfully engineered underground habitations that I have yet seen. A main entrance of good width takes you down some 39 steps to a depth of about 25ft, into a wide passage about 8 ft wide & some 60 yds long. Off

---

[1] Military Operations, 1916,II p. 442.
[2] N. Lytton, *The Press and the General Staff*, p. 47.

this passage on either side are about a dozen comfortably spacious offices. The whole of the interior is lined after a finished fashion with stout smooth boarding. The offices are all fitted with useful furniture such as tables, chairs & beds & above all, the place had been fitted throughout with electric light & an installation which provides perfect ventilation throughout. The Boche are wonderful engineers & these were probably one of their finest attempts at a dugout building but nevertheless when we were ready they had to move.

(McGowan, October 18th)

Starting at 6 a.m. on the following day, McGowan rode slowly on his horse through the congested traffic past Mametz up through Montauban, across the caterpillar valley to Longueval. Still standing miraculously amidst the ruins of Montauban was an intact painted terracotta figure of the Virgin Mary. At the cross roads about three hundred yards short of Longueval he was forced to dismount and send away his horse as the road was completely blocked. Along the ground beside it lay tangled rusty barbed wire in shell holes of muddy water. He had never encountered such shell torn ground as in the area to the south west of Delville Wood by Longueval village.

It had taken until early September to carry out the order of July 15th to take Delville Wood 'at all costs'. On July 15th the South Africans had gone in with 121 Officers and 3,032 men. As their tattered remnants emerged on the 20th they found themselves to be only 29 officers and 751 men strong. As McGowan would have seen it in October, Delville Wood presented a picture of anguished jutting tree stumps intermingled with trench lines strewn about with splinters. Such was the shelling that, although the wood is now replanted and the original rides re established it is unwise to stray off the marked paths, as unstable ammunition still lurks in the undergrowth.

Striking off on foot over what remained of the Longueval/Flers road, McGowan managed to locate 'Ferret' trench sheltering the Signals H.Q. of the 124th Brigade whom they were to relieve. Shells were dropping into Flers with unfailing regularity. Despite the fact that he wore a Military Cross, McGowans's opposite number of the 124th was neither affable nor obliging. Disdaining comment he adopted a superior manner. The antagonism appeared mutual as McGowan considered the man's operating methods cumbersome, wasteful and unsatisfactory. Excusing his rudeness because the 41st had been subjected to a week's enemy shelling, McGowan set about putting matters to rights to his own satisfaction as soon as he could.

Vacating 'Ferret' trench on October 12th, Brigade H.Q. moved up to 'Abbey Road' (running from Flers towards Eaucourt L'Abbaye). While reconnoitering further alleyways and spent trenches for his cables, McGowan chanced on a deserted trench leading nowhere filled with British and German

214

bodies in stages of decomposition entwined in their last fight. Not surprisingly, this graveyard had remained unvisited for days as the spot was heavily shelled.

Perhaps 'Division' felt apprehensive about the safety of the cables as orders came through that a visual signalling post be set up at the west end of Flers village. As usual McGowan's directions were muddled and confused and he braced himself to locate this dangerous station for himself. The Boche still hammered away on Flers but he and his men were lucky that time in returning safely to Abbey Road. Yet again, McGowan was unhappy about the preparations for a renewed attack, as usual the lines to Division were not complete, and there was no time to complete the cable laying forward to all the battalions along the walls of the communication trenches.

During the night of October 11th, companies of the 17th and 18th Manchesters and the 2nd R.S.F. had

Army Telephone Station on the Somme.

assembled for the forthcoming assault in 'Factory Trench', 'North Road' and 'Gird Trench' to the west of Guedecourt. They were supported by machine gunners from the 90th Brigade Machine Gun Company and the Motor Machine Gun Company in 'Factory Trench' who were to give overhead support to the attackers:

This was the situation at zero on October 12th 2.5 p.m. Before this there had been a continual bombardment of the enemy trenches by our artillery of all calibres, to which the enemy replied intermitently. During the afternoon on Oct. 11th a Chinese bombardment of the enemy's area was carried out, the enemy replying vigourously on our trenches. Zero was at 2.5 p.m. Oct 12th. Our artillery barrage opened at 2 hrs 1½ mins & 2 mins afterwards the enemy opened a very heavy barrage of arty. & H.G. fire, but only the front line for we behind were out on the bank

215

above Bde H.Q. watching it all in full view of the whole battle & never a shell near.

(McGowan, October 18th)

On the afternoon of October 12th a day of heavy showers, the plan of assault followed the same inexorable undeviating pattern, except that this time the attack was ordered to start in daylight. McGowan's narrative described how two hundred or so yards into no man's land, the 2nd R.S.F. were enfiladed by machine gun fire from the east and fired on by rifles stationed in 'Bayonet Trench' the machine guns were assumed to be devastated by the artillery barrage. Some parties of the Manchesters entered 'Bayonet' but could not sustain themselves:[1]

> Shortly afterwards the O.C. started to reorganise his battn. in the front line from which they had begun the attack, a somewhat difficult task due to the narrowness of the trenches & the confusion of Units & Coys. to say nothing of the enemy's barrage fire.

> The 17th Mchrs. attacked in two waves each of two companies. At zero the first wave advanced in good order & at this part of the line the enemy immed. opened a very heavy M.G. fire on the right flank, at the same time sending up red rockets which were immediately followed by a heavy artillery barrage on our front line & support trenches. The 1st, 2nd & 3rd waves of their right flank were mown down as soon as they crossed the parapet & within 50 yds of our own front line by enfilade M.G. fire & C.S.M. Ham who went over with the 3rd wave returned on his own initiative & stopped the 4th wave ordering them to remain in our front line trenches as a garrison in case the enemy counter-attacked. The left flank also came under heavy M.G. fire but pushed on & succeeded in occupying a shallow enemy trench about 100' to the front. There they were held up & all their officers being out of action the men joined up with the 2nd Beds Regt. on their left.

(McGowan, October 18th)

No one thought to hold back the 3rd and 4th waves which were attacking on the left and half right lead by Captain Sidebotham. They reached the enemy front line, but once the men had disappeared over the top, those back at the base knew little of them:

> Capt. Sidebotham was shot through the head while looking over the parados towards the enemy 2nd line & Lt. Dawson took command,

---

[1] *Military Operations 1916.* II p. 441.

216

entrenching & keeping in touch with the 2nd Beds. on the left. Fearing his R. flank was exposed he proceeded to patrol in that direction & was wounded in the foot. Lt. R. Jones advanced with a small party on Lt. Dawson's right & succeeded in pushing forward & establishing a line with a lewis gun on his left flank. He was at this point joined by an officer of 2nd Beds & an officer & a few men of the 18th Mchrs. All these officers were wounded & forced to retire. A party of the enemy at this time counter attacked from behind a clump of trees on our left, but were put out of action by our Lewis Gun.

Sniping was incessant from front & flanks also from the left & the right rear and all the officers being casualties the corporal in command ordered his men to fall back slowly which they did under cover of darkness in good order. *18th Mchrs* at zero this battn. less one company & 2 platoons left FACTORY TR & advanced in small columns covering the two battalion frontage. They encountered a very severe barrage immed. they left the trench but in spite of severe casualties they pushed forward in support of the 17th Mchrs.

At 5.45 p.m. the 16th Mchrs. were ordered to move up to the left of the sector to reinforce the 17th Mchrs. & was in position about 10 p.m. Our old line was then reorganised the remnants of the 2 R.S.F. & of the 18th Mchrs. held the right & Lt. Col. WALSH in command & the 17th & 16th Mchrs. the left, Lt. Col. KNOX in command.

The 18th K.L.R. was put at the disposal of G.O.C. 90th Bde. & placed in reserve in Flers trench, one company being used to carry up stores to the front line.

The above details were naturally obtained from front line survivors & not from observation from the rear & though not perhaps very accurate serve well to show what is the task in front of the attacking troops. This was the first attack our division had attempted in broad daylight & everything goes to prove that it was a mistake. Unless the artillery barrage is sufficiently strong & accurate to knock out every enemy M.G. a daylight advance is bound to prove disastrous, but when co-operating on a large scale with the French as was the case this time, *their word is law.* Watching the attack as I was from Bde Hd Qrs. (some 1,500 yds from the front line) all I could see through field glasses was a barrage of smoke from bursting shells through which isolated groups of men were staggering apparently to certain death.

(McGowan, October 18th)

In the mêlée, the acrid smoke and the noise of fire, McGowan's task of keeping open lines to the Battalion H.Q.'s and to the rear was herculean. After ordering his signallers who were packed like sardines to dig in at the Report Centre he ran into a barrage of gas shells. Knowing he should not linger, he nearly suffocated as he dashed through the fumes:

> Our new General is a peculiar man. He took it into his head to explore the front line the day after the battle & took Pemberton with him. From Pemberton's account it's a wonder either of them came back alive, for he wandered about across the open quite unconcerned. On Sunday morning not having myself seen the front line & also because I wished personally to see why it was so difficult to keep up commn. to the Rt. Sector now occupied by the 16th Mchrs. I set off to visit this Bn. Hdqrs. I found the trenches leading there battered to pieces & miles of cable lying at the bottom in a hopeless tangle, so ordered a completely new line to be run & carefully stapled to the floor of the trench. When I reached the 16th Hd. Qrs. I found them all huddled together in an extremely narrow open trench more demoralised than I have ever previously seen them. Four Officers including Megson had just been buried by a shell but were extracated without loss. It certainly wasn't a health resort & having seen what I wanted I made my way back to H.Q. thanking God that I was one of the H.Q. staff & that it wasn't my duty to hold such trenches.
>
> (McGowan, October 18th)

McGowan's eye witness account of the attack on October 12th was very factual. His narrative sent home was not embroidered with the terrible details of carnage, the cries of the wounded or the smell of the dead and decaying bodies of men and horses. Although he was not part of the assaulting troops, nevertheless his was dangerous work which he undertook with quiet conscientiousness and much courage. Although no tanks were used in their attack, two derelicts lay forlornly out of action by their H.Q. McGowan was surprised they looked so small.

> On the 13th (the day after the attack) there was a conference of Brigadiers at Carlton Trench & it was decided that the 89th Bde should be withdrawn to a rest camp W. of Montauban. They were not so badly hit as were the 90th but Gen. Lloyd thought we could stick it for a few days more & so as usual the spoilt children of the Division got the easy & the 90th the hard *apparently*.
>
> (McGowan, October 18th)

McGowan's anticipations did not materialise, as eventually the 89th relieved the 90th. In the change over he found the 89th Brigade mess not as companionable as theirs, the mess had been divided into 'A' and 'B' a necessary step because the bill of the 'A' mess the previous month had totalled £17. A large sum for impecunious young officers. But in the separation the two 'honourables' had turfed the juniors out of the only dug-out, while they sat down to a five course meal with the Staff Captain and Orderly Officers before retiring to rest in their spacious bunks. Not participating with their elders, the juniors had no means of knowing what was afoot.

It was a long weary tramp to the camp via Bazentin le Grand and the new Caterpillar Valley Railway. McGowan did not state the position of their camp but he described it as being to the rear of the original German front line: perhaps it was somewhere between Montauban and Mametz. After their efforts around Guedecourt their march exhuasted them, passing Bazentin le Grand Wood to their right, the ground fell to the south towards the deep chalky 'Caterpillar Valley' running between Longueval to Guillemont north west of Montauban. After the July fighting the valley was a land laid waste, the ground pitted with craters and dud shells of every kind all about. Although some road mending had taken place the way was choked with transport. Arriving at the camp at 3.30 a.m. they ate the cold food brought with them as the camp mess was not in a position to feed another mouth:

A more miserable rest billet than this I've never known. The weather turned wet & then bitterly cold. The erection of sheeting we first used for a mess became quite impossible fortunately an R.E. Coy. were erecting a number of wooden huts in the vicinity & we appropriated the first one finished as a mess, & by means of a red hot brazier we were able to keep reasonably warm. The signal office which consisted of a couple of sheets of corrugated iron over a trench with a wall of empty bomb boxes, also became impossible & I'd considerable difficulty in getting a tent to replace it. Apart from the actual discomfort the surroundings were so depressing. The camp itself was pitched on a shell-pocked patch just to the rear of the original German front line with remains of trenches & barbed wire to fall into & tear one's clothes against. After dark the whole vast quagmire was fit only for paddling in gum boots & nothing for miles around except mud stained soldiers, horses & motor lorries.

(McGowan, October 18th)

They were not required to go forward again as the whole Division was relieved by the fine and fresh 5th Australian Division on October 21st/23rd.

After waiting for the 16th Manchesters who had been left behind in reserve they departed from the camp by brigade column on October 22nd. It was a glorious morning for marching and glad they were to leave the battlefield.

But McGowan's mood was sombre. His usual optimism deserted him. He knew that their attack had been useless and many good men, among them his personal friends sacrificed unnecessarily. He begrudged the fact that now the division was no longer classed as 'A'. He knew it was not the bravery and quality of the infantry that led to their failure, that failure was due to the fact that the attack was made in broad daylight. Their division was sadly depleted after July and even now no leave was in prospect. He could forecast no end to it all. He was still a 2nd Lieutentant irked by the fact that others had been promoted around him, but was told that nothing could be done about it. Feeling very unsettled, he applied for a regular commission in the R.E's:

> The life of a regular R.E. Officer appeals to me, it's interesting, permits of travel & the possibility of living well within one's income & unless the war ends pretty soon I shall be little use to anyone at my old job & shall find it practically impossible to settle down to the brain-fag of a technical engineer or the humdrum strain of a commercial man.
>
> (McGowan, October 18th)

This bitterness increased on lamenting the small number left in his brigade. He noted that out of the thirty two officers present with each battalion eleven months before, fourteen now remained. The majority had been killed or wounded together with a large number of junior officers who had joined as reinforcements:

> Its a peculiarly true fact that in the army or for that matter in any business it's not the man with brains that necessarily gets on. No, if a man's sufficient of an aristocrat he'll rise to high rank whatever his interllectual (sic.) capabilities & whether he works or not & even if a man isn't an aristocrat if he's willing to kow-tow sufficiently to those above him he'll get on, but its not these two types that are running our active army at present. They are mostly the figureheads with hard working, clear thinking, subordinates who make the wheels go around. Then when it comes to the question of medals or awards its the figureheads who get them. Instance the fact that although the French presented 3 Legion of Honours to our Army for our part in the Frise attack of Feb 28th not one reached the 90th Bde. who were next to the French the whole time, a fact which greatly surprised the French General at whose instigation they were sent. Most probably they were distributed at G.H.Q. Also instance the fact that the only officer award

that came to this brigade for the taking of MONTAUBAN was one D.S.O. Of course for any particularly fine individual act gets it's due reward providing the individual lives & someone else lives to tell the tale, but for consistent good work few awards are granted in front of Divisional Head Quarters.

(McGowan, October 18th)

(In fact McGowan had been deservedly mentioned in despatches for his work in July).

Heald wrote on June 4th 1918 that everyone in High Command got a C.M.G. as regular as clockwork and he thought his regiment had been treated very badly in the matter of honours. He had been told that his name had been sent in for a Military Cross after the Somme, but nothing had come of it. The only thing they had received was Major Churton's D.S.O. Hodgkin's comments on medals only served to add to the discontent:

I see there is to be a 1914−15 Star, of the same design and colour of ribbon as the 1914 Star. What a brain must have conceived this! Neither the Old Army, nor the Territorial & New Armies will be pleased at being mistaken for one another.

(Hodgkin, November 22nd 1918)

At length when the long shadows of winter darkened the battlefields, the conflagrations of the Somme damped down. Joffre's proposed plan for the future with the agreement of Haig was simple. A continuation of the same tactics in the following February with a concession only to the severest weather. But on December 27th Joffre being relieved from his command, the armies were temporarily reprieved from the putrid mud.

Back home, the euphoric mood was changing. In 1914 Edmund Gosse had written to Lord Spencer: 'If we had ten sons we would give them all'.[1] By 1916 he and his wife lived in a constant anguish of anxiety about their only son Philip. But theatre lights continued to twinkle with hectic gaiety and Colonel à Court Repington the military writer for the Northcliffe Press wrote of the countless high life parties and aristocratic country house weekends he attended, commenting on the women he met who wore opulent clothes. On July 17th 1917 he observed:

'The only visible signs of war are that the men now wear usually short coats and black ties in the evening, that dinners are shorter and that servants are fewer and less good. There is a want of taxis and of petrol

---

[1] Ann Thwaite, *Edmund Gosse a Literary Landscape*, 1849−1928 O.U.P. 1983, p. 462.

and sugar in some places is rather scarce. The working classes are well paid and the food is abundant if dear. There is the minimum of privation and no general suffering from the war. The greatest sufferers are the middle classes, especially the humble gentlewomen with fixed incomes and those who have lost husbands and sons'.[1]

On October 23rd he looked in on Mrs Keppel and found her looking very well after her cure at Aix.[2]

When they returned on leave, the tommies who were given one shilling a day found that the ammunition workers received high wages spending their money lavishly. As inflation was mounting steadily (in 1918 the £1 was worth 8/3d) soldiers and their families suffered considerably.

Overshadowing the country were the unending pages of printed casualty lists which no newspaper propaganda could obliterate. Hardly a household on the land remained untouched; Britain was changing into a place where the streets were filled with old men, women, children and the walking wounded.

---

[1] Repington II, p. 34.
[2] Mrs George Keppel, mistress of King Edward VII.

CHAPTER 14

THE HINDENBURG LINE

In the aftermath of 1916, the armies in their water logged trenches resigned themselves once more to the wintry duties of suicidal raids and nocturnal patrols in the iced east winds. As the dark nights closed in, mad gusts tugged on the barbed wire, the burial parties with more leisure now, carved out the graves for their fallen comrades, their hands shrivelled in the frost. In the last month of the year Heald wrote: 'Our fellows are stiff with cold' and observed the men up to their knees in mud while the first snow flakes started to fall. The German trenches were as bad, some had extended, melting into large lakes, untenable and abandoned.

Working on the Divisional Staff, Heald enjoyed a well run mess. At H.Q. the French Liaison officer had engaged one of his countrymen to cook so they ate in fine fashion, Heald only had the doubt that the food was inclined to be too greasy and that he would get fat.

During that winter, both sides of the line indulged in spasmodic bombardments; on Christmas day the 56th Division kept up a slow one to stop the Hun fraternising. Never liking inaction, Heald could not keep away from the trenches. He had endured them for so long that he found it almost impossible to sit in a rear H.Q. without ascertaining for himself what was the reality for the forward battalions:

We attempted a small raid on the German trenches but the wire was not properly cut and the trench was thickly manned.

In the evening I went out and had a look at the posts we have established in the German lines. It was quite like old times crawling about with a revolver. The mud is very bad. However all was quiet.

(Heald, January 19th 1917)

I have had to stay in all day as the other Staff Officers are away. One of the Portuguese officers has been attached to me to learn intelligence work. He had to come over in mufti as he travelled through Spain, a neutral country. The Portuguese troops will come by sea. This officer is rather fat and swarthy and speaks no English so he has an interpreter with him. He is staying a week.

(Heald, January 20th)

Two months later when released on leave, he relaxed on the golf course with his friends and was entertained that week at one or two private dances.

Never missing a chance of a show he attended a mateneé of 'Zig Zag' at the Hippodrome featuring George Roby, and the same evening he saw a fine performance of 'Misleading Lady' at the Playhouse with the glamourous Diana Cooper, Weedon Grossmith and Malcolm Cherry in the leads. George Roby had not seemed at his best, probably he was free wheeling during the afternoon performance. Heald realised that he was quite sorry to leave home this time. Perhaps the grim compulsive absorption with the front which he shared with so many others was momentarily fading. In any case his position as a temporary Staff Officer did not make such a contrast between home and the misery of life in a trench.

With its ever brightening green, the cold spring of 1917 heralded the beginning of a fresh onslaught. Reluctant to face another 'Somme', before the enemy could strike again the Germans decided to make a strategic withdrawal to the prepared semi permanent fortified 'Hindenburg Line'. On February 4th the Kaiser had signed harsh instructions (called by a code name 'Alberich' the malicious dwarf of the Nibelung Saga) that the whole zone of retreat was to be devastated. Every tree was to be felled, all inhabitants to be removed and the wells filled up or polluted. The execution of these orders commenced on March 9th and the German Army was ordered not to engage the enemy while retreating.

McGowan's Brigade had been training in front of Arras during the winter months. On marching up the Arras road from the cobbled streets of Doullens during March he saw a complete scene of destruction in the path of the retiring enemy. Train and tramway lines were dismantled and all the cross roads had been mined.

In a strategic move further forward, the H.Q. of the 56th Division was now located in a château at Beaumetz les Loges. Without a pane of glass in the windows they shivered and shook in the cold March wind which blew sharp gusts of rain through the high empty rooms. It was the coldest place Heald had ever been in:

A very interesting day. Brooks our G.S.O.2. and I went round our new trenches which are those taken from the Germans. They have destroyed absolutely everything and partially filled in their trenches. They have blown up all their dugouts and every house still standing in Beaumetz. Two dugouts they had not time to destroy are fine examples of their thoroughness in work. One has a complete suite of rooms under the first floor. It is like a house in the earth. They have not retired far here. The line to which the main retirement has been made joins their old line at Arras, so we are more or less sitting in their old front line system. They are in a tremendously strong position on high ground and very well wired in. We shall find it a tough nut to crack. We have got any amount

of heavy artillery and already the Bosche is having a very unpleasant
time. His dugouts are wonderfully good though and very deep. It must
be very nice further south to have got away from the absolutely
devastated country. He had burned all the villages behind him in his
retreat so we shan't get good billets.

(Heald, March 21st)

After the flurries of sudden Spring snow the new forward trenches were
filthy and appallingly muddy. In his efforts to reconnoitre them thoroughly,
Heald dodged from bank to bank over the open ground, at times crawling on
his stomach to dodge the snipers and shells fired by the enemy who now
looked down on them from a nearby hill. This dreary performance lasted the
whole day while wearily he realised he had not brought anything to eat.
When eventually he gained the trenches his foot sank in about a yard each
step; but the contrary rain which he had relied on to screen his return
stopped, and the sun shone brightly down lighting up his way over the open.

In spite of knowing the strength of the new German positions, General
Nivelle (the French successor to General Joffre) insisted that the British
should carry out the proposed attack at Arras with increased forces.[1]

Accordingly, the engagements east of Arras from April 9th to May 15th
were fought by the British attacking the 'Hindenburg Line' now a deep
position of many strongly defended series of trenches. Trenches and dugouts
constructed thoroughly in the ways to which the Germans were so well
accustomed. All had wide strong belts of wire on steel angle iron pickets
about two feet apart forming formidable obstacles. Many of the trenches were
more than twelve feet wide at the top and interspersed with numbers of
fortified strong points.

The 56th Division (in VII Corps, under General Snow) lay to the extreme
right or south of General Allenby's Third Army which was destined for the
main role in the British attack. If Allenby could have broken through the old
defences to the north (at the limit of the Hindenburg line) he might have
achieved success in the flank and in the rear. But by this time the Germans
had almost completed an extended switch line, some five miles behind the
front system through Drocourt, intending to cover the rear of the old
defences north of Arras.

Heald had started a fearful chest cold, he could not throw it off. The
frontage allotted to the 56th Division was to the north west of Neuville
Vitasse, the 167th Brigade positioned to the right and the 168th to the left.

---

[1] J.E. Edmonds, *A Short History of World War I*, p. 216. For the strategy of the battles of Arras see pp. 227–238.

The anticipated attack had been delayed for twenty four hours and though he knew the forthcoming battle was at hand, Heald felt very pessimistic of its outcome. For a week before, the weather had been wintry, three inches of snow had fallen and as usual it seemed to him at Divisional H.Q. that little time had been allotted for proper reflection over the preparations. He was only thankful that for once he was not caught up in the midst of the customary preliminary bombardment.

On April 8th the H.Q. took up its position for the battle. Situated in a series of soaking wet rooms in a deep mined dugout thirty feet below ground there was an all pervading dank odour. Hating the atmosphere, Heald disliked the claustrophobic place intensely. Positioned just behind them, a battery of 8 inch howitzers nearly blew them out as they belched forth their shells. They were almost worse than the German guns. Heald did not stay there long, as he was ordered up to a forward O.P. as a liaison officer for Divisional H.Q. where he could report on the engagements. Close to the O.P. he had a little dugout contructed twelve feet underground, proof against anything except an 8 inch shell. He hoped against hope that this attack would succeed, never would he have such a wonderful view point again:

I started at 4 a.m. before it was light so as to reach my position before the Hun started shelling the tracks. The main attack started at 5.30 a.m. but we did not start until 7.45 as the other Divisions had to catch up to us. The day started with rain but was fine at zero hour. i.e. the time we started. I had a splendid view being only about 400 yards away. We had cut the barbed wire with artillery beforehand and attacked under cover of a creeping barrage, i.e. a line of bursting shells which moves in front of the waves of assaulting troops. Tanks also accompanied the leading troops and got over the front line trenches all right. Then most of them broke down. There was a big hill just over our left which our guns simply plastered with shells. We captured our first objective very easily and our share was to capture the village of Neuville Vitasse. The Hun did not put up much of a fight and surrendered freely. Then after a pause of four hours during which the artillery was brought up closer we attacked again and took another line of trenches. I went up into the German trenches to get a better view. They had been very much destroyed by shellfire. I could see very distinctly. It was very funny to see people wandering about over the open after trench warfare when no-one ever moved. A shell came and hit the entrance to my dugout knocking out five men. I had been lying on the very spot a moment before but had just gone down into the dugout. Lucky escape. The entrance to the dugout was blocked, but they soon dug it out.

We had very few casualties during the day and took more prisoners than casualties — about 700 in this Division. It was a very successful day for the British Army.

(Heald, April 9th)

Later on April 10th, the battle reports became discouraging. At intervals it was snowing heavily and the ground was freezing hard. Rumour had it that there had been reports of a cavalry attack further north and several further German trenches had been taken.

For a few wonderful hours on April 9th there had been the heartening gleam of success; the division captured Neuville Vitasse while the Cheshires valiantly patched up the wrecked communications. But on April 11th, in freezing winds and snow showers, the troops who had been denied the opportunity of surprise so essential for this action, found the enemy was now in readiness to receive them in their prepared positions. Though the 169th Brigade gallantly conquered the bastions of Heninel and Wancourt Tower, once more the gleam faded and the engagements soon degenerated into fruitless assaults with the resulting sacrificial casualties:

I went out early this morning to make a reconnaissance of our position, and to find out where the enemy were. We were on the high ground beyond Heninal I found our outposts in shell holes. It was a perfect morning a bit misty so I went ahead to reconnoitre. I found a line of trenches that had been dug by the Bosche and deserted by him. When I got further I saw them across the valley digging a new line of trenches and holding it quite strongly. I could not get nearer as they started sniping at me. I went back and got our outposts forward into the line of trenches I had found. Just as I had finished and was going away I felt a blow on my buttock. I wasn't sure whether I had been hit or not. I walked on back to battalion H.Q. and told the Colonel of that regiment what I had done. Then on looking again and feeling blood I found a bullet had gone right through my right buttock. I had bound it up and with the help of a couple of men managed to walk to the dressing station. Spent the night in the hospital train.

(Heald April 13th)

Good night. Leg a bit stiff but does not hurt. We have meandered to Abbeville. I am in bed in hospital. The fellow next to me has got a hole in his back as big as my fist. I am fed up with staying in bed.

(Heald, April 14th)

By 1917 the transportation of the wounded to England was well organised. Hospital trains (such as one of eight coaches built by the Great Eastern Railway and donated by the U.K. Flour Millers Association) were well sprung and contained operating theatres, dispensaries, kitchens, staff rooms, stores and washing facilities. The long heavy khaki coaches each had a central corridor flanked by hospital beds on racks which could be lifted out of the train on stretchers. Each coach had a small kitchen with water and hot drinks. Doctors and nurses were in constant attendance, and all ranks among the sick and wounded attested to the subtle spirit of sweet gentleness which seemed to permeate the strict discipline of the nurses and Red Cross workers. Blankets and bed linen used by ambulances in England were washed and ironed free by local laundries as well as by the servants in private houses near hospital depots. Because many drugs had beeen manufactured in Germany before the war, the British Pharmaceutical Society speedily had to reorganise supplies from elsewhere.

Happy to have received a 'Blighty one' at last, Heald found himself with other wounded on a very slow boat across the channel. His wound, easily healed, was a desirable passport from the battlefield. Now with the increasing fear of 'U-boats' they all had to wear life jackets, the vessel being escorted by two destroyers in complete darkness. In London he was taken to the comfort of the Samuelson, a private hospital at 58 Grosvenor Street where in a ward with five others who were very cheery, he had a kind and very pretty Irish nurse. Soon he'd be out of bed.

But April 20th simply records: 'Got pneumonia'. The privations he had endured had undermined his resistance and he was not fit to return to the front for a further four months. His convalescence was made pleasurable by a sojourn of five weeks in May and June at the home of Lord Hambledon at Moretonhampstead on the edge of Dartmoor. Apart from owning W.H. Smith & Co Lord Hambledon (1868–1928) was a generous philanthropist, one of whose interests lay in the administration of voluntary hospitals. The house designed by Lutyens lay in a lovely position in large grounds where the fourteen officers who were recouperating could fish and play tennis. There was no golf course.

Meanwhile on April 9th McGowan's Brigade had attacked the Hindenburg Line in front of Telegraph Hill in the Ficheux area. Like the others at first they had success and by 1.00 p.m. they saw that Neuville Vitasse was in their hands. Despite the winter weather they all enjoyed the exhilarating movement forward, it was a complete novelty to be chasing a retreating enemy. For this taxing work, commanding the Brigade Signals during the ceaseless changes in the disposition of mobile units, McGowan was mentioned once more in despatches.

However the later operations of April 22nd/23rd after the enemy had consolidated were by far the worst experience McGowan had so far encountered. His division was involved in three frontal attacks in twenty four hours, dusk, dawn and dusk again. Half it's strength having disappeared once again, there was a complete withdrawal. For this engagement the 90th Brigade received no honours. The attack had been judged a failure:

> For several hours on the night of April 22nd, the old German dugout in which our signal office was located was the scene of considerable activity and contained a glorious bag for the enemy had the front line broken. The G.O.C. 30th Div. (General Shea), his G.S.O. 2 (Capt. Maxwell) General Morgan 21st Bde., General Stanley (89th Bde), Gen. Lloyd (90th Bde), their three Bde. Majors, Two Staff Captains, and two Artillery liaison officers. The dugout was situated at the top of a steep slope leading to the village of Heninal. Sometime after midnight there was a wild report from Corps that the Boche had broken through the 33rd Div. front, and were pouring down the hill towards Heninal. Our General Lloyd, being at a loss for something to do, strolled out with an orderly and a torch (it was pitch black night). He was back almost before he was missed, to report no signs of life either German or British in what was left of the village. It was so much shelled that our troops religiously avoided it, except to sneak in for water at the dawn.
>
> (Memoirs of George McGowan, p. 53)

After continuous privations, McGowan's health had been seriously weakened. Struck down by a bad attack of hepatitis, in August of that year he was sent to No. 7 base hospital at Dieppe overlooking the harbour. From his window, as he watched the leave boats coming and going to England he realised that he was now the last of the original members of the mess of his beloved 90th Brigade. A week later he was transferred to the comfortable Lady Michelin Rest Home for Officers near by:

> It was here I met the popular actress Zena Dare, a private guest of Lady Michelin, who asked me if I would partner Zena in a mixed foursome on the tennis court. I must confess it was rather indifferent tennis. After a restful month at this delightful hospital, I was fighting fit again, but unfortunately had lost my brigade signal section, as Lieut. Wright of the 2nd R.S.F. who took my place had been confirmed as B.S.O. It was a big disappointment, but I'd missed the slaughter at Passchendaele, which in my reduced state of health I might not have survived.
>
> (Memoirs of George McGowan, p. 53)

CHAPTER 15

CAMBRAI

On his return to the western front on August 19th Heald sailed down the Solent from Southampton. It was a lovely evening with rather a high wind. He felt lucky to have got a good boat and that night he turned in early sharing his cabin with an Australian returning from leave:

> Arrived Havre about 3 a.m. but did not disembark until 8. Slept well. Spent day at rest camp. Beastly place. Obtained pass out and went and watched all Havre bathe. It was Sunday, mixed bathing. Apparently the whole family takes a tent and spends the day on the beach. Madame skipping about in the water as gaily as her youngest. Bathing costumes not smart. Had dinner at very French place. Quite good.
>
> Another lovely day. Went to Rouen by boat up the Seine. The scenery is gorgeous and the French populace still extraordinarily enthusiastic. Everybody turns out and waves flags, handkerchiefs etc. It must be the chief event of the day to come and watch the troopship pass. Our men like it. Vive l'Entente Cordiale. We landed about 5 p.m. I was posted to 5th Cheshires so that is all right. The first step towards getting back to the Division. Had tea at British Officers Club. They have English waitresses there, the W.A.A.C. They look very smart too. Went to No. 4 I.B.D. A huge camp from where drafts are sent to the front. I hope I shall not be here long.
>
> (Heald, August 20th & 21st)

After eleven days of inaction he wrote: 'Am going up the line tomorrow, thank goodness. Had a celebration dinner in Rouen'. With a large new draft of Welsh troops under his charge he entrained for the south, thankful not to be sent to Ypres as he had feared. There were only five to a carriage this time.

The battalion was resting in tents near Haplincourt and gave Heald a great welcome on his return. They had been caught up in a slough of despond in a night assault on Glencorse Copse and Polygon Wood on August 16th in an attack at 'Third Ypres'. The unseasonable August rains pouring down on the devastated intricate drainage system of Flanders marsh land had rendered the ground impossible for pioneer work. They told Heald that the mud was so tenacious and deep that movement was almost impossible. During the night the wiring parties, continually shelled, had suffered many killed and wounded and those who remained returned exhausted in the early morning. Two days later the depleted 56th Division had been withdrawn.

Like McGowan, Heald was supremely fortunate to have escaped the horrendous tragedy of 'Third Ypres', the closing phases of which between October 12th and November 10th are known by the abhorrent name of 'Passchendaele'. In spite of the division's grisly ordeal in August, it appeared that they did not realise the true nature of that terrible campaign. On Tuesday November 6th Heald only briefly mentioned success: 'We have made a successful push at Ypres and taken Passchendaele'. His entry might have echoed that of Haig written on the same day in Paris when the British Commander had taken the opportunity of calling on Joffre. Having contrasted Joffre's reduced living conditions compared with the customary grand châteaux he inhabited while commanding the French Armies, Haig merely stated: 'The operations were completely successful'... 'Today was a very important success'.[1] Although Passchendaele ridge had at last been taken on November 6th by the Canadians brought from Lens, it was a hollow victory for the hundreds of thousands of dead, and the drowning wounded whose trifling gains had been grieviously impaired by the enemy's increasing use of mustard gas.

At 169 Brigade H.Q., Heald still remained without a permanent job. He was irked that though he had been recommended as a G.S.O. III the previous January he had been passed over because he had been wounded. Still acting as a Liason Officer he accompanied Brigadier General E.S.D.E Coke in trench inspections. He knew the Brigadier General as he had accompanied him on various courses and had been at school with his brother. During September and October Heald was frequently in the front line; in spite of the divisional strength being so much depleted after Ypres, dangerous random patrols with ceaseless raiding parties were the order of the day:

> Went up to the trenches — had a very narrow escape. A piece of shell missed my head by about 2 inches and destroyed the notebook I had in my hand.
>
> (Heald, September 12th)

> Spent afternoon in an observation post. It was very interesting. On the enemy side of course all the villages are intact and the country looks lovely. On ours all devastated. On a clear day you can almost read the time on Cambrai church tower. The Boche must be living very comfortably now whilst we are in shantys.
>
> (Heald, September 20th)

> Went out tonight about six hundred yards in front of our trenches to tape out some barbed wire. It was raining very hard and the night so

---

[1] Blake, op cit. p. 264.

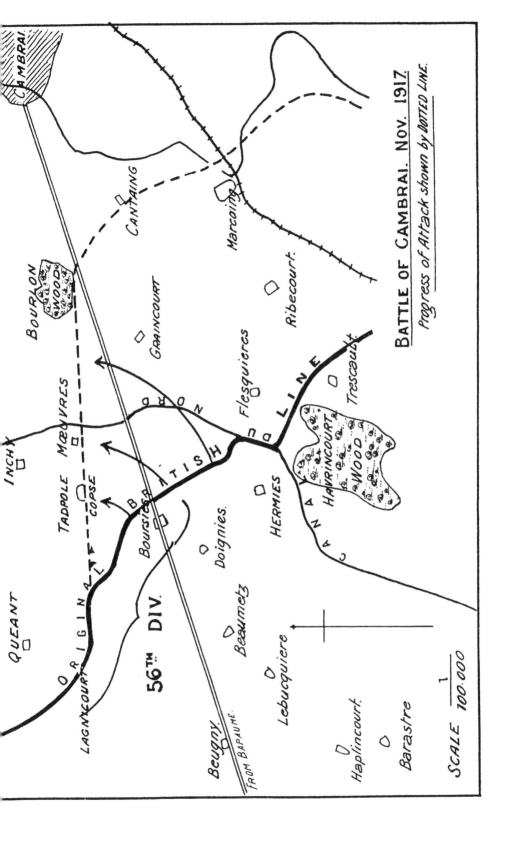

BATTLE OF CAMBRAI. NOV. 1917.

Progress of Attack shown by DOTTED LINE.

SCALE $\frac{1}{100.000}$

dark one could not see twenty yards. I had to measure the distance to make sure I was in the right place. When we were out there a raid started to our left. The Boche got alarmed and shelled us a bit but did no harm. I finished the work satisfactorily but got covered in mud wet through and my clothes torn. Was glad to get back as I was dead tired.

(Heald, October 8th)

A company of Cheshires did the wiring. I went up and saw everything was all right. It was completed throughout but the Brigade on our left did not link up with us having taped their line wrong in the dark.

(Heald, October 9th)

In many ways, the countryside to the south west of Cambrai resembled Salisbury Plain, being rolling and open downland composed of sand and chalk. It had remained uncultivated for two years and was now covered with a sparse growth of greyish grass. To the left lay the dominating protuberance of Bourlon Wood west of Cambrai. Adjoining the wood, Bourlon village and park were situated to the north west of it.

In spite of every effort to maintain secrecy by G.H.Q., as October lengthened it became increasingly evident that something was brewing. Reconnaissance planes had been kept to a minimum but Heald saw several R.F.C. 'dog fights':

There was a most exciting aeroplane fight over us this afternoon, between a British and a German aeroplane. They circled round each other for some time firing their machine guns. Suddenly the British seemed to turn over and come down in a spinning nosedive. We all thought he was done when just before reaching the ground he recovered and skimmed along about twenty feet up. The Boche followed him down to finish him off so we all got rifles and fired at the Boche which made him sheer off and our fellow managed to land safely. It seems that our man's gun jammed so he pretended to fall to deceive the enemy then he flew very low so that the Boche could not follow because of our fire. Very clever of him. He saved his life in that way. Went up the line at night to tape out a new trench in front of our lines.

(Heald, September 24th)

Soon showers of paper descended on the office and three American officers arrived for instruction; there was a devil of a lot of work to do. Heald rather liked being with the Americans whom he came across from time to time on the Staff:

234

We have got an American General staying with us. He is very old. He said before he came out he thought he knew the last word about war but now realises that he had got to learn all over again. There is one good point about these Americans they are very willing to learn and do not adopt the attitude that they have come to finish the war.

(Heald, January 6th, 1918)

Bad news was coming through from Italy where the Austrians and Germans had won a decisive victory at Caporetto on October 24th. The battle had been a rout and Heald thought it about time the Italians stopped running.

Much to his disgust, he was transferred back to Divisional H.Q. and still on a temporary basis. He hated being out of touch with his men:

The new G.S.O III arrived tonight. He seems a very nice chap. Apparently the Division were not consulted at all. It seems very hard lines that I missed my job last July and am still left. It was rotten luck getting wounded. I took the Corps Commander round the trenches to view the ground in front from our best observation posts. He never eats any lunch so I was rather hungry when I got back.

(Heald, November 12th)

In the overcrowded office there were too many staff. Heald felt very tired of the war, it seemed unending. One morning he walked up to the front line in the fog to dissipate his ill humour, and still yearning for exercise in the afternoon he went riding: 'I borrowed a horse which was a wild devil. It nearly got away with me once or twice. My arms feel as though they had been pulled out of their sockets'.

Before the battle known as 'Cambrai' began, it was an anxious time for General Sir Julian Byng now commanding the Third Army. Absolute secrecy was necessary for his system of attack which was a novel one. For once there was to be no long preliminary bombardment. Instead, five divisions of over three hundred tanks would cross the plain, this time on ground suitable for their capabilities. (It was a situation advocated by E.W. Swinton in the first instance). A thousand guns were to fire at zero hour on the enemy line while the infantry were to follow up the tanks to attack the Germans in a concentrated area. It was necessary for the artillery to fire with great precision so that the tank advance was not endangered.

At H.Q. on November 18th, Heald knew for sure that the battle would start two days later and that he had been designated as 'the eyes' of the Division. Accordingly he searched round the front line to the left for the best vantage point. The next day he wrote that the Boche had got wind of the attack, some

British prisoners apprehended in a trench raid had divulged some information with the result that the enemy had rustled up some machine gun reserves. But Heald did not think much harm was done.

On November 20th the early morning was cold and misty, many of the waiting troops in the open had been shivering in their blankets from 3.30 a.m.:

> "Z" day. A great day. I arose at 3.30 a.m. and went to a position in the front line from where I could see. The enemy evidently had a suspicion of the attack because he shelled heavily just before dawn. The attack started at 6.20 a.m. and went splendidly from the start. We used tanks instead of the usual artillery preparation and the enemy surrendered directly they saw them coming. I saw the whole show. Once I thought the enemy were counter attacking but it was only a long line of Boches coming out to surrender. Our cavalry have gone through and I hope are creating havoc in the rear. During the afternoon I walked across to inspect the Boche trenches — the famous Hindenburg line. I took a prisoner — a wounded Boche came and surrendered to me. The advance is being continued tomorrow. I expect we shall take Cambrai. It is raining and one can't see anything now. I got back about 6.30 feeling very tired. Apparently the Division was very pleased with the information I sent them.
>
> (Heald, November 20th)

Led by General Hugh Elles the commander of the Tank Corps in person, the initial tactics were brilliantly successful. Each tank carried on its nose one fascine made of about seventy five bundles of strongly compressed brushwood tightly bound by heavy chains.[1] In intricate manoeuvres each fascine was released with precision into the wide trenches of the Hindenburg lines, enabling the following tank to cross. Every detail of tank formations had been carefully prepared. As they crushed down the wire and silenced enemy machine guns the Germans fled in panic.

Positioned to the north of the Bapaume Road early on November 20th the 56th Division had carried out a feint using twelve full sized dummy tanks with dummy figures fashioned by the brigades amid an extensive smoke screen. Great ingenuity was used in the practise of drawing enemy fire by these convincing canvas dummies, and this make believe scheme caused considerable amusement. (About two hundred and fifty figures were deployed by each brigade). The silhouettes placed in irregular lines were manipulated by wires and tricked the Germans through the film of smoke at a few hundred yards distance. A motor bicycle in the front line trench was used

---

[1] C & A. Williams Ellis, op. cit., pp. 103, 104.

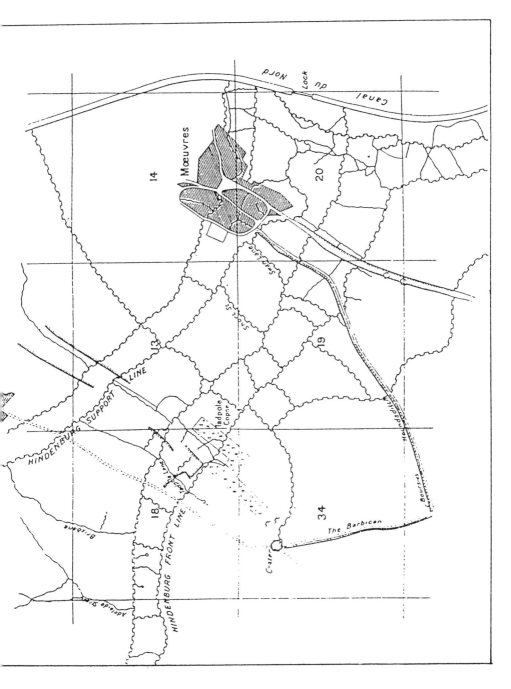

LOCAL MAP. FRONT OF THE DIVISION AT CAMBRAI 1917.

to imitate the noise of a tank. The division faced Tadpole Copse; Bourlon Wood lay behind the second enemy lines to the east:

> Again acted as forward observer for the Division. Visibility was very bad could not see very much. Our job was to work up the German front trenches to widen the gap. It is always a very slow costly job to bomb up trenches. We made about 1000 yards and took 79 prisoners. I went forward almost up to the captured position but still could not see much. The main attack is apparently held up and I don't think we shall get Cambrai now as the Germans are rushing troops up.
>
> (Heald, November 22nd)

The British captured Bourlon Wood a very important position on high ground. I expect we shall settle down and consolidate now. Our cavalry have not been in action at all. I think they have proved a failure. Probably their commanders are too old and have lost their initiative. The cavalry only block up the roads and are more trouble that they are worth.

(Heald, November 23rd)

CAVALRY CORPS HORSE SHOW.

Before the rain!

Darkness had closed in early on November 23rd, sunset being at 4.30 p.m. it was very cold and the intermittent gusts of heavy rain added to the general discomfort. The reasons for the cavalry delay seem varied and obscurely confused. In any case, was it wise to order up bodies of horse to jostle through the two confined narrow bridges over the Canal de l'Escaut in order to confront machine guns and tangled barbed wire? Some squadrons acted with utmost bravery, but as Heald said they cluttered up the roads.

After their remarkable beginning, the tank crews boxed up for hours within the confines of their hot and crowded machines had become exhausted. There were no further vehicles in reserve. Similarly the infantry (carrying a load of 72 lbs) were pressed to the limit of endurance. After the shock of surprise on November 20th, the Germans were increasingly gathering their forces for defence:

> Our division have done very well and have worked up the German front line to Tadpole Copse by bombing. This means we have taken the German's first system on a front of a mile. It is rather an exposed position. The enemy counter-attacked and cut off two companies of London Scottish. But we later retook the ground. The Germans behaved very badly towards our prisoners. They would not dress their wounds but left them to die.
>
> (Heald, November 24th)

An eye witness, Private Tom Sharp of the 5th Cheshires who was getting a meal going on four cookers in a nearby copse, recounted how terrible it was to see so many wounded of the London Scottish on their left fighting their way back. Sharp described Bourlon Wood as a thick dense place, riddled with underground passages, where the Germans when they allowed the London Scottish to enter it had sealed off all exits, and subsequently the companies from the rear. In the shelling, Sharp's cookers where blown to smithereens so there was nothing left to eat but 'hard tack'.[1]

The following day, Heald went up to Tadpole Copse to see the position for himself. The copse seemed a long way from their lines and he thought that all at once the rest of the men would be cut off. Crawling around he spied the captured German trenches which were well constructed with many deep dug-outs. On the following day the enemy strongly counter attacked the copse but the London Rangers who have relieved the London Scottish, bravely resisted in driving them off. Two days later Heald returned, but by now the Boche were ceaselessly shelling the place and the big crumps fairly made him jump out of his skin. In the flickering glare of the rumbling and bumping bombardment the trenches were rapidly disintegrating, their crumbling walls caving in on the dead and wounded:

> The enemy attacked in force this morning at 10 a.m. from Tadpole Copse to Bourlon Wood. He employed about five Divisions. After very severe fighting he was repulsed but he captured our front line, i.e. a portion of his old 1st system. He did not drive us out nor break through.
>
> Down South at the other end of the salient formed by our attack on the 20th he apparently broke through to a depth of 4 miles and the cavalry had to be thrown in to stop the gap.
>
> (Heald, November 30th)

---

[1] Letter from Tom Sharp to the Author, July 15th 1989.

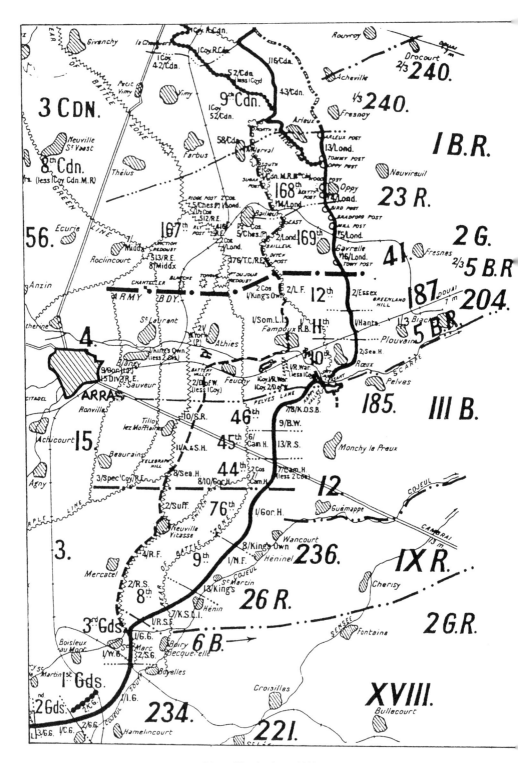

Line of Battle, Arras 1918.

After he had undergone a further heavy bombardment on December 1st in Tadpole Copse, two days later Heald slowly dragged back with the remains of the division and finally managed to climb into a cattle truck with one of the battalions. After the attack, they had plenty of rations to share around as divisional casualties stood at around one thousand six hundred and twenty. The winter weather becoming ever colder, caused their feet to freeze in their wet boots.

As November drew to its close, it had become obvious to him that the heavy fighting had become increasingly confused. In the high winds, with heavy rain occasionally turning into snow, the looked for capture of Bourlon Wood, (considered by the Generals to be of such importance) was a task far beyond the weary men who had no back up of reserves. The organised enemy counter attack of November 30th gaining hundreds of prisoners and guns, once more shocked the waiting people back at home who had so joyfully rung the bells for a victory on November 21st.

CHAPTER 16

ARRAS

At the beginning of December 1917 the 56th Division was transferred to the north of Arras to a quiet place on Vimy Ridge. From time to time Arras had been badly shelled and now few of the inhabitants lived there. It seemed to Heald like a city of the dead. Lining the square of the Place des Héroes only façades remained of the quaint tall old houses with their distinctive gabled roofs, while jutting out from the débris lay the ruins of the Hotel de Ville and belfry (burnt down in October 1914). From time to time during British occupation, military bands livened up the spacious 'Grand Place' with popular tunes. Four months later, Heald found himself well situated in a narrow side street:

> We moved in to a fine house — of course unoccupied by its owner. It is funny how the French like imitation things. The house is supposed to be decorated with oak panels and beams stained dark which is rather heavy. On examination it is all mainly plaster painted over. What look like solid mahogany pillars can be pushed about with one hand. They are hollow. I have got a very nice bedroom. We shall be extremely comfortable unless a shell hits the house.
>
> (Heald, April 24th 1918)

Once more it was Christmas, now the third that Heald had spent around the trenches. Seasonable snow, they could have well forgone, fell heavily as the customary Christmas orders came through to shell the enemy to prevent him fraternising. The yearly feast in 1917 was thought only reasonable, though the ration pudding was pronounced 'very good'.

For the first month or two of 1918, Heald's life with the staff grew more comfortable, although his office at Villers Château was very cold like all French châteaux in war time. In spite of its proximity to the front the family still occupied their proud mansion:

> A Countess lives here too. Her little son Hubert came and had a long talk with me. He told me all about his horse, dog, sheep and rabbit and was not a bit shy. His age was six years. Quite a jolly little chap.

> I have got a bed here with a mattress. It is lovely. I can't get up in the mornings. 'G' Office used to be the library. It is in a stone turret and is

tiled which makes it cold but there is an open fire and one or two easy chairs so at times one can almost imagine one is at home.

(Heald, January 9th, 10th)

Heald found little work to do and apart from riding he taught the son of the house to drill after which he solemnly stood on guard with the sentry. Two weeks later and for no good reason he could think of, Heald was sent off quite suddenly to 1st Army H.Q. It seemed a very long way behind the lines:

It may mean a job but I am sorry to leave the Division. I loathe change and have lost my ambition to get on the Staff. I feel quite lost here. Everybody is either a General or a Colonel and the place is stiff with red tabs. However, I have got a very comfortable billet with a real bed and sheets. It's an ill wind that blows nobody any good.

(Heald, January 22nd)

Throughout his long life Heald loathed new places, he felt much happier in treading the same paths amongst familiar surroundings. He much preferred a job with responsibility where he could judge for himself. At Army H.Q. there was nothing to do except man the telephone. While he was there he was taken to visit the Portugese Corps who held the sector Quinque Rue to Picantin in front of Laventie. The Portugese had been allotted a quiet and waterlogged sector where it was thought there would be not much chance of an attack. The South African General, Smuts who visited the front at the end of January considered the Portugese very weak and the spirit of the troops far from good:[1]

Went with Major Neame V.C. (who used to be one of our Brigade Majors so I know him) to visit the Portuguese front. They are extraordinarily lazy and have not put out a strand of wire, their sentries do not appear to look out at all and no work was going on. Apparently, it is their officers who are so bad. Their one subject of conversation is women. I believe the men would be quite good under British officers but that unfortunately is impossible for political reasons. The British have arranged to close in behind the Portuguese if they are attacked.

(Heald, January 24th)

In the event, Heald only endured about two weeks at Army H.Q. and was sent back to Division with a good report. Perhaps he had been on probation, as on May 14th he was at long last promoted to be G.S.O. III.

---

[1] Edmonds. *Military Operations* 1918 (1) p. 40.

Meanwhile for the rest of February he resumed the endless dreary tours of the trenches in front of Bailleul, visiting the forward posts at Oppy and the strong points around Mill Post. Near the unfordable river Scarpe the trenches were swampy, knee deep in mud and conspicuously overlooked.

During March an attack was continuously expected in their sector. Heavy fighting was taking place in the south, the Germans, having transferred up to fifteen divisions to the west after the collapse of Russia, were gaining ground. Yet apart from mutual molestations the Arras area remained initially relatively quiet. On one of the forward O.P.'s Heald could almost read the time on the church tower of Douai situated away to the east in the Scarpe valley. He thought it unfair that the Germans should have cushy billets while they awaited them in draughty huts.

Eventually at 4 a.m. on March 28th the long expected attack on the divisional front was launched. Starting with an intense and terrible four and a half hour barrage of gas and high explosive it was followed by waves of grey coated enemy infantry advancing shoulder to shoulder. All the advanced posts Heald had been nurturing were wrecked in the bombardment. One survivor came out of Mill Post and reported that the trenches were blotted out. The Battalions of the 56th mowed down the wall of attackers as they advanced up the Scarpe valley but eventually (though managing somehow to hold part of the lines) had to yield some ground in heavy fighting. At some points in the attack during the following month, in their turn the Germans used tanks. Hodgkin had sketched a German tank at Villers Bretonneux.

It was fortunate that it had been Heald's turn for leave on March 19th, as all leave was stopped on the 20th. He did not return to the division until April 4th, so missed the worst of the fighting. On return he found the 56th holding their old positions which they had occupied by Arras in 1917. Early on April 9th he inspected the line:

> It was most unpleasant. Thick mist and the Boche throwing heavy stuff all over the place. He nearly got us once — one dropped on top of the trench in which we were. He is using a lot of gas shell too, we had to wear our masks for a bit. We managed to get as far as Battn. H.Q. on Telegraph Hill and the Boche put down a barrage on the front line so we came back again. We came back via some caves just outside Arras. They are wonderful and will hold thousands of men. We walked right into the centre of Arras through them. They have been cemented up and lit by electric light. The passage under the town is through a sewer. The air is quite good in most parts. The Boche has broken through the Portuguese up north. It is the limit. They were to have been relieved tonight too.
>
> (Heald, April 9th)

GERMAN TANK

Sketch of one used at VILLERS-BRETONNEUX on 24.4.18.

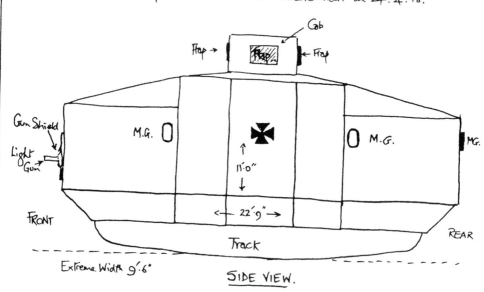

Cab

Flap → Flap ← Flap

Gun Shield

Light Gun

M.G. O

11'0"

22'9"

O M.G.

MG.

FRONT

Track

REAR

Extreme Width 9'6"

SIDE VIEW.

VULNERABLE POINTS:- The points most vulnerable to rifle & MG bullets are marked —

EFFECT OF BULLETS :- Armour-piercing bullets will penetrate the cab on top of the tank. This, & the flaps & all the apertures shown above are vulnerable against the 'splash' of ordinary bullets; that is to say small particles of molten metal formed on the impact of the bullet, splash through the joints of the flap & wound the crew. There is a space between the gun-shield & the front of the tank through which bullets can pass.

It is known that during the VILLERS-BRETONNEUX attack, our MG-& rifle fire wounded some of the German machine gunners & effectively kept down their fire.

EFFECT of ARTILLERY :- A direct hit will put the tank out of action.

CAPABILITIES:- The tank cannot cross a wide French (8ft. wide or over) or large shell holes.

MARKING :- The German tank is marked with a black Maltese Cross, similar to that used on German aeroplanes.

On April 14th Heald reported to the H.Q. of the 168 Infantry Brigade now billeted safely in the depths of the Ronville Caves to the south of the station. The entrance was effected by way of a number of shafts with steep steps. The caves, several centuries old, were named after various famous generals, one of these being Wellington. They were lit by electric light bulbs connected by wires running along the roofs of the passages through porcelain insulators. Some of these installations still exist today as proof of the fine workmanship by the British soldiers. Connected by long dank passages the caves were notorious for the fine white dust floating everywhere, irritating eyes and throats. One of the main passageways housed a light railway line carrying supply trucks, while to the east a long walkway led up to the old front line trenches. Small offices sparsely furnished with beds and desks accommodating the staff lead off some of the main passages. From time to time heavy shells aimed at the station exploded above them causing portions of the roof to fall in scattering further clouds of gritty chalk into the polluted atmosphere. Gas shells were feared particularly as it was thought their deadly poison might seep insidiously through the broken up ground. To provide some light entertainment the Divisional Band put on concerts in one of the larger caves. In the electric light the effect resembled a pantomime scene.[1]

Although Heald preferred to be closer to the men at Brigade H.Q. he hated the bizarre and claustrophobic caves where you could not tell day from night. Increasingly he longed for a bath. During most days he escaped thankfully into the open air, visiting the trenches with Brigadier General G.G. Loch with whom he had struck up a friendship. Since the attack in March, the situation of the division was fragile with the trench defences broken and undefined. Like troglodytes emerging nightly from the cave shafts, the Cheshires laboured unceasingly on trenches and wires:

> Spent the whole day with the General going round the trenches. In the evening about midnight I had to go up again to see if all preparations for a small attack we are going to do tomorrow are complete. Got back at 2.30 a.m.
>
> (Heald, April 18th)

> The attack was quite successful, and we rushed the Boche outpost line and captured a few prisoners and five machine guns. Was up in the trenches all day clearing up the situation. The enemy were shelling a good deal which rather frightened me at times when one came particularly close. About dusk the Boche counter-attacked and we withdrew to our original positions. We had arranged to evacuate these in

---

[1] War Record, *1/5th Battalion the Cheshire Regiment*, p. 79.

case of hostile attack the identification being the important point. We
were relieved by 169 Bde. and went back into support.

(Heald April 19th)

During the following weeks they continuously awaited a fresh onslaught.
But despite sporadic raids and sometimes heavy shelling the line gradually
simmered down. In the late spring suddenly the trees burst into leaf and the
gardens became clothed in green, camouflaging the desecration of war:

The General and I spent the day up in the line. It was wonderfully quiet
and as we had taken some sandwiches we had a good long walk. The
trenches were nice and dry and no shells were flying about so we
enjoyed it. In the evening a very heavy thunderstorm came down. That
will make the trenches a sea of mud.

(Heald April 29th)

As a change from tours of the trenches, Heald inspected the Citadel which
lay to the south west of Arras. Built by Vauban in 1670 this old and staunch
fortification formed a strong part of their rear defence system. The barracks
housed one of the most impressive vaulted stable blocks in France. Today the
Citadel is associated with sinister memories; at the south side of the fort lies
the 'Mur des Fusillés' a bleak and haunted enclosure where plaques are
displayed commemorating the names of two hundred Resistance fighters
executed there by the Germans between July 1941 and July 1944.

Meanwhile the trenches once more knee deep in mire made inspections a
wearisome business:

No sign of attack yet. In the evening I went out and taped out a line of
new wire to enclose our outposts — about 700 yards in front of our front
line. Everything was quiet and I rather enjoyed it. That sort of work is
always exciting as one may meet a Boche patrol. Not that one wants to.

(Heald, May 8th)

Even when promoted to G.S.O III at 56th Division on May 15th, Heald
never slackened his duty tours of the trenches: 'If you want to do a job
properly, do it yourself' remained his motto until the end of his days. On
May 5th, after a serious illness Major General Sir Amyatt Hull had resumed
command of the 56th. Even though Gommecourt had been disastrous, Heald
considered Hull a fine General and was pleased about his re-appointment. He
also felt that Hull thought well of him.

Heald by now had become adept at riding. It gave him a sense of freedom
and liberation to break away and gallop over the ever brightening summer

countryside, where life still had a semblance of normality. He tried to teach his horse Jerry to jump but the animal was very nervous and inclined to swerve; perhaps he had been kept too long cooped up in a stable. Realising that Jerry would be no good near gunfire Heald changed him for a little mare who jumped well; though later, venturing his luck in a jumping competition she jibbed at the first fence which was very ignominious.

Occasional other diversions occurred to break up the monotonous round:

> Spent the day in the line. I had to look at a portion that has been much
> damaged by shell fire. They had been shelling it just before I got there
> but were quiet when I was there. I had a splendid lunch with the L.R.B.
> (London Rifle Brigade) in their dugout in the trenches. Dr. Horn was
> there. He is attached to them as Medical Officer. He is a very cheery
> fellow and popular with all.
>
> (Heald, June 5th)

Heald invited Horn back to dinner at H.Q. He thought him an extremely nice fellow. By coincidence they both lived in the same town and two years later in 1920, Heald married Evelyn Shelmerdine (the authors mother) who was the youngest sister of Horn's wife. During a daylight raid on June 12th Heald was in the front line to watch the show:

> We covered the area to be raided with a ring of smoke. Our fellows
> (L.R.B.) killed about 24 Boche and destroyed three trench mortars. Our
> casualties sixteen, most of whom were lightly wounded. Dined with
> Harold Bibby, he goes on leave tomorrow.[1]
>
> (Heald, June 12th)

In reserve the 168th Brigade in high spirits held a sports meeting on the following day:

> It was a great show. Massed bands and flags flying and clowns some of
> whom were very clever, Two were dressed as Staff Officers and were
> very amusing. There were horse races and bookies calling the odds and
> refreshment tents. I enjoyed it very much. It was a lovely day. An
> aeroplane flew over and dropped a message "Cheerio 168 Brigade".
>
> (Heald, June 13th)

During the hot summer, the last of the war, Heald continued his careful supervision of the trenches, occasionally enjoying spells behind the line, playing tennis and travelling about. On July 28th he attended a sports

---

[1] Harold Bibby (later Sir Harold) was Heald's first cousin and his family owned the Bibby shipping line based in Liverpool.

meeting at Estrée Cauchy with his old battalion, lunching with Oscar Johnson who was still commanding 'A' Company.

Throughout the war discontent erupted about awards, it was a never ending topic:

> Orders have come through that one can't get a Military Cross except for an act of gallantry under fire. For continuous good service one can only get an O.B.E. Thousands have had the M.C. by now for the latter services. It does not seem at all right to change now.
>
> (Heald, August 18th)

At last, after the perilous German onslaught in the Spring there were signs that the Allies could retaliate. By the month, American forces had been arriving in increasing numbers to swell the ranks and in the Arras sector the enemy made a partial withdrawal. Taking this evidence as the sign of a crack, the 56th Divisional H.Q. moved forward to Bavincourt south of Arras.

> I was attached to 168 Inf. Bde to help their staff. In the evening we moved to battle H.Q.'s behind a railway embankment. The guide lost his way as guides nearly always do. However it was a bright moonlight night so we were able to find our way by map. We had quite a good dugout which was well protected against gas. The enemy shelled us with gas all night making a fearful smell. Our troops were attacking over unknown ground and at very short notice. We only got them into their assembly positions just before zero hour. Several tanks got put out of action by gas.
>
> (Heald, August 22nd)

> The attack started at 5.a.m and everything went well. We got all objectives and five hundred prisoners. I went over to the captured part. Everything quiet. I had a talk with a front battalion Commander—Col. Shaw— soon after I left him he was killed. He was such a good chap. I then went back to Div H.Q. which had moved to Blairville.
>
> (Heald, August 23rd)[1]

Their unrelenting attacks continued in fierce contest and though the divisional objective of Bullecourt was captured and re captured, as the battle ebbed and flowed the scent of hope increased for the 'big show' due for September 2nd:

---

[1] Lieut. Col. R.S.F. Shaw M.C., the 1/13th London Regt. (Kensingtons) was killed by a sniper amidst confused fighting.

Windy day and showery.

First reports indicate that the attack is going well. We have captured
Cagincourt and the cavalry are ahead. We have broken the Drocourt
Quéant line and are pushing ahead. A very peculiar situation will arise
tonight. We shall be holding a section of the Hindenburg line against the
Boche. The positions being exactly opposite to last winter.

(Heald, September 2nd)

The attack is progressing well and we have reached the line of the Canal
du Nord and secured the crossings thus opening the way for an attack on
Bourlon Wood. I and the Colonel went up on to some high ground
north of Quéant and saw the advance progressing. It was like an old time
picture of a battle. There was a Divisional Commander with his staff
with glasses and maps watching the battle. To the left front a creeping
barrage was going forward for the attack on Marquion and on our right
front small bodies of men were moving across the open with no
opposition. It appears as if there was a gap to our right front which the
Hun has been unable to fill. We know his divisions are disorganised as
parts have been identified on various parts of the front and that the
morale of his troops is very bad. We captured a despatch rider last night
bearing a message from the Regimental Commander to his General and
saying that his troops were done and that they would give in unless
relieved. There are opportunities for a huge victory if only we are quick
enough to push on and seize them. We have never had such a chance
before.

(Heald, September 3rd)

Heald's diary notebook until November 1st, when he returned from
October leave is missing without trace but he must have taken part in the
brilliantly successful attack by the 56th Division on September 27th.
Combining with the 1st Canadian Division in a dramatic sweep they crossed
the canal du Nord, the Canadians pressing ever forward, as the 56th
consolidated.

After his illness in Dieppe McGowan did not return to the 90th Brigade.
Instead he was sent to a sector near the original 1915 Cheshire positions at
Neuve Eglise where he found his new signals job rather dull. He enjoyed
making friends with a family in the village with whom he spent Christmas.
Shortly afterwards he was appointed as an instructor to the Australian Corps
school at Aveluy, subsequently becoming Acting Captain in charge of 10th
Corps H.A. Signals, responsible for all communications between corps and
brigades of heavy artillery. At the end of October after the armies had

progressed past the zone of enemy destruction, he found it comparatively easy to maintain excellent communications throughout the rapid advance; on reaching Turcoing Roubaix and Lille they could use the existing telephone lines. McGowan's expert knowledge so impressed Brigadier General A.H. Ollivant that the night before the Armistice at the request of Brigadier General B.C. Freyburg V.C. (a friend of Ollivant,) McGowan was detailed to report for briefing in a particularly novel stunt General Freyburg proposed to carry out on November 11th. McGowan was to accompany him with a walkie-talkie,[1] but he was much relieved that the Armistice operated from 11 a.m. on the 11th and that this new fangled scheme never materialised.

---

[1] McGowan, *Memoirs*, p. 54.

CHAPTER 17

ARMISTICE

During the collapse of the German forces in October and November 1918, the allies advanced with all the determination they could muster. In their efforts to delay their pursuers the enemy rearguard fiercely contested the major strong points; but the nightly glare of towns and villages in conflagration was proof of a full scale retreat. As the German tide receded from the occupied land the former invaders systematically destroyed railways, culverts, roads and bridges leaving bombs and booby traps in their wake. Up to the end the mobile line was a very dangerous one. Over eighty thousand British troops were killed in the battles of the final advance.[1]

Because of the speed of the advance and in order to lighten the transport and the load carried by the men, on November 3rd the 56th Division was ordered to dump their blankets and packs at Pyramid de Denain. Communications soon became a very serious matter and all the energies of the Cheshires as pioneers were concentrated on making the roads fit for transport. As a Staff Officer, Heald was taxed with the problem of supplies: He felt that much depended on the railways (though they couldn't keep pace):

It has rained for three days and cross country tracks are impassable. Things have got to such a state that motor lorries cannot get within seven miles of our front line, and we have to get supplies forward by horse transport.

I hear that the German delegates arrived at Paris and presented proposals which Foch immediately rejected. They have been given 72 hours to accept or refuse. They have not got a hope unless the Allies fall out amongst themselves. I think there will be peace within a week. I rode up today on my mare and the ground is sodden. One very noticeable feature is the way all the civilians greet one. Very different to the ones in the rear who only want all your money. They all look fairly well fed. The American food mission has done extraordinarily good work. There seems to be a large number of men among them.

(Heald, November 8th)

---

[1] The author's father-in-law, Lieut. Col. J.A. Wolff, R.H.A. was killed by shrapnel while reconnoitering forward gun positions south of Valenciennes on October 23rd.

The poet Wilfred Owen was killed by machine gun fire while helping his company across the Sambre Canal on November 4th.

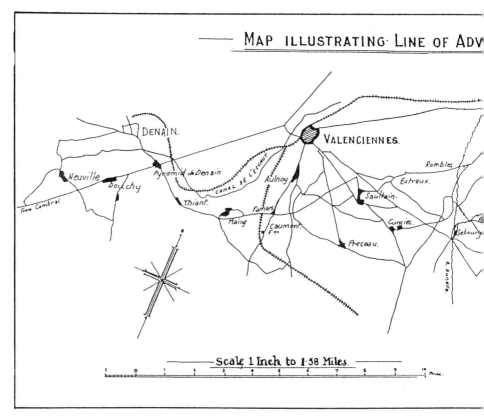

Scale 1 Inch to 1·58 Miles.

We are still advancing and have reached the Mons Montegne road. We can't go any further as we can't feed ourselves until the roads are repaired.

Div. H.Q. moved to Fayt le Franc a very nice little village — quite untouched by the war. The inhabitants are extraordinarily pleased to see us and the old lady where I am billeted was pathetically anxious to know if my room was good enough. It has a bed and clean sheets — quite good enough for anyone. There are quite a lot of cows and hens in the village and they gave us a huge cream cheese that was delicious. According to the inhabitants the Boche army is losing all discipline. They tell tales of how the men assault their officers. We found three German officers with their throats cut today. The inhabitants also say that the Boche retreat is getting disorderly and the men refuse to fight. The war is indeed nearly over now. I doubt whether we shall have any more fighting.

(Heald, November 9th)

It is a lovely autumn day, slight frost in the morning and a bright sun. This village is a charming spot. We again advanced and caught up to the Boche who had left some machine guns to cover his retreat. His men though are almost a rabble and refuse to fight. They chuck away their

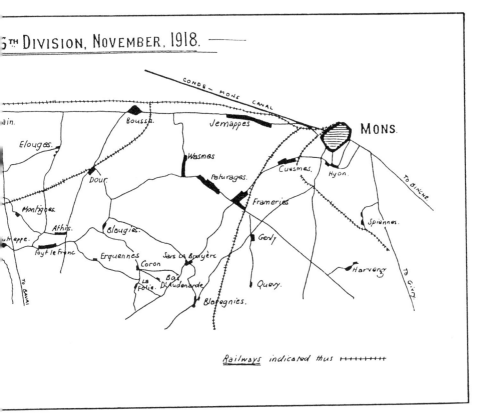

arms and shoot their officers if they attempt to coerce them. Revolution has broken out in Germany and the Kaiser and Crown Prince have abdicated. It is the end. The civilians are extraordinarily bitter against the Boche and tell us most gruesome tales of how badly the Germans treated them. For instance in November 1915, they took 600 men from this district and herded them together to make them work for them. They tried to make them sign a declaration that they were willing to work for Germany but they all refused so the Germans took them out into the fields, took off their clothes and left them for the night. They have behaved like devils, they have stolen destroyed and burnt everything they could lay their hands on. I had a long ride to our forward positions and stopped and had some coffee at a Nunnery. The Nuns simply tumbled over each other in their efforts to serve us. They hated the Boche. This is the country that Marlborough fought over in Queen Anne's reign. I rode over the battlefield of Malplaquet this afternoon and saw the monument erected to it with the head of Marlborough on. This evening we have heard that the Germans have sent a wireless message to their delegates to accept our terms, also to request us to send food to Germany. If true it is peace at last. It seems incredible, I can't realise that the last shot had been fired.[1] I feel so

---

[1] The casualties of the 56th Division totalled nearly thirty five thousand men.

glad it is over. To be a soldier is not my metier. There will be some wonderful rejoicings in London tomorrow night. I should like to be there. We are still carrying on with our usual arrangements for the advance to proceed but I have lost all interest in the war. The work for which I joined is finished and I don't feel myself bound to the Army any longer.

(Heald, November 10th)

At 11 a.m. today hostilities ceased. We captured Mons early this morning. The Americans captured Sedan. It is rather appropriate to have got these two places on the last day of the Great War. The British Army started at Mons and has finished there. The Americans have wiped out the Sedan capitulation of 1871.

We mess in the Curé's house so we asked him to dinner with us. He produced a couple of bottles of extraordinarily good Burgundy which had been buried since the commencement of the war. He is a well educated man and very interesting. We managed to put up quite a good dinner.

(Heald, November 11th)

Lovely day. It is pleasant not hearing the sound of guns. We are going to form part of the army of occupation and march to the Rhine in a few days. Very interesting I expect. Our armistice terms were published today. I think we have let the Germans down very lightly. However it looks as though they are going to punish themselves by red revolution. We shall have to guard against our men getting infected.

(Heald, November 12th)

At the end of October McGowan with some signallers had entered Lille. Only recently liberated, on October 18th the city with its beautiful boulevards and magnificent buildings greatly impressed him; there were few outward signs of damage, except for the German habitation, but he found the silent streets almost uncanny. Because the enemy had removed or destroyed such machinery as they could from the factories, industry was dead; all the railways were paralysed as bridges and junctions had been totally destroyed.[1] McGowan only saw one pair of scraggy horses in the whole city; the citizens had to carry their belongings about by hand or wheel them about

---

[1] The first train of military supplies reached St. André station on October 25th. From that date. 20 wagons of civilian supplies reached Lille per day. A.M. Henniker, *Transportation on the Western Front.* H.M.S.O. 1937, p. 458.

in makeshift hand carts. As yet, it seemed the dazed population did not realise that after four years the bulk of their troubles were over:

They appear 'timide' but ready enough to talk when spoken to. They are suffering from morale weakness rather than physical illness. As a result of being for so long under the thumb of their Prussian captors. Although the prices they had to pay for luxuries such as wine, butter, eggs etc. were fabulous (wine 40 frcs. a bottle, butter 65 frcs. a kilo, etc.) yet they've evidently been kept supplied with the necessities of life sufficient to keep them from starvation through the Amercian mission.

I went into one shop to get some lace and was very surprised to find it cheaper than any I've ever bought before. Unfortunately they'd only a very small stock left, just what they were able to hide from the Boche who was requisitioning all he could find for his gun powder factories. They are now selling it at its pre war price & I took advantage to get a fair stock for I'll warrant it will be double the price as soon as British troops get established in the town.

I'll be sending you some of it along very shortly, so you'll know where it has come from. The girl in the shop was most interesting to talk to, very quiet and apparently well educated. She would hardly talk about the Boche in reply to my questions but what she did say showed heartfelt bitterness.

(McGowan, October 29th)

By November 11th the inhabitants appeared to have become accustomed to their newly found liberty. Hodgkin noted that all the damsels seemed very pleased to see them and that newspapers were selling like hot cakes, their headlines blazoning the tidings of a white flag party sent to General Foch:

From LILLE we went on to ROUBAIX, a town of very magnificent but very uncomfortable marble houses with stained-glass windows & so on: Second Army are installed here: Then on to a village called WILLEMS & to TOURNAI. This was only taken a day or two ago & all the civilians were out in their best clothes welcoming our troops marching through. The town has been rather battered by shell fire on the outskirts & the Boche has destroyed all the modern bridges across the Canal but has left the old Pont des Irons for some reason.

(Hodgkin, November 11th)

Continuing their itinerary, they enjoyed a most excellent dinner at Marchiennes followed by 'Games of chance'. Having disposed of the father of all fleas, Hodgkin spent a very good night in a bed with real sheets. Leaving next day they went through Douai:

> Where there is rather a quaint old tower on the Town Hall & some very picturesque little spots down by the Canal. The centre of the town is destroyed deliberately, otherwise, except the Station, the Town is fairly intact. Then onto LENS which for sheer desolation & destruction on a grand scale surpasses anything I have seen this war. It is like all the villages of the SOMME battlefield gathered together: there is no house that approaches the name in the whole town. This place has probably had more gas discharged onto it than any other place in the war zone.
>
> (Hodgkin, November 12th)

> Then on through JORCHAZ & ABLAIN ST. NAZAIRE. Coming in from the Boche side so to speak, one realises how tremendously the VIMY RIDGE & the heights of LORETTE dominate the area: these ridges both stand up like whale-backs & provide the most perfect observation for miles. We got back to JAVY for lunch, & discovered that the *ARMISTICE* had been signed yesterday & that hostilities had ceased at 11.00 a.m.

> Also that last night, the men, knowing this, had been very reluctant to come out for night operations in the rain & had only been induced to do so after Hamilton had been to see them personally. Regrettable from a disciplinary standpoint, but very natural from a human one.
>
> (Hodgkin, November 12th)

Ending his journey through the battle area he heard that the Fifth Army was shortly to be disbanded and that his unit was to be concentrated around St. Omer. It gave him furiously to think: 'This is a horrible fate.'

> I finally got into the box car that was taking stores to VALENCIENNES, broke a spring in DENAIN, patched it up with a block of wood & some wire (in spite of the driver who appeared to write off the car as hopeless & who immediately the mishap occurred, folded his hands together, said Kismet (or words to that effect) & prepared to do nothing) dropped our stores in VALENCIENNES, & fetched up at ANGRE, in Belgium, over the worst pavé roads I have ever travelled on, at 10.30 p.m.
>
> (Hodgkin, November 13th)

> To my exceeding delight a wire came in from Corps today asking for officers with a knowledge of German for service with Second & Fourth

Armies. I at once put my name down, & am now living in terror lest some gilded Staff Officer should call upon me to give him a sample of German! I walked over to Corps at SEBOURG today to see how the land lies, but did not get much further. Red tape is still abundant, especially in XXII Corps.

(Hodgkin, November 14th)

On November 15th a party of three officers and one hundred men of the 1/5th Cheshires commanded by Captain A.H. Joliffe, was chosen to be part of a detachment of the 56th Division to make a state entry into Mons. Having arrived at Mons on the previous day to attend the celebrations, Heald was surprised at the flourishing air of the town just liberated by the Canadians on November 11th:

It is so different from the other towns we have passed through. It has plenty of shops which look fairly well filled and seems to be full of civilians — men as well as women. It is decked out with flags. It is a mining town in reality, but I don't think the mines are working at present. Of course the roads are very bad, the Boche has blown up craters at every road junction.

(Heald, November 14th)

Today the British celebrated their official entry into Mons. Troops were formed up in the Grande Place and lined all the principal streets. General Horne, the 1st Army Commander, then entered and the Mayor received him outside the Town Hall where a raised dais had been prepared. They each made speeches, the band played, the populace waved flags and cheered, and funny Belgian gendarmes in tall plumed hats rushed about and preserved order. The detachments from all troops in the 1st Army marched past. It was quite an historical event because the British Army fought its first fight at Mons in August 1914 and recaptured Mons on the last day of the war in November 1918. I was very pleased at being able to attend though it got a little wearisome, however the sun shone and everybody put on their best clothes and the place was a mass of red (staff officers and generals).

(Heald, November 15th)

Meanwhile Hodgkin had walked over to his old battalion at Athis near Mons to lunch with Lt. Col. W.A. Churton and those who had stayed behind: 'I said I wanted to come back to my Battn., now that Gen. Foukes has no excuse for keeping me any longer, & the Col. said he would consider how he could fit me in.' (Lieut. Col. Groves had been invalided back to England earlier that year). But alas, once more Hodgkin was to be disappointed as six days later he learnt that the battalion was already overstocked with officers and there was no place for him:

> I am very sick: having been persuaded from rejoining during the last 3 years by my General, I am now, when the said General has at last given me leave, prevented by force of numbers. I am afraid it looks as if I shall never get back to them again until we return to peace conditions: by which time I expect to have forsaken Cheshire for good.
>
> (Hodgkin, November 21st)

After the Mons parade, Heald went off on leave with Hartley of his battalion to Paris; he described the city as brilliantly lit and full of cars, people and gaiety. They stayed at an hotel near the Louvre and spent their time exploring, dining in restaurants and attending theatres and the opera:

> The prices are simply wicked and I hope we charge the French in the same way when they come to London. The place is full of American officers, perhaps that accounts somewhat for the inflated prices. We saw the King on his drive through, the weather was wretched but all Paris turned out to see him and gave him a great reception. There was very little ceremony. Paris is a very beautiful city, the buildings, and spacious boulevards and squares impressed me very much. At one point we came across a place where they were cutting a boulevard right through a thickly inhabited portion of Paris up to Notre Dame — through buildings and all. They stage a very fine ballet at the Opera certainly the finest I have seen.
>
> (Heald, November 22nd-29th)

On February 21st 1917, Hodgkin had been sent to Paris for a course on gas, the capital had regained its verve and gaiety after August 1914 when the Grands Boulevards had rapidly emptied, the shops had put up their shutters and vehicles had disappeared from the streets. At the onset of war, the luxurious Meurice was hurriedly transformed into a hospital and the glittering Ritz uninhabited. Across the wide and empty Place de la Concorde flocks of sheep were driven to the Gare de l'Est for enrailment to the front.

Hodgkin stayed at the Grand Hotel, Boulevard des Capucines and dined at the Restaurant Brufant (Boulevard de l'Opera) and at the Café de la Paix: 'Here was the most amazing mixture of respectability and the reverse, and a number of comparatively pretty girls who ought to have known better. I think I rather like Paris.' He also visited the Folies Bergères and was taken to dinner at Maxims. He noted that the attentions of the ladies were very pressing all through his visit.

Once the Armistice had been signed, it became a taxing affair to occupy the troops whose sole idea was to return home as quickly as possible:

> I assembled the Company today & gave them all the information available about Demobilisation. I fear a lot of them think they will be spending Christmas at home. So I did my best to dispel this illusion by reading to them a most excellent lecture originally delivered by some big-wig at G.H.Q., which set out very clearly what the Government proposes to do. I have a kind of feeling (why I don't in the least know) that Government is really going to do this demobilisation business well. Personally I am in no hurry to get back. I should like to see the thing out right to the end if possible "and damn the experts"!

> We have also begun to get our Education Scheme on a business footing. Have already got several prospective lecturers (myself among them, I blush to say) & some searchers after knowledge. The people who really need it, the labourers and so forth, are, needless to say, entirely unmoved, & we shall have to think out some cunning scheme by which they may be entrapped.
>
> (Hodgkin, November 22nd)

In the grim December weather Heald was exceedingly bored and applied himself to lessons in German and French. Towards Christmas a number of festivities were arranged by the local inhabitants anxious to make the army welcome, Heald was invited to a dance in the house of a Belgian lady when the 'Bow Bells' their Divisional Band supplied the music:

> All the girls were Belgian and very few could talk English. Their dances were very old fashioned and none had danced during the German occupation. However it was all very jolly and although the girls were not attractive in looks they were animated. The floor was stone which made dancing a little heavy. We all enjoyed it immensely, it was such a change from this dull little village.
>
> (Heald, December 8th)

Just over a fortnight later the XXII Corps gave a dance in Mons for the town celebrities. Though Heald enjoyed the evening, he found the Belgian girls not too light on their feet. After returning at 3.0 a.m. he noticed that no longer could he dance all night as he used to without feeling tired; perhaps his fatigue was caused by the heavy footed Belgian girls and the effort of speaking nothing but French.

Heald did not specify the old fashioned dances in Mons or whether the waltzes were fast or slow. Before the war the Boston waltz from America became popular, while the Argentine Tango 'discovered' in Buenos Aires around 1910 had taken European ballrooms by storm. But above all it was rag time which had captured the imagination and Irving Berlin's 'Alexander's Ragtime Band' rocketed around the world. With 'Rag' came the one step, a smooth walk with a step to every count of the music. In London the Savoy Hotel, quick to take advantage of the new craze installed a ragtime band 'Murray's Savoy Quartette' consisting of banjo, banjo and vocalist, piano and drums.[1] A magnet for those on leave from the trenches, the heady freedoms of the new dances were far more attractive than old fashioned string orchestras playing the lancers and veletas. In private houses and at other balls where programme dances took place, the names of the tunes were often printed on the programmes at the side of the relevant dance. Orchestras in 1913 and 14 played such popular waltzes as: 'Among the Daffodils', 'Dearest', 'The Girl in the Taxi', and the haunting 'Destiny'. The one steps (ragtime) included, 'Sumuran Girl', 'Hitchy Koo', 'Midnight Choo Choo', 'Temptation Rag' and 'You Made Me Love You'. All the tango tunes had Spanish names: 'Seducción', 'Y Como le Va' and 'El Choclo'. Many a flirtation blossomed in the romantic atmosphere of these heady rhythms which continued to be played throughout the war.

Hodgkin also managed to amuse himself in a light hearted way. He went off to Brussels where he stayed in a hotel with Davies, a friend from his unit. Providing one had the money to pay for them, there seemed no lack of any of the ordinary commodities of life except soap, an article which had not been obtainable for years:

> We walked about till dinner-time & dined expensively & not too well at the Merry Grill: I do not care for passé ladies in tights dancing 'Foxtrots' and similar things in front of me while I eat my beefsteak. Afterwards, Davies, having a passion for dancing, tried to find a place where he could indulge himself, but failing to do so he finally joined me at the Gaiety, where we saw an extremely fourth-rate variety show: we could'nt stick it out to the end.
>
> (Hodgkin, December 4th)

> Davies tried to get some breakfast this morning in a Hotel, but can't understand much French: so the landlady, quite a cheerful soul &

---

[1] S. Jackson. *The Savoy — Romance of a Great Hotel*, Muller, London. 1964, p. 24.

passably young, suggested that she should come & ask me about it. So I was roused from my heavy slumbers by much knocking on the door, & finally by the sight of Davies' long face, accompanied by Madame (or M'mlle) in her dressing gown. I burst forth in my best french, with the casual clad Madame, overcome with laughing (whether at me, or at her costume, or at the whole situation I don't know) said that she had no bread in the house. So Davies got his breakfast elsewhere.

Croquis Serbe

Serbian soldiers, 1917.

Later we all set forth for a walk round the city (for details see any guide book): quite a nice place. The Town Hall is magnificient: so are the names of the streets: e.g. "The Street of Herbs to make Soup with" & "The Street of the Animals without Ferocity". We bought a little lace from an extremely pretty damsel in a shop in the Passage du Nord, had lunch in a restaurant in the Boulevard Anspach & then "home" by box-car again. Altogether, my impression was that the Englishman was regarded more of a curiosity than anything else. The Americans seem to be all that matter. Considering that England had driven the Boche out of Belgium I thought the people might reverse the situation: but apparently they think otherwise'.

(Hodgkin, December 5th)

In London where Hodgkin spent Christmas leave, people of all kinds packed the city to overflowing. Prices had gone sky high and a coat and breeches he had ordered two months before cost him £13.11.0. During his leave he noted he saw the back of President Wilson's head:

Left VICTORIA at 8.00 a.m. & was held up for two hrs. to let the President's train go through & after an inconcievably beastly journey

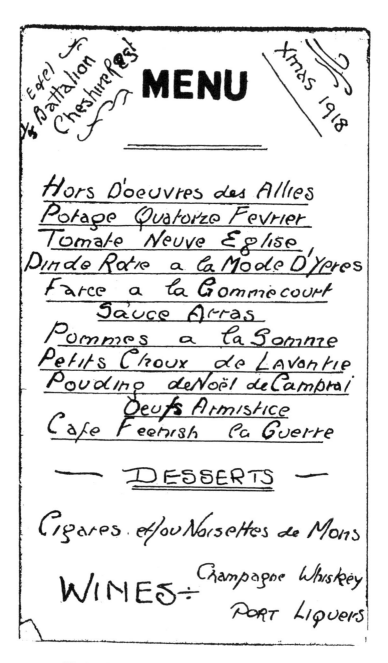

The last Christmas dinner overseas at Spienne near Mons.

arrived at CALAIS & put up at the Officers Club in the Rue de La
Riviére: a very poor place compared with the Grand Hotel. Here the
night was made hideous by several American Naval Officers & one
temporary gentleman of our army, who thought it fit & proper to sit
down to talk with the Club waiters (soldiers) & drink all night.

(Hodgkin, December 31st)

On the last Christmas Day overseas at 8 p.m. the 1/5th Cheshires Officers'
dinner was held at the school room at Spienne near Mons, where 36 officers
sat down. Turkeys had been brought from Paris, excellent beer from Mons
and the men feasted on plum puddings to their hearts content. Private
Edward I. Ireland whose father was a Chester florist, waited on 6 officers
whose names he wrote down on the back of his buff coloured menu. Among
these were: Lieut. Col. W.A.V. Churton, Staff Capt. T. Heald and Capt.
Hartley.[1]

On New Year's eve a splendid victory ball took place at the imposing Hotel
de Ville in the Grand Place at Brussels:

I and Coke the Staff Captain of 168 Inf. Brigade went to Brussels. We
got there about 4 p.m. and had tea at a large Hotel, "the Palace". Then
we had a look round the shops which were brilliantly lit and apparently
had plenty to sell. Prices are extraordinarily high but have diminished
lately by about half. Bacon was about 11s.0 a pound, butter about 8s.0 a
pound, and meat about 7s.0 a pound. Apparently during the war they
had no rationing and consequently the rich could get whatever they
wanted whilst the poor went without. Wine is also prohibitive. In the
evening we went to a ball given by the 4th Canadian Division at the
Hotel de Ville. It was almost a State function. The invitations for
civilians had been given by a lady of high social standing and
consequently tickets were much sought after. Crowds of Belgians
besieged the place during the preceding days to try and get tickets.
Apparently their social positions for the next ten years depended on
obtaining permission to go. The doors were very well guarded and only
bona-fide ticket holders got admission. It was a fine spectacle. Dancing
was going on in three rooms, including the famous Gothic Hall where
the British danced before the battle of Waterloo. All the Belgian
notabilities were there in their war paint and there were some very
pretty girls too. I was told that a lot of the women had gone to Paris to
procure their gowns. Of course it was overcrowded and the dancing very
old fashioned but I enjoyed it immensely. The Prince of Wales was there

---

[1] A miscellany of Private Ireland's papers is at Chester Castle.

looking very boyish. He has got a very clear complexion. He started the dance with a Belgian lady wearing a coronet, I don't know who she was, but later on he got some nice girls as partners.

We left there about 11.30 p.m. and went to a nightclub where one sits at small tables round the room, and dancing goes on in the centre. There were lots of girls there and no introduction necessary. We saw the New Year in amid scenes of great hilarity. About 1 a.m. we left and went back to the Palace Hotel for supper, and eventually left Brussels at 2 a.m. in the car getting back here about 5 a.m. It was the best New Year I remember having spent anywhere.

(Heald, December 31st)

The Gothic Hall with it's rich wood carving and Michelen tapestries would have made a magnificent setting for the ball on this glittering occasion. Many of the principal rooms in the town hall had painted ceilings of renown, and on the walls portraits could be seen of European Royalty. Heald's dance programme with it's black and gold ribbon in one corner, featured the waltz every third dance, interspersed with the one-step and the two-step. At 10.30 p.m. there was a sword dance. There was only one fox-trot. Heald had not written any names of dancing partners in the appropriate spaces of his programme. Perhaps he had not been introduced to any of the women of quality who were present. In contrast to all the formality, a night club with it's intimate style of dancing, was still something of a daring novelty. After they had been requested to leave their caps, sticks and 'Sam Brownes' at the vestiaire the officers would probably have paid a fairly costly cover charge. But who cared on that hectic New Year's Eve when at last the long years of war were over? Heald did not mention any vaudeville show on that occasion, but no doubt the welcoming girls, the music and flowing champagne were compensations enough.

Hodgkin had also been invited to a ball in Brussels, to be given at the Concert Noble by the Corps Commander and Staff of the XXII Corps on January 28th 1919 at 10.00 p.m.: 'Am I to go in boots, shoes, pumps or gum boots?' he asked himself on January 19th. It was a difficult decision. In the end he chose none of these:

I cannot & do not want to "Jazz" & all the other extraordinary dances of today. Nor do I intend making a pilgrimage to Waterloo: Wellington said that he could not recognise the place when he came to re-visit it a few years after the battle, so there is even less chance for me now.

(Hodgkin, January 31st)

Armistice

Jazz as opposed to ragtime had become popular by the end of 1917 and for some time the modern dances were referred to as 'Jazz dances'. Dominic la Rocca and the 'Original Dixiland Jazz Band' appeared at the Hammersmith Palais in 1920. Being one of the outstanding white American bands of the period it was chosen by the Savoy Hotel to play at the Victory Ball held to celebrate the signing of the Versailles Treaty.[1] In peacetime did Hodgkin ever become converted to these new and extraordinary dances?

> I have been having some trouble with some of my men who tried to
> adopt the "strike" method when working under a Staff Sgt. of another
> company. They did not like the work (at a stores dump) & the S.Sgt.
> bullied them. So they stopped work until ordered to continue by one of
> my officers. So I had them all up, told them what fools they were, put
> them in close arrest for the night with the "mutiny" to ponder upon,
> and brought them before the CRE in the morning: who repeated what I
> said previously & let them all off with a caution. The S.Sgt. also got a
> few words said to him. I hope, & think, that it is all over now: but this
> demobilisation muddle has made things very awkward & the men of all
> units are in a very disturbing frame of mind. Not that there is in the
> least likely to be any serious trouble (although a Canadian mounted
> policeman exchanged some shots with some of their own men out looting
> a ration dump the other night), but one feels that it is not very far
> beneath the surface. There ought to have been no talk of demobilisation
> at all until the time had come to proceed with it thoroughly.
>
> (Hodgkin, January 19th)

When at last the time came for demobilisation, Hodgkin found himself formed up in the square at Mons where the troops were told off in batches according to their various dispersal areas in England:

> We Officers received a lecture from the Colonel Commandant on the
> various processes of the journey & the necessity for strict discipline, & I
> found myself appointed O.C. Train in command of roughly 30 officers
> and 950 other ranks: I hope I shall survive.
>
> (Hodgkin, February 11th)

Writing alone at 1.30 a.m. in the mess after a farewell dinner with his friends, he came near to ending his narrative:

> I don't want to go one little bit now that it really comes to the point. If
> only they would make the Army a well paid profession nothing would

[1] *S. Jackson* op. cit. p. 26.

267

induce me to leave it for the ramshackle business of civilian life. We are due to go to BOULOGNE: the train is booked to take 16½ hours but usually takes 50 I am told!

Later

I am now veritably demobilised and in England. Our journey to BOULOGNE was got over in about 24 hours. Leaving MONS at 4.0 a.m. we all of us made the journey in cattle trucks, warming ourselves with stoves looted from a neighbouring train & lying down amongst the reserve supply of coal. Of the intense discomfort of the demobilisation camps at BOULOGNE & of the super-efficiency & rudeness of the officials who conducted them I have no patience to write. We stayed 3 days here & then took ship to England to wit FOLKESTONE.

(Hodgkin, February 11th)

Heald had left the 56th Division for demobilisation on February 2nd. Since the Armistice he considered he had quite a pleasant time with not much work. He had been treated as one of the family by some hospitable Belgians and had managed to improve his French a lot; but the war was finished and he wanted to get home again. Somehow he managed to escape the first part of demobilisation which comprised the four day journey from the concentration camp at Mons in the open cattle trucks to the embarkation camp at Dieppe. The extraordinarily cold weather resembled that of February 1915 the first winter of the war:

I got a car to Amiens, and after a good lunch there caught a civilian train for Sergneux which is as far as it is possible to get tonight. The civilian train has the windows broken and no lights but with the help of a candle the journey passed off all right and I got to Sergneux about 8 p.m. I stayed the night at a small railway hotel and had to have the sheets of my bed changed they were so dirty.

(Heald, February 2nd)

Caught a train about 11 a.m. and reached Dieppe about 1 p.m. and found that the embarkation camp was about four miles out. Luckily I got a lorry to take me and my kit there. Stayed the night in an empty hut — plenty of blankets and a wood floor so quite comfortable.

(Heald, February 3rd)

Armistice

Was put in charge of a party of men and marched them to the boat at Dieppe. Luckily got a cabin. The boat sailed at 10 p.m.

(Heald, February 4th)

Passed a good night and fairly smooth crossing We landed at Southampton about 8.30 a.m. and after a lot of sorting the men out for their various dispersal areas was put in charge of a team going to Wimbledon. On arrival it was snowing hard and we had to go to a camp about two miles out. It was a beastly journey but at the Dispersal Camp they put us through in about twenty minutes and we were demobilised. On the whole the arrangements for demobilisation worked very smoothly from Dieppe onwards.

So ends my experience in the Great War.

(Heald, February 5th)

After the Armistice McGowan wrote that his life was one long picnic, including six months in the army of occupation on the Rhine with ample time for exploring the vicinity and for ten days leave at Nice in the south of France. In spite of this he found it a demoralising existence and he was not demobilised until June 1919, when the boat journey from Rotterdam was the roughest sea trip he had ever experienced. Although his civilian position with Siemens awaited him, when he reached Harwich he felt sick at heart with depression, and more so the day he discarded his uniform and became a mere civilian once again. In this mood he turned down an invitation for a long weekend houseparty for the 90th Brigade at the house of General Lloyd in Surrey. He imagined that out of uniform he could not hold his own against some of the aristocrats of the brigade and would display his ignorance in the matter of dress and etiquette. In later life he very much regretted this lost opportunity.

In the aftermath of the war, the humdrum convalescence of peace irked many who survived their dead comrades. Some finding it difficult to settle amongst those who had little knowledge of their traumas, emigrated to find new experiences, McGowan to Australia and Heald to Egypt.

While working for the newly formed Imperial Chemical Industries Ltd., Hodgkin was sent to Canada from May to November of 1928. The company required him to look for potash deposits in Nova Scotia, for phosphate mines in Quebec, to do research in lignite mines and in petrol manufacturing in northern Alberta. No doubt his inventive mind, combined with practical skills were invaluable while working in some of the more remote regions. His photographs portray camping expeditions and fishing in the wilds. Much of his spare time in England was spent in handcrafts, he constructed his own

269

boat and published a book called *The Archer's Craft* having fashioned a perfect bow.

For Heald the prospect of civilian life in a northern law practice with a father with whom he was not in tune was intolerable. Business opportunities in Egypt at the end of the war were good, the Lancashire textile mills enjoyed favourable trade spinning and weaving Egyptian cotton, and the price of raw cotton which had more than doubled between 1918 and 1919 had enriched both the pashas and British merchants. There was however an underlying current of unrest, particularly among the student and labouring population who were determined on self rule.

On his way to Cairo, Heald paused in Vienna where he witnessed the city's pangs in the aftermath of defeat. The spectre of starvation walked the streets while hollow eyed women in their desperation for food solicited any likely male passer by. Owing to astronomical inflation Austrian bank notes became increasingly worthless by the day and valuable antiques and objets d'art could be picked up for a song.

Later in Egypt Heald's path crossed that of Field Marshal Viscount Allenby (nicknamed 'The Bull') formerly G.O.C. of the Third Army and the 56th Division at Gommecourt. Allenby had recently become British High Commissioner, his task politically was tortuous and Egyptian independence of which he was in favour seemed long in arriving. His situation was made even more complicated by a British Government who pursued no cohesive policy concerning the Protectorate which had been set up in November 1914. The Anglo Egyptian and European communities did not generally favour Allenby. They considered that he preferred the Egyptian point of view and that he was not harsh enough in his measures to stamp out crime.

Troubles were increased when British and European residents as well as Egyptians were randomly murdered during periods of unrest. Martial law had been in force since 1914 and remained until the arrival of partial independence in 1922. At regular intervals mounted cavalry patrolled the streets to keep order and on several occasions Heald had to repel intruders who had tried to break into the bungalow where he lived.

Sultan Ahmed Fuad (proclaimed King in 1922) who had succeeded his brother the Sultan Hussein Kamel in 1917 was not popular among the Egyptians. He had been brought up in Italy and had hardly any practical knowledge of the country. He spoke little Arabic and scarcely concerned himself with his people's welfare. Heald saw Fuad being paraded in procession along the course before a race meeting and had the impression that the Sultan was scared stiff of assassination. European ladies bidden by the Sultana Nazli to receptions at the Abdin Palace were given a glimpse of the baby Prince Farouk (born in 1920) being rocked in a golden cradle. He was a fair and beautiful child with blue eyes.

In his leisure time, besides playing golf and winning the Egyptian championship at the Gezira Club, Heald learnt to speak and write Arabic. His teacher was an erudite Egyptian sheikh with whom he struck up a close friendship.

At the residency surrounded by its extensive gardens, Allenby and his wife lived without ostentation, although a good table was always kept for their large collection of guests. Sometimes Allenby could be seen the little the worse for drink. His beloved only child Michael had been killed aged twenty on the Western Front. It was a grievous blow and affected him deeply. Was Allenby like so many haunted by a far off vision of the line?

Nightmares of bombarding shells raining on Ypres, on the Somme, at Arras and at Cambrai haunted Heald for many years. He suffered recurrent dreams that he was buried beneath the debris. When he was very old and the dreams had faded he once remarked: 'If you have been through the Somme, nothing is quite the same again.'

APPENDIX I

THOMAS LANE CLAYPOLE HEALD was born in Southport in 1889. Educated at Shrewsbury School he qualified as a solicitor before 1914. In August 1914 he enlisted in the ranks as a private in the 5th Battalion the Cheshire Regiment (T.F.) and left for France as a 2nd Lieutenant on February 14th, 1915. Apart from being wounded in 1917 he served continuously on the Western Front until February 1919, ending the war as a Staff Captain, he was awarded the M.C. and was twice mentioned in Despatches. Leaving England in 1919 he went to Egypt to join a cotton business returning home in 1924. Subsequently in 1932 he resumed his profession as a solicitor. Given the rank of Lieutentant Colonel, in 1937 he raised the 6th Battalion the Manchester Regiment (T.F.) which he commanded until 1940. Reaching the age of 50 he was appointed O.C. Troops on ships sailing both in and out of convoys throughout the world. He was a first class amateur golfer winning the Egyptian Championship in 1922 and the Lancashire Championship in 1924. He went round the old course at St. Andrews in 84 shots (net 68) at the age of 83. He died in 1980 aged 91.

ADRIAN ELIOT HODGKIN born in 1890, was educated at Repton School. In 1909 he gained a classical scholarship to Keble College, Oxford, where he obtained an Honours Degree in Chemistry and won a rowing blue. In 1913 he was employed as a research chemist with Brunner Mond at Winnington in Cheshire. Having been commissioned into the Territorial Force in 1910, in August 1914 he was mobilised with the 5th battalion the Cheshire Regiment. After being wounded in 1915 he returned to the Western Front where he worked with the Inland Water Transport, Royal Engineers, later becoming a Chemical Adviser at 5th Army H.Q. in 1916, and in 1917 at 3rd Army H.Q. he was awarded the M.C. After the war, Adrian Hodgkin continued his work as research chemist until late 1926 when he was appointed Assistant in the Technical Dept. of Imperial Chemistries Ltd. In 1937 he became the first chairman of the newly formed plastics division which had been inaugurated under his guidance. On September 1st 1939, with the rank of Major, he joined the Chemical Warfare Training Battalion Royal Engineers, subsequently becoming Assistant Director of Chemical Warfare at G.H.Q. France. During a two year break from the Army, again working at I.C.I., in 1942 he invented a hand thrown plastic anti tank grenade known as 'Hodgkin's grenade'. Recalled once more to military service he joined the Civil Affairs Staff Centre and was promoted in 1944 to Brigadier when he became Deputy Director (exec.) Civil Affairs Military Government, under Major General G.W.R. Templer at 21 Army Group, North West Europe. Brigadier Hodgkin was awarded the O.B.E., he was made an Officer of the Legion of Merit (U.S.A.) and an Officer of the Order of Leopold (Belgium). He was a Fellow of the Institute of Chemists, a Fellow of the Chemical Society and a member of the Leander Club. In 1947 he retired from I.C.I. He died in 1972.

GEORGE McGOWAN born in Eccles, Lancashire, in 1892, was educated at Grove Park School Wrexham. In 1908 he was apprenticed at the National Telephone Company's central telephone exchange in Manchester, later in January 1914 joining Siemens Brothers at Woolwich. In response to an appeal by Lord Roberts he joined the 6th Battalion (T.F.) the Manchester Regiment as a private in 1910, and in November 1914 was gazetted as a 2nd Lieutenant in the 2/5th the Cheshire Regiment (T.F.). Subsequently he transferred to the 1/5th in January 1915 and served with them on the Western Front until November 1915, when he was appointed Signals Officer to the 90th Brigade of the 30th Division. He ended the war with the rank of Captain. He was awarded the M.C. and was twice mentioned in Despatches.

After the war McGowan emigrated to Australia where in 1920 he became a fruit grower in Tasmania. Later he moved to Victoria in order to start a cider manufacturing business under the name of "Mac's Cyder". He remained a Cider Maker until 1982.

APPENDIX II

THE 1/5th BATTALION, THE CHESHIRE REGIMENT (T.F.)

The 1/5th Battalion the Cheshire Regiment (22nd Regiment of Foot) had its origins in the Old Chester Volunteers properly established in 1860. It was formed by the amalgamation of the old 2nd (Earl of Chester's) and 3rd Volunteer Battalions.

On the formation of the Territorial Force in 1907 a Cheshire Infantry Brigade was formed. Part of this Brigade was the 5th (Earl of Chester's) and 3rd Volunteer Battalions. Its H.Q. was at Chester. In January 1915 the 5th Battalion became the 1/5th Battalion. Having left for overseas on February 14th, on February 18th they received orders to join the 14th Brigade of the 5th Division 2nd Corps, 2nd Army.

The 14th Infantry Brigade comprised:

1st	Battalion	Devonshire Regiment.
1st	,, ,,	East Surrey Regiment
1st	,, ,,	Duke of Cornwall's Light Infantry
2nd	,, ,,	Manchester Regiment
1/5	,, ,,	(Earl of Chester's) Cheshire Regiment T.F.

On February 2nd 1916, the 1/5th Cheshires as Divisional Troops joined the newly formed 56th (London T.F.) Division. In the first part of May the Division became part of 7th Corps, 3rd Army. The Division consisted of:-

167th Brigade
1/1st	Battalion London Royal Fusiliers.			
1/3rd	,,	,,	,,	,,
1/7th	,,	Middlesex Regiment		
1/8th	,,	,,	,,	

168th Brigade
1/4th	Battalion Royal Fusiliers			
1/12th	,,	London Regiment (Rangers)		
1/13th	,,	,,	,,	(Kensingtons)
1/14th	,,	,,	,,	(London Scottish)

169th Brigade
1/2nd	Battalion Royal Fusiliers			
1/5th	,,	London Regiment (London Rifle Brigade)		
1/9th	,,	,,	,,	(Queens Victoria Rifles)
1/16th	,,	,,	,,	(Queen's Westminsters)

275

Divisional Troops

Pioneer Battalion 1/5th Batt. (E. of. C.) Cheshire Regiment.

Three Field Companies of Engineers, three Brigades of Artillery, and Units of R.A.M.C. and A.S.C. (Not listed, as not specifically referred to in the text).

APPENDIX III

List and approximate weights of Officers Kit and Equipment annotated by Captain A.E. Hodgkin in February 1915

a. FIELD KIT

	lbs	
Valise	15.0	
Riding breeches	2.½	
Thin Jacket	3.0	
Blanket	3.¼	
Boots	5.0 (about)	
100 rounds	2.¼ (in boxes)	
Bucket	1.0	
Towel	1.½	
2 vests	1.¾	9.0 lbs when
3 prs. socks	1.¼	weighed together
Putties	1.¼	
2 collars	0.¼	
Cholera belt	0.½	
2 candles	0.½	
Kit bag	1.0	

35lbs when weighed together

b. EQUIPMENT

S.B. Belt
Sword
Revolver
Field Glasses
Waterbottle
Compass
Haversack
(containing
  pencil box
  notebook
  ¼ lb. tobacco
  wirecutters
  oil bottle
  cleaning rod
  30 rounds
  2 field dressings
  2 handkerchiefs
  1 pipe)

15lbs

c. RUCKSACK

	lbs.	
Rucksack	1.¾	
Oilskin (& strap)	4.½	
Burberry	3.½	
Canteen	2.0	16lbs
20 rounds	2.¼	
Muffler	1.0	
Balaclava helmet	0.½	
Shirt	1.0	
1 socks	0.½	
(+ diary		
notepaper		
& small towel)		

GLOSSARY

Bivvy
: A makeshift tent to hold a few men; a water proof sheet being supported by a central ridge pole three feet or so above the ground.

Bivouac
: Also loosely used for a dug-out.

Blighty One
: A wound sufficiently serious to be sent back to Blighty, i.e. England and home.

British Warm
: A warm short army overcoat worn especially by officers from 1901.

B.S.O.
: Brigade Signals Officer.

Centime Nap.
: Nap. short for Napoleon. A card game in which each person (halfpenny) receives five cards and calls the number of tricks he expects to win. One who calls 'five' is said to go "Napoleon" if he wins them all.

Chinese Attack
: A short bombardment followed by a sham attack made with dummy canvas figures to represent infantry pulled up by wires. The figures sometimes being half hidden by a smoke haze.

Cholera belt
: A wide belt often of flannel to be wound round the stomach to alleviate kidney and bowel pains.

Crump
: Big high explosive.

D.G.A.M.S.
: Director General Army Medical Services.

F.O.O.
: Forward Observation Officer (Artillery) Duty to observe the correct fall of shot from a gun.

Grenadiers
: At the early part of the 17th century every line battalion had its grenadier company carrying a large pouch of grenades to cover the advance to the battle or lead the way to an assault. Although Grenadier companies were abandoned by the British after the Crimean War the name persisted. In the first World War, about twenty men in each or any of the four infantry companies of a battalion were trained as bomb throwers and acted under the command of an officer.

G.S.O.
: General Staff Officer

Hard Tack
: A dry hard biscuit resembling a dog biscuit.

Maconachie
: A tinned ration consisting of thin sliced vegetables chiefly turnips and carrots in their soup or gravy.

Medicine and Duty
: A pill was given to a soldier who reported himself sick without obvious cause together with orders to report himself to his platoon sergeant for duty (and a cursing).

P.B.I.
: Poor Bloody Infantry.

R.F.A.
: Royal Field Artillery.

R.F.C.
: Royal Flying Corps.

R.H.A.	:	Royal Horse Artillery.
R.S.F.	:	Royal Scots Fusiliers.
R.T.O.	:	Railway Transport Officer.
S.B. Belt	:	Sam Browne belt. Officers' brown leather belt with brass fittings, usually with one shoulder strap but sometimes two.
Shrapnel	:	The Shrapnel shell did good service in the Peninsula War and at Waterloo. So called after their inventor, a British officer, one Colonel Shrapnel. Bullets were enclosed in the shell which was burst by a small powder charge set going by a time fuse when close to the target. The bullets then proceeded with the velocity which the shell had at the time of opening.
Unico	:	Thought to be a type of small patent stove with solid fuel tablet.
"Very" or "verey" light	:	Fired from a special pistol capable of sending different coloured light signals.
Whizz bang	:	Small field gun shell with short range, low trajectory.
Whoofer	:	Medium sized high explosive.

BIBLIOGRAPHY

Á Court Repington,	*The First World War 1914–1918*, II vols., Constable, London, 1920.
Alison J.M.,	*Raemaekers Cartoon History of the War*, John Lane, London, 1919.
Babington A.,	*For the Sake of Example*, Methuen, London, 1975.
Ed. Blake R.N.W.,	*The Private Papers of Sir Douglas Haig*, Eyre and Spottiswood, London, 1952.
Blunden E.,	*Undertones of War*, Cobden Sanderson, London, 1929.
Bonham — Carter V.,	*Soldier True, The Life and Times of Field-Marshall Sir William Robertson, Bart. 1860–1933.* Frederick Muller, London, 1963.
Boraston J.H.,	*Sir Douglas Haig's Despatches*, Dent, London, 1919.
Brice B.,	*The Battle Book of Ypres*, John Murray, London, 1927.
Brophy J. and Partridge E.H.,	*The Long Trial, [Songs and Slang of the British Soldier, 1914–1918]*, André Deutsch, London, 1965.
Callwell C.E.,	*Experiences of a Dug Out 1914–1918*, Constable, London, 1920.
Churchill W.S.,	*The World Crisis*, V vols., Thornton Butterworth, London, 1923.
Churton W.A.V.,	*The War Record of the 1/5th (Earl of Chester's) Battalion, the Cheshire Regiment*, Chester, 1920.
Crookenden A.,	*History of the Cheshire Regiment in the Great War*, 2nd edition, Evans, Chester, 1939.
Crouch L.W.,	*Duty and Service*, privately printed, Aylesbury, 1917.
Crutwell C.,	*A History of the Great War 1914–1918*, Clarendon, Oxford, 1934.
Dearden H.,	*Medicine and Duty*, William Heinemann, London, 1928.
Edmonds J.E.,	*History of the Great War based on official documents, Military Operations 1914–1919*, H.M.S.O. London, 1949.
Edmonds J.E.,	*A Short History of World War I*, O.U.P., London, 1951.
Gardner B.,	*Allenby*, Cassells, London, 1965.
Ed. Gordon Lennox, A.,	*The Diary of Lord Bertie of Thame, 1914–1918*, Hodder and Stoughton, London, 1924.

Graves R.,   *Goodbye to All that,* revised edition, Penguin, Harmondsworth, 1967.

Guard W.J.,   *The Soul of Paris — Two Months in 1914 by an American Newspaperman,* Sun Publishing Co., New York 1914.

Ed. Hart-Davies R.,   *Siegfried Sassoon Diaries,* 1915–1918, Faber and Faber, London, 1983.

Hockley A. Farrer.,   *Death of an Army,* Arthur Baker, London, 1967.

Houlihan M.,   *World War I, Trench Warfare,* Super Source Books/Ward Lock, London, 1974.

Illustrated War News   Illustrated London News & Sketch Ltd., 1914–1917, London.

Ingram A.F. Winnington, *The Church in Time of War,* Wills Gardner & Co., London, 1915.

Ed. James R.,   *Winston S. Churchill, His Complete Speeches,* vol., III, 1914–1922, Chelsea House Publishers, London, 1979.

Keegan J.,   *The Face of Battle,* Penguin, Harmondsworth, 1986.

Kennedy A. and Crabb
G.,   *The Postal History of the British Army in World War I,* Charlwood, Epsom, 1977.

Laffin J.,   *Surgeons in the Field,* J.M. Dent, London, 1969.

Langley M.,   *The East Surrey Regiment,* Leo Cooper, London, 1972.

Lewis C.A.,   *Sagittarius Rising,* [Reminiscences of flying in the Great War] Penguin, Harmondsworth, London, 1983.

Lidell Hart B.H.,   *A History of the World War, 1914–1918,* Faber and Faber, London, 1934.

Lloyd George D.,   *The War Memoirs,* VI vols., Ivor Nicholson & Watson, London, 1934.

Loraine W.,   *Robert Loraine,* William Collins, London, 1938.

Luard K.E.,   *Unknown Warriors,* Chatto and Windus, London, 1930.

Lytton N.,   *The Press and the General Staff,* William Collins, London, 1920.

Macdonald L.,   *Somme,* Michael Joseph, London, 1983.

Macpherson W.G.,   *History of the Great War,* Medical Services, Diseases of the War II, H.M.S.O., London 1923, Surgery of the War II, H.M.S.O. 1922.

Magnus P.,   *Kitchener, Portrait of an Imperialist,* John
Murray, London, 1958.

Manchester Guardian
History of the War   1914–1920, (IX vols.) Manchester.

Marshall–Cornwall J.,   *Haig as Military Commander,* B.T. Batsford,
London, 1973.

McGuinness J.H.,   *The First Hundred Years, the Story of the 4th*
Battalion The Cheshire Regiment, privately
printed, Evans, 1959.

Middlebrook M.,   *The First Day on the Somme,* Penguin,
Harmondsworth, 1984.

Miscellaneous papers.   Chester Regimental Archives, Chester Castle.

Pearl A.H.,   *Paris Sees It Through, A Diary 1914–19,*
Hodder & Stoughton, London 1919.

Pierrefeu J. de.,   *French Headquarters 1915–1918,* Geoffrey Bles,
London 1924.

Ed. Raleigh W. and
Jones H.A.,   *The War in the Air,* Clarendon, Oxford, 1928.

Rigby B.,   *Ever Glorious,* the story of the 22nd Cheshire
Regiment, published by the Regiment, Chester,
1983.

Royle T.,   *The Kitchener Enigma,* Michael Joseph,
London, 1985.

Russell A.,   *The Machine Gunner,* Kinneton, London, 1977.

Sassoon S.,   *Memoirs of an Infantry Officer,* paperback Faber
& Faber, London, 1966.

Simpkins P.,   *Air Fighting 1914–1918,* Imperial War
Museum, London, 1978.

Smith G.V.,   *The Bishop of London's Visit to the Front,*
Longman's & Co., London, 1915.

Smithers A.J.,   *The Man who Disobeyed, Sir Horace Smith —*
Dorian and his enemies, Leo Cooper, London,
1970.

Ed. Strahan F.,   *The Core of the Apple,* Memoirs of George
McGowan, Cider Maker 1892–1982,
University of Melbourne, Melbourne, 1982.

Swinton E.W.,   *Eye Witness,* E. Arnold, London, 1915.

Terraine J.,   *The Road to Passchendaele,* Leo Cooper,
London, 1977.

Terraine J.,   *The Smoke and the Fire,* Book Club Associates,
London, 1981.

Times History of the War, XXII vols., London [1914–21].

Tuchman B., *August 1914,* Papermac, Macmillan, London, 1983.

Vaughan E.C., *Some Desperate Glory,* Frederick Vaughan, London, 1982.

Ward C.M. Dudley, *The Fifty Sixth Division, (1st London Territorial Division)* John Murray, London, 1921.

Wilkinson A., *The Church of England and the First World War,* S.P.C.K. London, 1978.

Williams Ellis C and A., *The Tank Corps.* George H. Doran & Co., New York, 1919.